"I Will Be Meat for My Salish"

The Buffalo and the

Montana Writers Project Interviews

on the Flathead Indian Reservation

Sun Buffalo Cow ran very fast along the other trail to the top of the cliff. She said, "I go into [change to] the form of earth buffalo. **I will be meat for my Salish.**" She jumped headlong from the high rock to the foot of the cliff.

The people came and saw the dead buffalo. They said: "Our Mother spoke true words. Here is herd buffalo fallen from the rock. It is warm meat. It is good."

from "Sun Buffalo Cow Sacrificed Her Life"
told by Lassaw Redhorn, François Skyenna
and Dominic Michell

"I Will Be Meat for My Salish"

The Buffalo and the Montana Writers Project Interviews on the Flathead Indian Reservation

written by

Bon I. Whealdon and others

edited by

Robert Bigart

drawings by

Dwight BilleDeaux

co-published by
Salish Kootenai College Press
Pablo, Montana
and
Montana Historical Society Press
Helena, Montana

Copyright 2001
Salish Kootenai College
PO Box 117
Pablo, MT 59855

All rights reserved. No part of this publication may be reproduced or transmitted in any form or by any means, electronic or mechanical, including photocopy, recording, or any information storage or retrieval system, without permission in writing from the copyright holder.

Demers cattle drive map on page 194 by Wyatt Designs, Helena, Montana.

Interviews from the Works Progress Administration Papers, Special Collections, Renne Library, Montana State University, Bozeman, MT, are reproduced with permission of the library. All rights reserved.

Base maps of the Flathead Indian Reservation reproduced with permission of the Confederated Salish and Kootenai Tribes, Pablo, Montana. All rights reserved.

Cover art and the drawings between chapters are by Dwight BilleDeuax. They are reproduced with permission of the Salish-Pend d'Oreille Culture Committee, St. Ignatius, Montana. All rights reserved.

Pictures of Bon Whealdon are reproduced with permission of David Whealdon, Louisville, Kentucky. All rights reserved.

Library of Congress CIP data:
I will be meat for my Salish : the buffalo and the Montana Writers Project interviews on the Flathead Indian Reservation / written by Bon I. Whealdon and others ; edited by Robert Bigart ; drawings by Dwight BilleDeaux.
   p. cm.
Includes bibliographical references and index.
ISBN 0-917298-84-5
   1. Salish Indians—Hunting. 2. Bison, American—Montana—Flathead Indian Reservation (Mont.) I. Whealdon, Bon I. (Bon Isaac), 1889-1959. II. Bigart, Robert.
E99.S2 I2 2002
639'.11643'0978683—dc21

2001055138

ISBN 0-917298-84-5
10 11 12 13 14   6 5 4 3 2

Disclaimer

The interviews recorded in this book are a valuable source of information from Salish elders over sixty years ago, but the written records that survive have been filtered through interpreters and writers. Most of the interviews that were originally given in Salish were gathered by Bon Whealdon. The interpreters are identified in the research reports. The translation from Salish to oral English probably impacted the information, but translating the oral English to written English altered the contents further. Stilted, "primitive" English was often used in place of articulate Salish. Also, offensive English terms such as squaw, papoose, savage, primitive, etc. were introduced by the writers to make the results more colorful.

It is not possible in the twenty-first century to separate the veneer of the writers from the oral information given by the Salish elders. We need to point out, however, that some of the language used in the Montana Writers Project research reports is offensive to Indian people. The knowledge of the Salish elders recorded in these research reports is valuable, but we must object to some of the "dressing" added by the writers.

Salish-Pend d'Oreille Culture Committee
Confederated Salish and Kootenai Tribes
St. Ignatius, Montana

Editor's Acknowledgments

The editor would like to thank Elaine Peterson and Kim Scott of the Renne Library, Montana State University, Bozeman, MT, for permission to reproduce materials in the Works Progress Administration Papers and for their patient help while I was doing research for this book.

Corky Clairmont generously drew the cattle brand illustrations that appear in the text.

The Confederated Salish and Kootenai Tribes provided the base maps of the reservation that appear in this book.

Special thanks are due Joe McDonald, Corky Clairmont, and Johnny Arlee, of Salish Kootenai College; Marie Torosian and Tom Smith, of the Salish-Pend d'Oreille Culture Committee; Dave Moore and George Price, of the University of Montana, Missoula; and Martha Kohl, of the Montana Historical Society, for reading the manuscript and making corrections and suggestions.

I appreciate the help of each of the readers. They have greatly improved this book. I should emphasize, however, that none of the readers necessarily agree with all the statements in the book or all the language used. As editor, I am responsible for the introduction and other interpretive material added to the book. I have also tried to correct typographical and spelling errors in the research reports. Those mistakes or problems that remain, however, are my responsibility alone. I hope that they are few and far between.

Robert Bigart
Salish Kootenai College
Pablo, Montana

Contents

Introduction	1
Part 1: Salish Buffalo Legends and History	19
Chapter 1. Buffalo in Salish Culture and History	21
Chapter 2. Salish Buffalo Legends	47
Chapter 3. Buffalo Behavior	61
Part II: Flathead Indian Reservation Buffalo	67
Chapter 4. The Pablo-Allard Herd by W. A. Bartlett	69
Chapter 5. Origins of the Flathead Reservation Buffalo Herd	103
Chapter 6. Management of the Flathead Reservation Buffalo Herd	115
Chapter 7. The Buffalo Roundup, 1907-1909	125
Chapter 8. After the Roundup	141
Part III: Biographies and Other Subjects	147
Chapter 9. Others Aspects of Salish Culture and History	149
Chapter 10. Horses and Cattle	183
Chapter 11. Biographies	199
Biographical Glossary of Flathead Indian Reservation Names by Eugene Mark Felsman and Robert Bigart	235
About the Writers	267
Name Index	275

Introduction

The economic history of the Salish-speaking tribes of the Flathead Indian Reservation pirouettes on buffalo. Before the arrival of white people, the buffalo were a commissary for the tribes. They provided food, clothing, shelter, and much more. After the Salish were forced to move off the eastern Montana plains by the Blackfeet during the late eighteenth century, the Salish continued to foray east on buffalo-hunting expeditions that met with opposition from the Blackfeet and other Plains tribes. These semiannual plains buffalo-hunting trips precipitated continuing bloody warfare that cost the lives of many Salish men, women, and children and almost destroyed the Salish tribes.

The buffalo were also integral to the economic changes engulfing the Salish during the nineteenth century. When overhunting destroyed the plains buffalo herds, the Salish were forced to find other means of economic survival. In the 1870s, a small number of buffalo were brought to the Flathead Indian Reservation. These animals became the nucleus of Michel Pablo's and Charles Allard's herd, which protected the buffalo from extinction, provided economic support for tribal members who worked with the buffalo, and prefigured one of the principal economic foundations of the Flathead Reservation in the twenty-first century—cattle ranching.

"I Will Be Meat for My Salish" includes interviews with Salish elders about both the earlier period of buffalo hunts and the later experience with the reservation buffalo, as well as other accounts of Salish life and culture. The Flathead Indian Reservation of western Montana provided the location for the stories told below; the Montana Salish tribes, especially the

Upper Pend d'Oreille Indians, provided the actors. The Flathead Reservation is home to five Indian tribes—four Salish-speaking tribes and one Kootenai-speaking tribe. The Salish-speaking tribes on the reservation are the Upper Pend d'Oreille or Upper Kalispel tribe; the Bitterroot Salish tribe, often called the Flatheads; part of the Lower Pend d'Oreille or Lower Kalispel tribe; and part of the Spokane tribe.

During the early nineteenth century the Salish tribes lived in the northern Rocky Mountain region now part of western Montana, northern Idaho, and northeastern Washington. They spoke closely related Salish languages and were on the eastern edge of what anthropologists call the Plateau Culture Area. Their economy was built on hunting, fishing, and gathering. They exploited a variety of seasonal plant foods and hunted large and small game in the Rockies and on the plains. Hunting emphasized buffalo, but also included elk, deer, and other game. The streams and lakes abounded with fish. Fields of edible roots and fruit were harvested in their season. Changing resource availability and competition from other Indian tribes, and later whites, forced dramatic changes. In fact, one hundred years of wrenching change provide the context for the interviews published in this book.

About the Montana Salish Tribes

Between 1780 and 1883 the Montana Salish faced a growing crisis from strange, new diseases and intense pressure from expanding military powers on the plains. A series of epidemics of smallpox and other diseases greatly reduced the Salish population and military forces. At the same time, the Salish found themselves confronted with aggressive and better-armed Plains tribes, who in turn were being pushed west by eastern tribes retreating in the face of the expanding United States. The much larger Blackfeet tribes took advantage of Salish weakness and forced the Salish to move west of the Continental Divide. In the early 1850s the Salish tribes, only about 1,500 strong, found themselves confronted by the Blackfeet confederation, which numbered over 9,000. The Salish refused, however, to stop regularly crossing the divide to hunt buffalo despite frequent attacks against them by members of the

Blackfeet, Sioux, and other Plains tribes. Add to this mixture the Salish wealth in high-quality horses, the shortage of horses among the Plains tribes, and the superior access of the Blackfeet to guns and ammunition: the Salish faced a crisis.

The Salish responded by creating a series of informal strategic alliances with other western tribes, such as the Nez Perce, Coeur d'Alene, and Spokane, and the new white immigrants to the area. These alliances allowed the tribal communities to adapt and survive. While the leadership worked to gain new spiritual powers from the Christian missionaries, the tribes' alliance with whites helped guarantee members' access to guns and ammunition for protection against the Blackfeet and other Plains tribes. The tribes also replenished their population by incorporating new members through adoption and marriage. The loss of young men due to war resulted in a surplus of marriageable women. Their husbands came from outside the tribes and brought new members to the tribes or created alliances when they left the tribes. White traders and western fishing tribes provided a ready market for the dried meat and leather products produced by the Salish tribes. Even more importantly, intertribal alliances made possible larger travel parties, which gave protection against attacks.

The alliances also brought some problems, however. The Salish tribes had always been willing to share the resources of western Montana with whites and allied tribes. The early white settlers in the Bitterroot Valley helped guard against Blackfeet raids, but they brought with them a strange new ideology. As their numbers increased, the white people acted as if they owned the place. They claimed exclusive use of traditional camping areas, gathering sites, and grazing fields. It was hard for the Salish to see how the whites could be so stingy, and act so dishonorably, and yet feel they were superior. But some whites were able to rise above these prejudices and treat their Indian neighbors with respect. Chief Charlo, for example, had a number of white friends in the Bitterroot whom he visited regularly.

By the 1870s, life became especially challenging for the Salish leadership. The shrinking buffalo herds resulted in intensified fighting with the Blackfeet, Sioux, and, sometimes, the Crow. At the same time, the Blackfeet and Sioux were fighting the whites. Maintaining the Salish alliance with the whites to avoid destroying the tribes in a two-front war was critical. Keeping peace with the whites while on buffalo hunts was especially hard. Alcohol was too readily available, and many trigger-happy whites were whipped into a frenzy of fear against Indians. A slight misstep could result in tribal extermination, so the leadership worked hard to keep the peace. Chief Charlo and the other Salish leaders even ended their alliance with the Nez Perce in 1877 when the Nez Perce fought against the whites.

The strategy of forming alliances had allowed the tribes to survive against much larger and more powerful enemies, but in the 1880s, a new period was beginning. After the buffalo were gone in 1883, the primary threat for the Salish was economic rather than military. The loss of the buffalo forced the tribes to move from a hunting and gathering economy, with some farming, to a ranching and farming economy, with some hunting. By 1880 many Salish had small farms or did seasonal work for other farmers. While most planted their crops and then spent much of the growing season hunting, big game in western Montana was in serious decline. It was also harder to hunt what little game remained as sports hunters, beginning in the 1880s, used state game laws in the name of conservation to stop commercial hunting and seriously limit subsistence hunting. Hunting seasons and other regulations were not designed to accommodate the rural whites and Indians who relied on game for most of their meat supply during the year.

The changing situation called for a new strategy. The Salish leadership continued to work with the whites but also made a special effort to preserve their independence. The most immediate problem was how to remain economically independent. The community turned its attention to developing cattle ranching and grain farming. During the 1880s and 1890s the missionaries provided some technical help and trained the young people in English, math, and trades while the federal government provided limited development aid such as wagons and plows, and usually expected labor in return. The Flathead Agency—acting for the federal government—did provide emergency support for the old and infirm and food assistance during some crop failures, but the federal government never actually supported the tribes.

By not becoming dependent on government rations, the Salish leadership was able to limit the power of the agent to dictate to the tribes. For example, the government was never successful in enforcing a pass system to control tribal members leaving the Flathead Reservation. The Salish brought the agent a copy of the treaty and showed him their treaty-right to hunt in traditional Salish hunting areas off the reservation. Since the tribes did not rely on rations, the agent could not coerce them by manipulating the food supply. The tribes adapted successfully to the dramatic economic changes on the reservation between 1883 and 1904. By the early 1900s the reservation was about as well off economically as other rural Montana communities. In other words, the tribes were not poor.

Chief Charlo and the Bitterroot Salish tribe tried to maintain an independent Salish community in the Bitterroot Valley, but they were unsuccessful. In the 1870s and early 1880s, the government tried threats of military force to get Charlo to join the other Salish and Kootenai tribes on the Jocko or Flathead Reservation, but it only increased his resolve to stay in the Bitterroot. During the mid-1880s the Bitterroot Salish had received government help in developing their farms, and they had had some success. Charlo and the other Salish leaders worked hard to get along with the Bitterroot Valley whites, and relations were generally friendly through the period. The drought of 1889, however, wiped out the farms of the Salish and many of their white neighbors. In 1889 Charlo reluctantly agreed to move north to the reservation, but bureaucratic ineptitude delayed the removal until 1891.

The extensive changes in the tribal economy on the reservation and in the Bitterroot Valley did not result from any desire to discard traditional Salish culture; rather, they were unfortunate, but necessary, adaptations to declining resources. The changes must have been painful in many ways, but the alternative of dependence on the government or missionaries would have been even more unsettling. By 1904, on the reservation the tribal community was expanding, and the tribes were still united enough to make collective decisions and work to protect tribal interests. Some cultural activities had gone underground or were lost, such as buffalo hunting and some religious ceremonies, but the community was able to preserve many traditional ways.

The next dramatic challenge occurred in 1904 with the passage of the Flathead Allotment Act. This began a period when oppressive government policies combined with agricultural and economic depression to almost destroy the tribes. The most devastating change forced on the tribes was the allotment policy. This policy divided up tribal lands into individual parcels or allotments. After twenty-five years, each tribal member was to get a patent on their land, and the tribes would be dissolved. Assigning allotments, or individualized landholdings, was not necessarily negative, but the allotment policy also included the forced sale of the "surplus" lands to white settlers at bargain rates. These land sales at below-market rates depleted tribal assets.

Tribal leaders fought the allotment policy through every avenue available. The files in the National Archives in Washington, D.C., are full of their objections and arguments. The records also contain copies of the government responses admitting that the allotment policy was imposed on the tribes without their consent.[1] In 1904, W. H. Smead, the Flathead Agent who was in favor of allotment, needed an armed guard when traveling around the reservation. Nevertheless, the land sales to whites began in 1910 and they soon made the Salish a minority on their own reservation. This combination of coercive social engineering to force tribal members to become small, independent farmers and robbery by the federal government had social and economic consequences that still impact the tribes today. As any businessman will tell you, future prospects are reduced if one is forced to sell assets for twenty-four cents on the dollar—which is what happened to the tribes.

Allotment was not the end of this economic onslaught. Between 1910 and 1935 the government issued forced, or involuntary, land patents that removed trust restrictions on land sales, and used other policies that deliberately crippled the economic foundation of the tribes by pushing tribal members to sell land and live off the proceeds. Some sympathetic white senators gave tribal representatives access to hearings in Washington, D.C., and early white tribal attorneys, including Burton K. Wheeler and Albert A. Grorud, sometimes worked for free, but the tribes won only a few defensive victories during this period.

The agricultural depression in Montana that started in the late 1910s aggravated the situation by destroying many of the farms and ranches owned by tribal members. Hunger and poverty became part of the reservation landscape. The combination of drought and predatory government policies caused considerable factional conflict within the tribes. For a time, two different tribal organizations, the Flathead Tribal Council and the Flathead Business Committee, fought each other and the federal government at the same time. This factionalism and the continued impact of the government and missionaries seriously damaged tribal community and values. The white educational system available to the tribes taught young people English and some useful trades but also tried to coerce the students into accepting white values and social norms.

Even during these dark and perilous days after 1910, the tribes found dedicated leaders, such as Marie Lemery, who worked hard to protect the Salish people. These leaders fought against the use of tribal money to build an irrigation system that largely benefited white homesteaders, against land patents forced on allottees who wanted to remain part of the tribes, against use of tribal money to fund the Bureau of Indian Affairs, and against the use of the Kerr Dam to subsidize local white irrigators. The leaders wrote and traveled to Washington, D.C., to make their case. They hired white lawyers to lobby and pursue cases in court—and, in some instances, such as ending the use of tribal money for the Flathead Irrigation Project—they were victorious.

They fought against great odds, but they did not give up. While they won only a few of the battles, they never lost hope or their belief in the justness of their cause. In 1935 the New Deal reversed government policies with the Indian Reorganization Act, from trying to disband the tribe to protecting tribal assets and strengthening tribal culture and self-government. The tribal leaders could finally switch from defensive action to rebuilding. Many assets had been lost or stolen, and much damage had been done to the social fabric of the tribes; but in the late 1930s, the tribes found leaders to begin the long work to repair the destruction wrought between 1904 and 1935. Some of these leaders came from prominent tribal families such as the Charlos and McDonalds, but others, such as Eneas Conko, also played important roles.

Factionalism and poverty in the early twentieth century had inflicted serious cultural damage on the tribes, but the tribal community survived physically and had protected enough economic assets to begin building and healing. The tribal leadership continued the fight for survival. They fought efforts during the 1950s to terminate the tribes and abrogate the 1855 Hell Gate treaty, which established the Flathead Indian Reservation. The termination movement would have ended the legal status of the reservation and the tribal government without tribal consent. Today, the tribes' survival is no longer as threatened, and new cultural and political leaders continue to develop strategies to meet the challenges of the twenty-first century.

About the Interviews

The story of the Salish tribes is one of a brave and determined community's ability to adapt and survive while preserving important parts of its culture and values. The interviews of Salish tribal elders included in this book give us a collection of snapshots of the drama of Salish survival through the 1940s. Preserved during the late 1930s and early 1940s by a number of workers for the Montana Writers Project, these interviews with Salish elders were themselves the result of a strategy for economic survival—this time on the part of the federal government in response to the Great Depression.

Part of the Federal Writers Project, which in turn was a branch of the U.S. Works Progress Administration, the Montana Writers Project provided jobs for unemployed writers, editors, researchers, and clerical workers at the height of the Great Depression. One of the principal goals of the Federal Writers Project was to develop state guidebooks with historic, geographic, and cultural information about each state. The Montana Writers Project focused on publishing *Montana: A*

State Guide Book in 1939. They also published a collection of stories about the Butte mines, a book of Assiniboine Indian legends, a book of photographs of Montana, and a humorous history and almanac of the state. Other projects were incomplete in 1943 when the Montana Writers Project was closed due to World War II. These included a history of livestock grazing in Montana, a history of the buffalo in Montana, collections on the traditions and cultures of Montana Indian tribes, and the folklore of Montana ethnic communities.

H. G. Merriam, the legendary English professor at the University of Montana in Missoula, was the first director of the Montana Writers Project. He resigned after nine months, frustrated with bureaucratic red tape and problems finding and supervising writers in rural Montana. The Montana Writers Project had six other directors before it closed in 1943.[2]

The Montana Writers Project was a collaborative effort with field workers around the state gathering local material that professional writers used to assemble books. Some of the field workers were assigned to collect oral histories and then send the written research reports to the Montana Writers Project headquarters, which moved around between several Montana cities during the life of the project. At state headquarters the handwritten reports were typed and the originals discarded. Other field workers were paid to go through newspapers and published sources to make transcriptions of relevant materials. These research reports then served as the sources for writers to compile written histories or guidebooks.

During the course of the Montana Writers Project, extensive files of research reports were compiled for each Montana Indian reservation. Unfortunately, the Flathead Reservation files have disappeared. Only the second copies of some of the Flathead Reservation research reports in the files about buffalo and livestock have survived. This book includes the surviving research reports that relate to the Flathead Indian Reservation and are based on interviews. Research reports transcribing newspaper sources or other published sources are not reprinted.

Most of the Flathead Reservation research reports still extant were produced by Bon I. Whealdon, and many record interviews he conducted with Salish elders in the 1920s, before the Montana Writers Project began. Whealdon was an interesting character in his own right. Raised in a Quaker family in Washington state, he moved to the Flathead Reservation as a young man and worked as a farmer, logger, and cemetery keeper over the years. Beginning in the 1920s, he befriended Salish Indian elders in the Ronan area and recorded their stories and tribal traditions. Many of these interviews were later submitted to the Montana Writers Project.[3] The elders whom Whealdon interviewed over sixty years ago are no longer available to share their experiences with us, but through the research reports published here, we can catch a glimpse of the world they knew.

The first part of the book includes stories about traditional Salish uses of the buffalo, the importance of the buffalo to the Salish, and the organization of Salish buffalo hunts on the Montana plains. Many of these stories revolve around the bloody conflict with the Blackfeet tribes, especially the Piegan, who objected to sharing the buffalo with the tribes from west of the Continental Divide.

Part II of the book includes those interviews that relate to the Pablo-Allard buffalo herd on the Flathead Indian Reservation as well as an excerpt from an unfinished Montana Writers Project manuscript on the same subject. The Pablo-Allard herd played a critical role in the survival of the buffalo species after the buffalo were exterminated on the Great Plains in the 1880s. The origins of the herd are obscure. The primary sources and oral traditions record various accounts of how the herd started. Despite these conflicts, all the available Montana Writers Project interviews about the origins of the herd are included in this collection in chapter five. Regardless of the confusion about how the herd started, its importance for the survival of the species is well documented. The herd prospered and grew on the reservation until the early part of the twentieth century when the federal government used allotment to try to force the tribes into a small farm economy and shut down the free range on the reservation.

After the United States government rejected his offer to sell the buffalo to them, Michel Pablo sold his part of the herd to the Canadian government. Between 1907 and 1909 the buffalo were rounded up, loaded on trains at Ravalli, Montana, and shipped to Canada by rail. The roundup was a great show that attracted much attention from newspapers, photographers, and artists. Many of these interviews—reproduced in chapter seven—convey the color and excitement of the event.

Chapter four in Part II does not consist of interview transcripts, but reproduces part of "The Story of the Buffalo," an unfinished manuscript by W. A. Bartlett. No biographical information has been located about Bartlett, but he was hired by the Montana Writers Project to produce a manuscript about the buffalo based on the interviews, research transcripts, and other material gathered by the Montana Writers Project field workers. The manuscript is now part of the Works Progress Administration Papers at Montana State University in Bozeman.[4] The selections included here relate to the Pablo-Allard herd and include information from interviews that have not survived.

Part III of the collection includes the Montana Writers Project Flathead Reservation materials that emphasize other aspects of Salish culture and history than the buffalo. These valuable interviews preserve oral tribal knowledge from sources who are no longer living. Chapter nine includes the results of a series of interviews with Salish elders in the 1920s by Bon Whealdon, which an unidentified Montana Writers Project worker had edited for an unpublished book of Salish (or Flathead) stories titled "Sunlight and Shadow: The Story of the Flathead Indians." Only fragments of this unpublished manuscript, which covered a variety of topics about Salish culture, have been located. According to one source, Whealdon originally had sixty-eight interviews or stories in this manuscript. Only the fifteen published in the *Hot Springs Sentinel* in 1954-56 and one kept by his family were extant in 2001. All of these are reproduced here.

The final chapter is composed of biographies of Salish tribal members and white men who married into the tribes. Much of the biographical information came from interviews of family members collected by Montana Writers Project field workers for a history of livestock and grazing in Montana. Thus, they emphasize prominent cattlemen, but since these men include the ancestors of many of the members of the Confederated Salish and Kootenai Tribes living in 2001, they were deemed worthy of inclusion.

The sources of the Montana Writers Project interviews published in this book are varied. Most are now preserved as part of the Works Progress Administration Papers in the Merrill G. Burlingame Special Collections, Montana State University Libraries, Bozeman, Montana.[5] The fifteen research reports by Bon Whealdon reproduced in chapter nine were published in the *Hot Springs Sentinel* (Hot Springs, Montana) in 1954-56. One other research report written by Bon Whealdon was preserved by members of the Whealdon family and was provided by Jack Whealdon and Wallace Evans. The biographies in chapter eleven are of cattlemen who were tribal members or married into the tribes. These were microfilmed as part of the Western Range Cattle Industry Study by the Colorado Historical Society in Denver.[6]

Editorial Procedure

The manuscript research reports have been minimally edited for grammar, typographical errors, and clarity for this book. Quotations from published materials have been checked against the originals and corrected, except for those few sources that could not be located, which the editor has footnoted. The workers transcribing published sources frequently altered the wording while keeping the meaning the same. Many of the interviews have been translated from oral Salish to oral English. The writers of the interviews then translated the spoken word into written English. There is no way in 2001 to determine how much the meaning of the interviews was altered in the translation and transcription process as only the English typescripts have survived.

In those research reports where the Montana Writers Project writer is speaking, no quotation marks or indents are used. When the research report is written as the interviewee speaking, quotation marks are used but the text is not indented. Longer quotes embedded in the text are indented without quotation marks. Short quotations embedded in the text are identified by quotation marks.

Unfortunately, the Montana Writers Project did not establish a standard format for field workers to use for footnotes or source notes. The notes, therefore, are reproduced here as they were found in the manuscripts, except for adding the label "Notes," and moving them to the end of the interview. This may be confusing in some places, but rewriting the notes into a standard format ran the risk of changing their meaning. Notes added by the present editor are clearly identified as "Bigart Notes."

The one exception to the editorial policy outlined above is chapter four, which reproduces an excerpt from W. A. Bartlett's "The Story of the Buffalo." "The Story of the Buffalo" was treated as an unfinished manuscript. In addition to typographical and grammatical editing, all references to published sources or Montana Writers Project research reports were checked for accuracy and corrected. The footnotes in this chapter were written by Robert Bigart from notes in the manuscript.

Other editing notes:

● The manuscript has not been edited to remove derogatory terms such as "barbaric," "squaw," etc. An effort has been made to keep the editing neutral.

● Names have not been corrected. Where the spelling in the text might hinder the reader, the conventional spelling follows in brackets, i.e., McCloed [McLeod].

● Some tribal, personal, and geographic names and other words have variant spellings that did not seem to hinder readability. In these cases the names were left as spelled in the surviving manuscript, i.e., Pend Oreilles [Pend d'Oreille], Bitter Root [Bitterroot], Finlay [Finley], Michel [Michael], MacDonald [McDonald], tepee [teepee], pemmican [pemican], etc.

● Readers should remember that the date listed in the header note is the date the report was submitted to the Montana Writers Project, not the date the interview took place. Many of the interviews, particularly those conducted by Bon Whealdon, occurred in the 1920s.

Notes

1. For a detailed study of the politics behind the forced opening of the Flathead Indian Reservation in 1910 see Burton M. Smith, "The Politics of Allotment," *Pacific Northwest Quarterly,* vol. 70, no. 3 (July 1979), pp. 131-40. (Reprinted as a separate monograph by Salish Kootenai College Press, Pablo, Montana, in 1995.)

2. See Jerre Mangione, *The Dream and the Deal: The Federal Writers' Project, 1935-1943* (Boston: Little, Brown and Company, 1972), especially pp. 86-87 and 385.

3. For more information about Whealdon and the other writers represented below, see the biographical sketches at the end of this volume.

4. The Flathead Indian Reservation buffalo and grazing history research reports were transferred in 1943 to Merrill G. Burlingame, a history professor at Montana State University in Bozeman. See folder "Federal Writer's Project—Montana," Merrill G. Burlingame Papers, collection 1220, Merrill G. Burlingame Special Collections, Montana State University Libraries, Bozeman, MT; and Elaine Peterson, *Guide to the WPA Records at Montana State University-Bozeman* (Bozeman: Montana State University Libraries, 1996).

5. Works Progress Administration Papers, collection 2336, Merrill G. Burlingame Special Collections, Montana State University Libraries, Bozeman, MT. The research reports are in boxes 16, 47, 51-52, 61-62, and 128-30. The Bartlett buffalo manuscript in chapter four is in box 127.

6. All the Flathead Indian Reservation–related biographies were also found in the Montana State University Special Collections except the sketch of John Silverthorne, which is in reel 25, file "Missoula County—Livestock History #2." Microfilm copies of the Western Range Cattle Industry Study are available at the Mansfield Library, University of Montana, Missoula, and the Montana Historical Society Library, Helena.

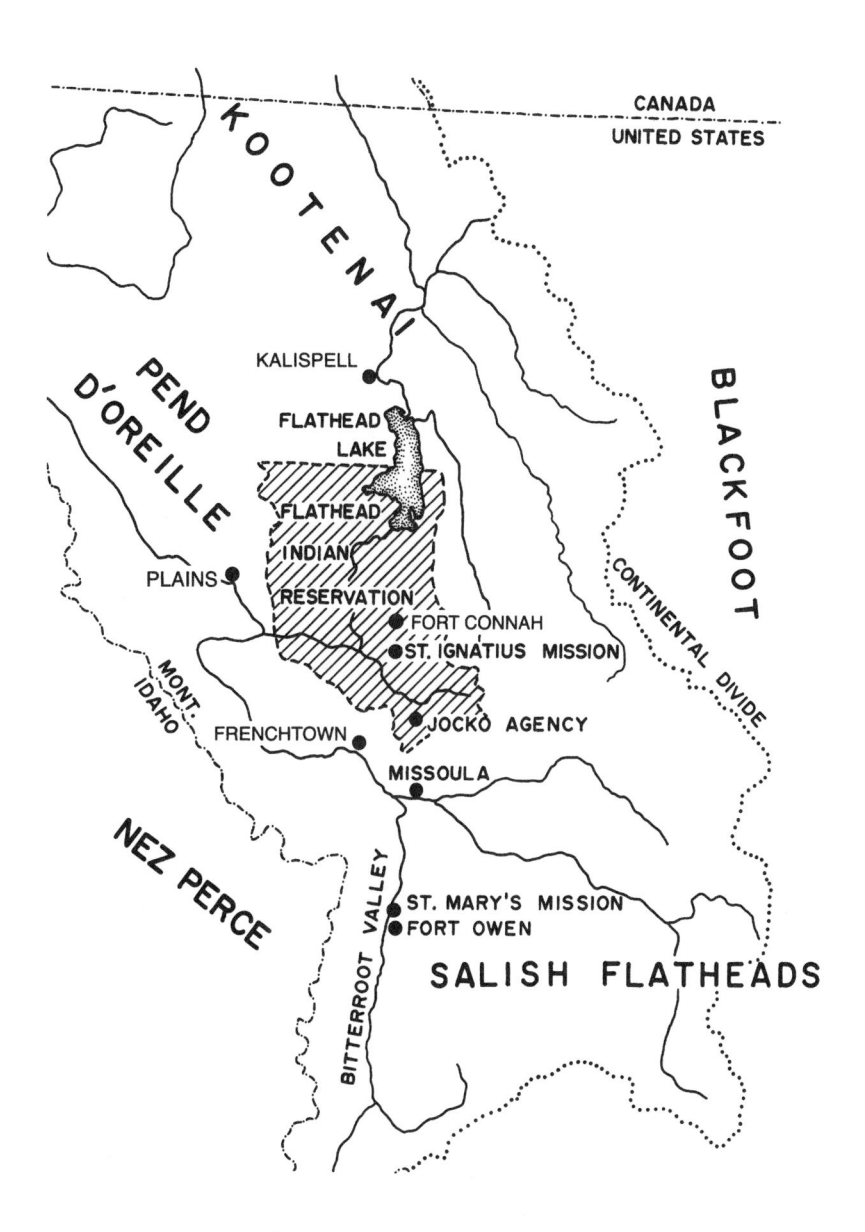

**Flathead Indian Reservation
Showing Tribal Territories, Surrounding Towns,
and Historic Sites, ca. 1850**

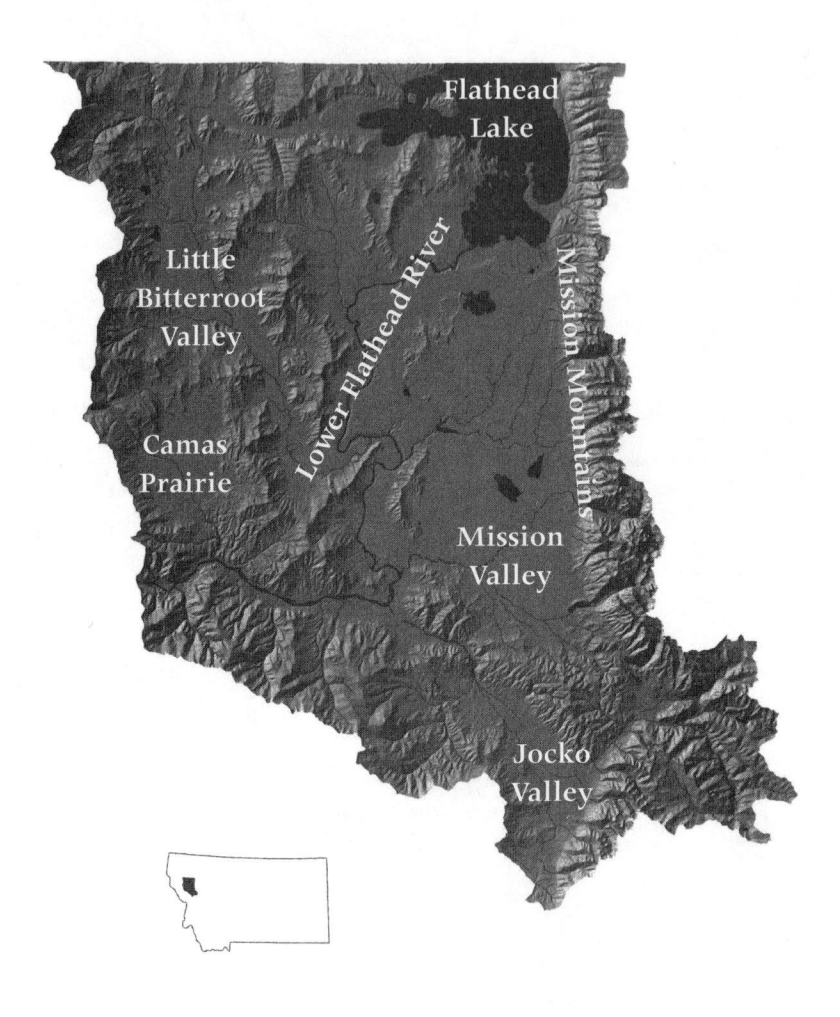

Basic Flathead Indian Reservation Geography

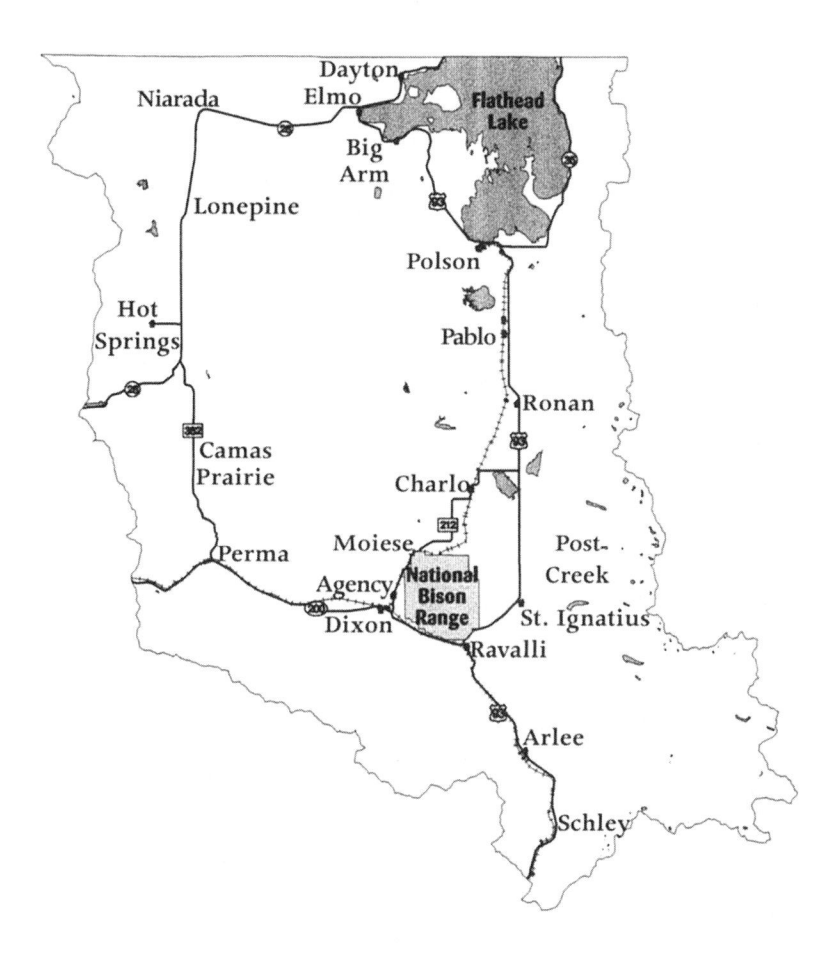

**Flathead Indian Reservation Showing
Towns, Highways, National Bison Range,
and Railroads**

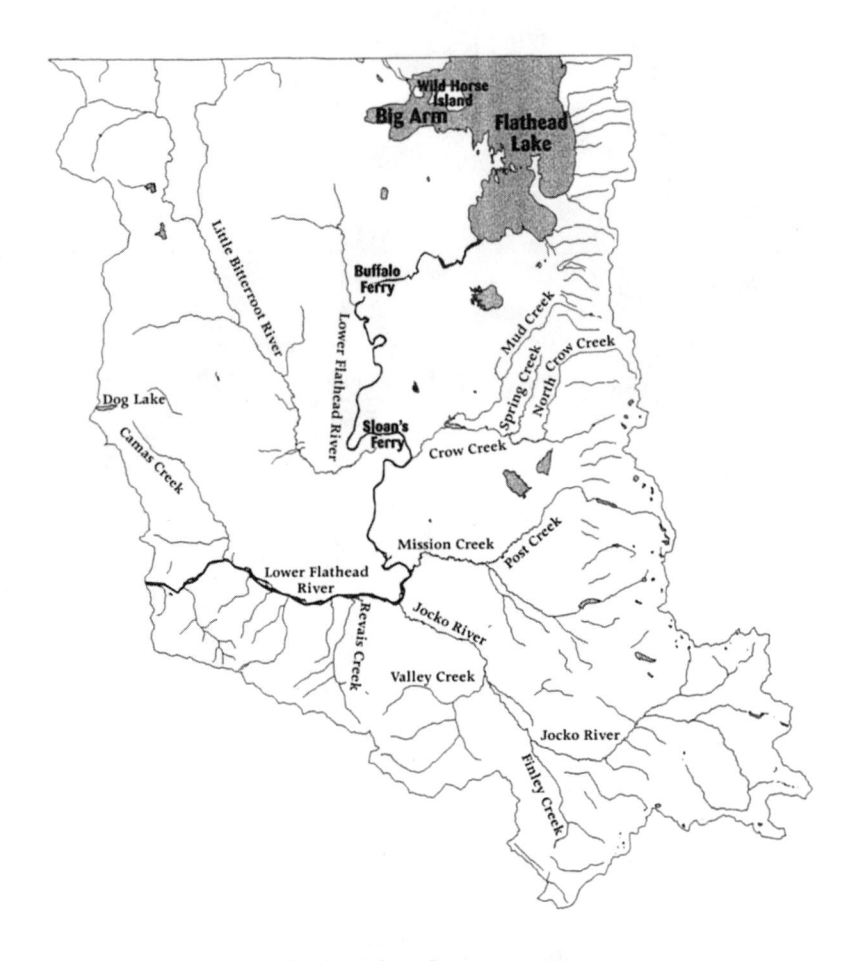

**Flathead Indian Reservation
Showing Selected Creeks, Rivers,
and Lakes**

Part I

Salish Buffalo Legends and History

The buffalo was a generous provider for the Montana Salish Indians; but the buffalo was not only an economic commodity for subsistence. In many of the interviews for the Montana Writers Project, tribal elders emphasized the importance of respecting the buffalo and all of the plants and animals that supported the Salish people. The Salish lived well, but they had to take care, as future abundance was not assured. Hunting success could change overnight as herds moved; crops of wild plants were dependent on weather and could fail during droughts; and enemy tribes on the plains violently contested Salish hunting rights.

These interviews indicate that the Salish were expert hunters who studied the land and game carefully. They were geographers, biologists, and scientists of the first order. But they were also a prayerful people, who readily asked for supernatural help in their daily efforts to survive.

The Blackfeet or Piegan, the Sioux, and often the Crow Indians carried on a long-term military campaign against the Salish to try to keep them from hunting buffalo on the plains. The Salish were also rich in horses much coveted by their plains enemies. Hunting the buffalo in eastern Montana was as much a military operation as an economic activity. The Salish, however, refused to consider ending their buffalo hunts.

The interviews indicate the importance of the buffalo to Salish sustenance. They also reveal aspects of the intertribal warfare that made it such a dangerous activity.

The buffalo were frequently featured in the legends or supernatural stories that taught values to the young. The legends collected here emphasize the religious importance of the buffalo to the pre-reservation Salish people.

Chapter 1

Buffalo in Salish Culture and History

Dancing and Singing for Buffalo or Other Game

Told by: **Dominic Michell**
Writer: **Bon I. Whealdon**
Date: December 18, 1942

Sometimes it was difficult to locate sufficient buffalo for meat and robes. The animals were upon the prairies, but for reasons unknown, the hunters were unable to find the roaming bands.

The shaman, who had as helper, or guardian spirit, the buffalo, was called upon to tell the people where to hunt in order to find the animals. If a buffalo shaman was not available, there was in each hunting party some hunter with shamanistic power, or spirit affinity with the buffalo.

Such a leader began his preparations for divination by a short fast, alone in his own teepee. During this period he meditated upon the power or gift imparted to him by his helper. He also prayed much that Amot Ken (God) grant him clear vision.

As he emerged from his teepee, carrying a buffalo robe, or, perhaps, the skull of that animal, he began singing his buffalo song. The hunters joined him in the dance and song. Often there were prayers offered for the success of the quest.

At any time during the dance, song, or prayers, the shaman might become in accord with his mystic helper, and receive the vision. When he did, silence fell upon the others, while he told them just where to go on the morrow, how many animals they would see, how many they would kill, and who would be fortunate in the hunt.

Some strange tales regarding these buffalo shamans have been told. Frequently in the giving of these revelations, the words seem to issue from the old buffalo skulls used during the ceremony.

At other times, the shaman employed an ancient Salish tongue, understood by only the oldest members of the party. At other occasions the message might be spoken in the Sioux, Crow, or Blackfoot languages, which caused the people to believe that their shamans were, at such times, controlled by the departed members of those tribes.

Notes

This same phenomena was observed at the Coast Chinook shamanistic meeting, on the Lower Columbia River, in 1876.

The Chinook shaman, who like his fellow Indians present at the time, had never seen a Sioux nor knew any of that language, yet when he was entranced, to the astonishment of white spectators who had lived among the Sioux, he delivered a lengthy harangue in the Sioux tongue.

All of which, leads the writer to agree with Shakespeare's statement, "There are more things betwixt heaven and earth than are dreamed of in our little, every day philosophy."

Tribal Hunt Rules
Told by: **Harry H. Burland and Oliver Gebeau**
Writer: **Bon I. Whealdon**
Date: December 15, 1941

When an Indian killed a buffalo, the skin or robe was considered the personal property of that particular hunter, as were the choicest cuts of meat. Then in accordance with tribal rules regulating the hunt and its spoils, the rest of the carcass was evenly shared among the other members of the party.

Generally as the scene of slaughter was some distance from the camp, the butchering was done by the hunters, and the meat packed upon ponies for the return trip. If near the encampment, the women who were skilled butchered the animals. They did most of the cutting of the meat into long thin pieces and they placed them upon the pole racks to dry.

When properly cared for, the average buffalo provided about 525 pounds of pemmican, which was placed in parfleche containers for the winter diet.

The bones were cracked, the marrow scraped out and put into the bladder bags. The rich tallow, an essential article of the Indian's menu, was melted and drained into the skin bags.

Buffalo Story
Told by: **Dominic Michell**
Writer: **Bon I. Whealdon**
Date: November 13, 1941

"Now, I am an old man, but when I was a young boy, my people were still crossing the mountains, so they could hunt buffalo upon the prairies in Eastern Montana. I remember of going with my parents during two winter hunts. Then the buffalo became so few that our people stopped going, but from their talks through the years, I have learned much about buffalo hunts.

"It is natural that many white people, and younger Indians too, have mistaken ideas about the things our old people did long ago. Some of these very good people think that the Indians rode out upon the plains and slaughtered the buffalo just for fun; like the city folks—called 'sports'—go into our mountains now to see how many elk and deer they can kill.

"The old Indians did not raise grains, vegetables and fruits. Their foods were meats, fish, berries and roots. The buffalo furnished them meat, robes for bedding, skins for teepee coverings, clothing, foot gear, sinew for sewing, bone splinters for sewing awls, and many other articles they required. To obtain these things, they killed buffalo; and that was the only reason for the two hunts each year.

"To needlessly kill buffalo was a very grave crime. Then, too, before the good Fathers came, our Indians believed the buffalo was a very strong spirit power, and was a good friend to Indians who protected the herds.

"Now, you can see why the buffalo was so important to my people—the Indians. It was food, shelter, clothing and religion. It must be protected by tribal laws, some of which must be very strict. A hunter must not start a prairie grass fire, as that might stampede the buffalo over cliffs. He must not still hunt, or do any other act to scatter a herd. When he killed a buffalo, the best parts of the flesh and the hide were his; then the ones hunting with him took certain pieces of meat, so no one suffered for food.

"The main hunt, engaged in by every able-bodied member of the tribe, was conducted during the summer time. Then the buffalo had full, firm flesh, with plenty of fat, needed in the Indians' diet. During warm weather, the hair upon the buffalo becomes very thin, so the pelts taken then are very valuable because they can be dressed on both sides. The bulk of hides to be made into teepee covers, pack-bags, articles of rough clothing, some moccasins and shields were obtained during the big tribal and ceremonial hunt.

"Buffalo hunting during winter months was neither a tribal nor ceremonial affair. A small band under the leadership of a sub-chief, or some good hunter, camped and hunted, where and when the leader deemed advantageous, free from all the tribal regulations. There were many of these independent groups, who hunted the bison during the cold months. Then the pelts were in prime condition, and the longer thicker hair on hides made warmer robes.

"White buffalo must have been very scarce in Montana. My father, during all his hunting life when buffalo were plentiful, never saw a white one, but he said that his grandfather had been in a hunt, where one had been killed with arrows. The robe from a white buffalo was considered very, very valuable, and all tribes thought it possessed the greatest medicine power. There was much jealousy among hunters. To stop the quarreling among our tribesmen, the main chief finally took the white robe, and divided it into many small pieces, one of which he gave to each member in that hunting party. My father carried his grandfather's square of robe in his medicine bundle. It was very old, and the hair had aged to a dingy yellow color. I am very sorry that someone, knowing of its history, stole it, some ancient arrow heads, and a spear from my cabin two years ago."

Moses Delaware added, "Our old people believed the white buffalo was son of the first Salish chief and a buffalo cow, and that is why it had great buffalo, as well as human, power. I do not believe that, because I am a Christian Indian, who can read and write. There are many stories about the strange birth of the white buffalo calf. I hear that the old Crows, Piegans and Cheyenne have stories like the ones my father told."

Note
Peter Pierre and Moses Delaware were interpreters. The concluding paragraph was written by Moses Delaware, at the time of the interview, several years ago.

Buffalo—Central Figure in Many Indian Beliefs and Ceremonies
Told by: **Oliver Gebeau**
Writer: **Bon I. Whealdon**
Date: September 15, 1941

"Yes, we venerated the buffalo? Why not, since it furnished our main supply of food, clothing and shelter? Did not the buffalo, Ekona, seeing the needs of the Indians long ago, give them its earth counterpart, the buffalo?

"We must be grateful, and show our appreciation in thanks, prayer words, songs, story, and dance, for these things are pleasing to the buffalo, Ekona.

"The buffalo, Ekona, was glad when the hunters carried in their medicine bags, tokens, remembrances of buffalo—pieces of bones, horn, fragments of robe or a few strands of buffalo hair. Doing this was strong medicine for a hunt, and the carriers always killed much game.

"Beating upon tom-toms, covered with buffalo hide, were the only sounds that appeased 'Thunder-bird,' and turned away its anger.

"During the old, real buffalo dance the warriors wore buffalo heads for masks and often, buffalo robes.

"When the Indians grew careless, and no longer carried the tokens, the buffalo, Ekona, permitted white hunters to slay the mighty herds. In the spirit country are all the buffalo, roaming the plains in that land."

Notes

Old Indian beliefs as related by Oliver Gebeau to Bon Whealdon, June 10, 1941.

The buffalo, Ekona, was evidently a spirit being, and was overseer of the herds. Gebeau is not sure that he has the right name. Since "Ekone" was an old Chinook Indian name for a good guardian spirit helper; and since, in youth, Gebeau was familiar with the Chinook tongue, I think he is giving the Chinook instead of Salish name for a buffalo spirit-being.

Bon I. Whealdon, Sept. 12, 1941

The Buffalo Provided the Flatheads with Food, Shelter, and Clothing

Told by: **Oliver Gebeau**
Writer: **Bon I. Whealdon**
Date: September 15, 1941

"I asked my grandfather, the aged James Finley, why the buffalo were so important to the early Indians. He was silent for a long time, then he put his pipe away and spoke.

Son, you are like a white man; you eat, think and live as he does. You will scarcely understand me when I tell you just what the buffalo gave my people in the days before the white man came. My heart sorrows that you do not know the old ways of your people, but I will tell you.

The buffalo provided us with food, shelter and clothing. It was fresh meat for the camps, while on our hunting trips on the plains east of the mountains. Then we cured great quantities of the flesh for the long Montana winters. Of course, in those days there was an abundance of deer and elk, but buffalo meat was preferred by all Indians.

Then there was the tallow, and the marrow from large bones. These gave us the grease element in our diet of meat and roots. I recall the women boiled or roasted the bones and when they had cooled, we sat near the campfires, cracking the bones and digging out the rich marrow.

We had another use for the tallow. Our warriors were very particular about the care of their hair. They knew that the scalps must be kept in a healthful condition in order to grow good crops of glossy hair. Whenever they found time, they took either raw or cooked marrow from buffalo bones and massaged it into their scalps and hair. Son, you smile, but I tell you our Indians had thick growths of black hair. It was not thin and gray like the hair of breeds and whites. Our hair did not fall off, leaving bare spots to shine like late snow patches on Elk Mountain.

Our teepees were covered with tanned buffalo hides. It took 9 or 10 skins to make a covering for an ordinary teepee. The teepees were conical shaped, with fire spot in the center directly under the flap opening at the top, so smoke could pass out. There were always buffalo mats with hair on for day purposes and other robes for blankets. The teepees were very neat, warm and comfortable.

Buffalo hides, because of their thickness, made the best, longest wearing soles for moccasins. It required a buffalo hair robe to make a shirt-like blouse for a warrior. When the cold weather came, the hair side was worn next to the body. When the days were warm, the warrior would turn the garment hair side out.

Son, you wonder how the Indian women sewed together the buffalo skins to make teepee coverings, articles of clothing, bags and moccasins, since they had not the white man's needles? When we cracked the buffalo bones, pieces came off in splinters or slivers with sharp, tapered points. These our sewers used as awls, in puncturing the hides along seams to be coarsely laced.

Elk sinew was often used as cord or thread in sewing, but we liked the stout sinew from big buffalo tendons better than that from any other animal.

Buffalo bladders were used as small bags in which to store small articles. From buffalo rawhide was made the pipe bag, which contained the medicine smoke pipe. Then there were other buffalo bags—flint bags and saddlebags.

While on hunting trips, we used dried buffalo dung cakes for fuel. We had no wood on the prairies, and the dung fuel was better anyhow, as it furnished plenty of heat and did not give off much smoke to attract the Piegans, who hated our people.

Note
    Interview with Oliver Gebeau, aged, ex-Indian policeman, granted to his daughter, Lizzie Barber and Bon Whealdon, June 10, 1941.

Buffalo Story: Indians and the Buffalo
Told by: **Dean A. L. Stone**
Writer: **Mabel C. Olson**
Date: January 28, 1942

    "Although Duncan McDonald did not belong to their tribe, the Selish Indians among whom he lived were very fond of him. From the time he was 12 years old they took him on their buffalo hunts, and sometimes even on their war expeditions.

    "In hunting the buffalo, their garb was limited to a G-string and moccasins; they did not want their movements encumbered by clothing. Their weapons for the hunt were bows and arrows. Often the arrow, even though aimed at a vulnerable spot, was too light weight to be fatal. And even when the Indians used their favorite method of hunting, and drove a whole band of buffalo over a cliff, the fall was not always sufficient to kill all. So the old men and squaws followed the hunters and with their clubs finished off the wounded animals.

    "Two such clubs are exhibited in the museum of the Journalism Building at the University of Montana. They were found on land which Henry Edgar took up, at the confluence of the Flathead and Clark's Fork rivers, near Paradise. They are round, smooth, and taper slightly to give a hand hold. One, of dull black stone, is notched for about six inches at the tapered end, perhaps to keep the wielder's grip from slipping. The notches are even and not very deep. The other, shorter club is of a dun-colored stone. Both are heavy.

    "For the Indian the buffalo supplied most of his needs. The hide, scraped and tanned, made his tepee. His carpets were the buffalo skins with the fur left on. His blankets were buffalo skins, scraped or not. His leggings, however, were made of elk-hide.

"Sometimes the hunters, in order to sneak up on a herd of buffalo, covered themselves with a buffalo robe, slipping it off only when in the midst of the herd.

"The ceremonial tepees of the Indians were decorated with picture writing, which, together with two or three groups of painted rocks, composes almost the sole written record of the Selish tribe. The younger generation of Indians lost interest in the picture writing, and Duncan McDonald was almost the last who was able to translate the stories. Felix Vandenberg is another who can. Nearly 80 now, he is still straight as a die. At one time he was one of the tribe's prize dancers.

"Their legends and stories of wars and the hunt were transmitted in council by word of mouth by the old men to the initiates. Each of their dances is historical or illustrative of a legend. As the dance is performed, the old men related the chapter of history the dance illustrated.

"It is difficult in this day to get from the Indians much detail of the buffalo hunt. The old ones do not prove very fluent when interviewed. I have talked to old Louise Finley on the Flathead Reservation without securing much copy.

"Lambert Demers, an Arlee merchant, grew up among the Indians, and can give considerable material on the hunt. He is a nephew of Jack Demers.

"Father Taelman, of the Colville Mission, the last of Father DeSmet's band of Jesuits, was at one time the supervisor of St. Ignatius Mission, and was of course in constant close touch with the Indians. He visits here about once a year. But, like Duncan McDonald, he is apt to evade questioning with, 'Sometime, my son; not now.'"

Bull-Boats

Told by: **Dominic Michell**
Writer: **Bon I. Whealdon**
Date: October 28, 1941

"My son, I am growing old, often my memory of things that happened in the days of the long ago, sleeps. Then later, perhaps, it awakens.

"When last we talked, I thought I had told you how my father and his people made some use of every part of the slain buffalo, but yesterday evening as I sat by my teepee fire, I pondered over our talk. Then came the picture (thought) of buffalo skin boats.

"Long before the white men came, our people used skin boats in which to cross streams. I have never seen them in actual use, but when I was a small boy, Salish Indians had buffalo skin boats among their possessions. I asked our old ones: 'What are these?' My grandfather's father answered:

> These are the hides of buffalo. Several were sewed tightly together, and the seams were frequently smeared with a mixture of fir-pitch and tallow to keep water from seeping in. When our people, during a journey, came to a wide creek, or a river, they did not want their women, babies and supplies to get wet. At that time, they had no horses. They made a strong framework of tree limbs, or poles, which they bound together with buffalo thongs. Over this, they drew the cover of hides.
>
> This work gave them round shaped, but secure, well balanced boats into which could be piled tribal and individual belongings. Then if the stream was not too deep, two men in each boat would pole them across. Trips were made, until all the squaws, papooses and equipment were safely landed. Usually, if in a hurry, the men swam across.
>
> Sometimes, buffalo ropes, or thick strips of elk hide were tied together, and used in pulling the little vessels across the stream.

Note

Source: Notes from conversation with Dominic Michell, Thompson's residence, Ronan, September 1926. Verified by Mr. and Mrs. L. E. Thompson.

Memories of Buffalo Camps

Told by: **Louise Roberts, daughter of Mary Finley**
Writer: **Bon I. Whealdon**
Date: September 29, 1941

"When my mother, Mary Finley King, was a young girl, she used to go with her people on buffalo hunts east of the mountains. They would go to those regions in Montana that are now called the Sun River country, Judith Basin, and often to that part called the 'Crow Indian Reservation.' Mother enjoyed telling my sisters and I about the journeys, and I shall never forget her stories regarding camp life and the work the women so gladly attended to. She used to remark, 'Our white friends think Indian women are like slaves, doing all the hard work, while the lazy men sit around. They protected us. They worked hard bringing in meat, so Indian women were pleased that they could attend to the camp work.' I know my mother's Indian words, but I must tell her stories in our words.

"Enough of our people would go together, so we were able to defend ourselves against surprise attacks by enemies. The Piegans and their cousins, the Bloods, were dreaded most of all. Sometimes, the Crow and Snakes were upon peace terms with us. The Colvilles, Flatheads, Pend O'reilles and Kootenais, in fact all the Indians from the west side, were friendly, and frequently made a common encampment.

"When a camp, always near a water supply, was established for the season, the women and older children immediately began preparing for the buffalo meat and hides the hunters would soon bring in. As we had passed through the mountains upon our trip over, we had cut a large supply of lodge poles, which had been strapped to the pack ponies. These we now barked (pealed off the bark), and dried in the hot sun a while. We liked birch poles better than any of a pitchy nature, but could not always get them.

"We made use of these poles in building drying racks for the meat. The poles were tied together with strips or thongs of buffalo rawhide. These pole platforms had to be off the ground in order for air, heat and smoke to circulate among the pieces of meat, so that they be thoroughly cured.

"Then if it was a summer camp, far from wood fuel, we children would gather great quantities of dried buffalo cakes—buffalo chips, the pioneers named them—out on the adjacent prairies. These we carried in buffalo-skin bags to camp, where we would stack them close to the racks. This fuel gave off sufficient heat for drying, and yet not such a big volume of smoke as might attract prowling enemies.

"We felt quite safe around camp, for always the chief left a guard of warriors with us, and then, if it was necessary, our mothers knew how to fight.

"When the hunters came riding in with loads of meat, we all helped in cutting it into pieces—not too thick—for curing. Then we must watch our fires that they gave off a slow, even heat. Often, just a smudge to keep away flies and other insects was all that was needed; the hot, penetrating sunshine doing the curing process.

"The meat, while curing, gave off a pleasing aroma, and we children could scarcely wait until the racks were emptied. Sometimes, the old women, who were always poking around among the racks, would catch us tearing off thin slices, then they would smack our fingers with sticks, and scold, telling us, 'You steal like Piegans.' That made us feel badly, for, at that time, we thought all Piegans were like wolves.

"When the meat was dry, we packed it in bags made of buffalo or elk hides, or in our little bags of buffalo-stomach. The meat was for our winter use.

"I liked to pound the dried meat into a coarse powder, then mix it with dried huckleberries or sarvice berries and a small piece of tallow. It was a nice tasting food, somewhat like the white peoples' mincemeat. Any meat was good with berries, even the flesh of young bear.

"Then there were piles of raw buffalo hides to be dried and scraped. Our way was to put the hide with the hair to the ground, and make small openings round the edge of the hide. Through these holes we drove very stout wooden pegs. As we pegged, we stretched the skin, so that when it was dry it was not badly shrunken. Then with bone scrapers (generally elk bone) we removed every bit of fat and flesh from the hide. When all this first work was finished, we had buffalo rawhides, very stiff and hard. Later as we had time and need, we softened some; others we tanned for new teepee coverings. We also made fine warm robes for beds. No usable part of a buffalo, or any other animal, was ever wasted.

"Life in camp was really very pleasant. Our Indians were very tender with the children. The father taught the sons, and the mother the daughters. We were taught to respect and care for the old. We must not lie. We must be brave. Our parents liked to talk with us, and often they would play games and laugh like happy children.

"The teepees had been set up in a circle. This gave better protection against enemies. If there was any danger of a surprise attack, our horses were driven into the circle for the night. Two or three warriors were always on guard. I remember lying on my bed-robe, and seeing the warriors pass on their way about camp. Often they would be softly singing the buffalo song. It was kind of a prayer, and was named 'Calling for buffalo.' Then there was a night bird, I do not know its right name, but it always sang during clear nights on the prairie, just like its heart was filled with happiness. We called it a very old word meaning, 'Friend in the night.' We thought it was sent to tell us that everything was alright. I believe the stars over the plains were brighter then than now. I liked to lie and count as many as I could see from my side of the teepee. Often I would see Mother Sun's dead sister, Old Moon, and I wondered if the poor thing would ever find the Sky-teepee, where she could lie down and sleep."

Note
Source: Notes from conversations with Mary Finley's daughter, the late Louise Roberts, cultured Flathead ward and friend of the writer, Bon Whealdon, September 22, 1941.

The Story of the Buffalo
Told by: **Will Cave**
Writer: **Mabel C. Olson**
Date: September 25, 1941

"The general belief is that even in the early days the buffalo did not live anywhere near Missoula. This belief has been refuted by the stories told by old Indians who at one time made their homes not far from there, and by the more material evidence of buffalo remains. I myself have found buffalo skulls and horns near the site of the Milwaukee depot.

"In 1870 three buffalo roamed the hills in the Bitter Root Valley, east of Stevensville.

"Duncan McDonald, who was an authority on western Montana history, and who treasured the stories told him by Indian patriarchs, said the bands which at one time fed in the Bitter Root, Missoula, and Grass Valleys were not driven out, but were seen making a voluntary exodus up the Big Blackfoot.

"Fifty years or more ago, McDonald told me this story, which may be pertinent in that it points the belief in the presence of the buffalo.

"'As is well known, the Selish and the Blackfeet were hereditary enemies. On one occasion 25 or 30 Indians were encamped south of Missoula, about where the golf club now is located. One morning, shortly after daylight, they saw what they took to be several buffalo on the hillside above them. All the hunters of the camp set forth in excited pursuit. But when they reached the spot where they had thought the buffalo to be, they found no trace of them. Mystified, they scanned the country all about, to discover that they had been tricked. Their tepees were ablaze, and when they dashed down the mountain, they found their women and children dead, killed by the wily Blackfeet, a few of whom had donned buffalo skins, to draw the warriors away from their camp.'

"Samuel Scott, who built Scott House in Deer Lodge, was an experienced buffalo hunter. I have heard it said that in the late [18]60s and possibly the early '70s, after the country was becoming settled, he would go up the Cottonwood, cross the range, and on one side or other of the summit he would bring down a woods buffalo. These were generally considered to be somewhat smaller than the prairie buffalo, and were thought to have wandered at one time from the original range on lower land."

Buffalo Milk Saves Indian Child

Told by: **Shot-His-Horse-In-The-Head**
Writer: **Bon I. Whealdon**
Date: December 3, 1941

"My father was a buffalo hunter. When he was a very young man, he hunted the buffalo with bow and arrow, and with a lance, or spear. That was before the 'Black Robes' came to Spetlemin (the Bitter Root Valley). As he grew older, he and the other hunters were able to trade buffalo robes to the traders for guns and ammunition. With these weapons of the white men, our people had a surer way of defending themselves against surprise attacks by the Piegans.

"My father liked the winter hunt for robes more than he did the summer tribal hunt. He had many friends among the Salish people, as well as among the Nez Perce and Coeur d'Alene. In the camp were four Coeur d'Alene warriors, the wife and infant child of one of them, and my father. They were hunting in the Judith Basin country. It was an easy matter to get robes, which they traded to a post near old Fort Benton.

"The woman with the little baby had not been well since the time of her confinement. She gradually became weaker. The men got her medicine from the trading post, but it did not help her. Soon she died. The men buried the woman near her teepee. Then they moved the other teepees to a new place, as our Indians would not remain in, or near, a teepee which had been visited by death.

"The little baby was very hungry for its mother's milk. It was not old enough to eat strong (solid) foods. It cried all the time. The men felt very sorry for the small child. They asked: 'What shall we do to feed this boy baby? It must not die.'

"Then one hunter said: 'To the north, within four days walk, is a camp of Salish and their families. One man in that party has as wife, my sister. She has a small baby. We must take this one to her. She has milk. She will let it suckle.'

"The father said: 'It is good that we take my son to your sister's breasts, but the child is weak for milk now. It will soon die.'

"Then the other replied: 'Some buffalo cows still have late calves at their sides. Now we shall find such a one. We shall drive her into the deep snows of the ravine; then she can not travel. We shall press out her milk into a skin bag. We shall feed the milk to the boy child. We shall carry him to the camp of the Salish.'

"The cow could not run on the snow crust. She sank down, and could not move. The hunters on the snowshoes came quickly to her and put their buffalo ropes around (tied) her. Digging away the snow, they pressed her milk into the skin bag.

"The father said: 'We must not kill this buffalo cow. She gave out milk for my son.' They took their ropes from the cow. They stamped a way for her through the snow to the open hill.

"They dropped warm milk into the mouth of the babe. It drank and fell asleep. They froze the rest of the milk. They traveled on snowshoes, carrying the boy child. When the little fellow cried, they made fire to warm the frozen milk. In three days walk they came to the north plain, and on the fourth day they came to the Salish camp. The woman had much milk. She said: 'The infant shall warm under my robes. It shall have one taste of my breast. It shall suckle as my own.'

"The men were very happy. They said to the woman: 'It shall be as your (own) child. It shall suckle you. It is good.'

"The boy grew to be a very strong man. The people all called him, 'Man-of-Three-Mothers.'"

Buffalo Story
Told by: **Lassaw Redhorn**
Writer: **Bon I. Whealdon**
Date: November 18 and 19, 1941

"When I was a young boy, and was with my people on the summer buffalo hunt in the Yellow Stone River country, fall time came very early that year. As they had sufficient meat cured for winter, the main body of the tribe decided to return to Spetlemin (the Bitter Root) and to Sinaxelemin (the Flathead Valley). The remaining group divided into several bands for the winter hunt. My father's band moved a considerable distance toward the north to establish its winter camp, and to be where there was good grazing for the ponies. On account of the deep snow, horses could not be used to any advantage during the winter season, but regardless of that, they must eat.

"After camp had been established in a sheltered spot, we were all busy as beavers rustling in a wood supply. This fuel was augmented by great piles of 'buffalo chips.' Then the men and women began making snowshoes. The snowshoes manufactured by our people were of different size and shape then the ones the Piegans, Bloods and Crees made. We used birch to form the frame or foot-hoop, which I remember correctly was about 11 or 13 inches wide and 3 ft. long. Across this was woven a network of buffalo rawhide. Then several broader straps were fastened across this surface to hold one's foot to the snowshoe. These snowshoes were very necessary for the winter hunt, when the drifted snow filled every gully and ravine.

"We did not do our heaviest hunting until the very coldest weather had settled down over the region, for then the fur was primest. The buffalo fed upon the hillsides from which the wind had blown the snow. It was pitiful the way the herds congested at each opening searching for the grass.

"Our hunters would select one of these spots, and at the given signal would rush out toward the herd yelling at the top of their voices to start the stampede. Frightened out of their wits, the animals would break into a run to the snow filled ravines. The poor things were too heavy to travel on the snow crust, and very soon were deep in the snowdrifts, unable to go ahead or back out. The hunters on their snowshoes appeared to literally skim across the crust to their victims. With arrow, lances, and the few guns they had, the Indians soon dispatched the entire herd. The hides were quickly jerked off from the great bodies. The carcasses were left to rot, or to be eaten by wolves and coyotes.

"The fur traders with their insatiable demands for robes, and then, more robes, were of course responsible for this wholesale slaughter of the herds. Prior to the appearance of the fur traders, our Indians had always conducted winter hunts to procure the needed robes, but it was a rule among all the Montana tribes, that during no season would there be a needless or excessive slaughter of the brutes. But when it was learned that there was a profitable market for robes; and that white men with the sanction and protection of the soldiery were everywhere annihilating the herds, then naturally the Indians planned to get the cream of the robe crop. I am sure that was the beginning of the end for the old way of life—the buffalo.

"White men and Indians were not the only foes of the buffalo in Montana. In those days the wolves were very numerous. There were several families of wolves. I have seen them. I have seen their destructive work, but I do not know their right names. There were ferocious ones, steel gray in color, and the great white ones, and always the sneaky, cowardly coyotes, but these latter did little harm. It was different with the true wolves, whose delight it was to follow a buffalo herd for days, or until an old, sick, or injured buffalo no longer able to keep up with its kind, lagged behind. Such a one was sure of a hideous fate. The wolf pack, often as many as 40 in number, would crowd around the poor creature and then whet their appetites for the anticipated feast by torturing it in a hellish fashion. One day near Sun River I scared a pack from its victim to find it was an old cow with nose, eyes and tongue eaten off while her hide was torn into shreds, her tail gone. Evidently the fight had lasted for hours, for strewn about the arena were the carcasses of eight wolves the brave old she had stamped to the death. The wolves are very wise. They would not attack a herd of buffalo, for the monarchs would unite their defense efforts to stamp them out. The offensive coyotes, when driven by hunger would occasionally find, kill and devour a young calf, isolated from the herd by death of its mother."

Note

Harry H. Burland was interpreter.

Exterminating a Montana Buffalo Herd in 1836
Told by: **Frank McCloed [McLeod]**
Writer: **Bon I. Whealdon**
Date: September 19. 1941

"My truthful old grandmother, Mary Finley, daughter of one of that group of five white men who first settled in what is now Stevens County, Washington, often related the story that follows:

When I was 15 years old, my father, my Indian mother and I went with a strong party of our buffalo hunters into eastern Montana. We always went at that season, while our friends, the Flatheads, were there upon the same errand. With our combined forces, we were able to hold our own against the murderous Piegans.

We made our camp at the mouth of the north fork of Sun River. Early the morning after our arrival, our men left camp for a hunt on the prairies. Empty handed, they returned late that night. They informed us they had seen many large herds stampeding in a northerly direction, but that they were unable to get within killing distance of the animals. They said the buffaloes were so numerous that the pounding of their hoofs made a noise like the rumble of thunder.

The second day passed with the same dismal report at night. We were all discouraged as the season was far along when we arrived, and we were anxious to obtain our meat, so we could return to Washington before the snow filled the passes.

That evening our medicine man went a short distance from camp, and made medicine in order to see what the morrow held for us. You children smile at that, but we had absolute faith in his words, as he had never failed to rightly advise us in every tribal emergency. When he returned he was so agitated he could scarcely speak. Finally he managed to tell us that we would get all our supply of meat from one great pile of bloody buffalo the following day. There were no doubts in our minds, our man had seen a true vision.

The third morning, our hunters rode away in hope, nor were they to be disappointed. They succeeded in sheering what we called a small herd up North Fork Canyon. Their intention was to kill just the amount that was needed. However, the herd swung up along our side of the canyon. The trail terminated in a narrow cliff. The buffalo could not turn around and make their way back to safety. Over the side they literally poured in a 300 foot drop to the jagged rocks below. Our men rode up the canyon to see a ghastly sight. There, in one great pile of mangled, dead and living bodies, were hundreds of the animals. Blood in tiny streams was running from the gruesome mass. A few head, their fall having been broken by the mound of under bodies, were rising unharmed. They disappeared over a ridge. The badly crippled ones, our hunters mercifully shot.

The women were summoned to the tasks of butchering and curing. The Flathead camps were told to come get their meat. Still there were hundreds of carcasses left to rot. As closely as we could count them, there were more than 600 head killed.

We felt badly over this unpremeditated manner of killing buffalo, for the Colville Indians and the Flatheads never needlessly slaughtered.

By the time we had finished drying our meat, the weather had become very disagreeable with all indications of an early snowfall. We made hurried preparations to cross the mountains, as we did not care to winter in that region.

The morning set for leaving, we arose about 4 o'clock to find that snow, 5 inches in depth, had fallen during the night. While preparing the early meal, we saw an Indian, crawling upon elbows and knees, toward our camp. At first we thought he was a scouting Piegan and our warriors brought their guns in positions to shoot, when the man called for help in the Salish tongue.

We found he had been shot through his right hand, left wrist and calf of one leg in a skirmish with the Piegans, and, though his horse had been killed, he had managed to crawl to our teepees. We dressed his wounds and furnished him a saddle horse. We took him to the Colville, Washington, country. He was with us nearly a year, when he suddenly disappeared. We all missed him, as he was a splendid, helpful chap.

Fifty years later, while visiting my people in the Flathead Valley, I was introduced to an elderly, crippled Indian in the home of August Finley. I noticed he kept watching me rather closely. At last he asked me if when I was a girl, I had been called "Mary Finley" and had I been with a camp of buffalo hunters on Sun River, where a herd had gone over a cliff? I told him he was correct; whereupon he told me he was the Indian the Piegans had shot, and how we had saved his life.

Buffalo Hunt, Battle with Piegans and Indian Magic
Told by: **Harry Burland**
Writer: **Bon I. Whealdon**
Date: September 14, 1941

"About the year 1840, François LaMousse, a descendant of the Iroquois Indians who had settled among and intermarried with the Bitter Root Valley Indians (Salish) was admitted to the ranks of bison hunters. He joined a small party of the latter Indians for a hunt across the Continental Divide in the Piegans' hunting region. When their presence there was discovered by Piegan scouts, their warriors soon surrounded the little band from the Bitter Root.

"The Salish were in danger of being massacred, when François LaMousse, the only Christian in the group, knelt in prayer to his God for succor. The Bitter Root medicine man realized that only a severe storm would drive the Piegans to the temporary refuge of their own teepees. He took his sacred otter robe from his medicine bag. This he hurriedly dipped into a nearby stream, before he commenced twirling it in the air. All the while, he 'made medicine,' invoking the cloudless skies to pour out rains and winds.

"Immediately, according to legend, a terrible electrical storm with rain and hail, did occur. Dismayed, the Piegans scattered, thus enabling the Salish to retreat to a place of safety.

"Thereafter, round many a council fire, the Salish long debated the question: 'Who made the effective medicine that brought the storm, François LaMousse with his Christian prayers, or the Salish medicine man by invoking his unseen helpers?'"

Note
Related to Bon I. Whealdon by Harry Burland in 1930.

Old Chief Michell Michell's Story of Buffalo Hunt and Battle
Told by: **Chief Charley Michell, son of Michell Michell**
Writer: **Bon I. Whealdon**
Date: September 29, 1941

"I was among the hunters 1840, when our party was surrounded by the Piegans, and would have been exterminated, had it not been for either François LaMousse's prayers to his God, or for our medicine man's invocations. Though I have given much thought to the matter, I know not which one brought the storm that scattered the enemies. The good Black Robes, when they came, told us we must not give heed to the older ways, as they came from a great evil spirit. We now follow the white man's Christian way, but we do not forget what happened long ago, for they were true happenings. This I know that when we were about to be killed by the Piegans, both men made medicine, each [in] his own manner. Then quickly came dark clouds, rain, wind, and the lightning tore at the sky, while the earth shook.

"Once before, we had been saved by 'Indian medicine.' We had been warned by Coyote and by Quas-auee (Blue Jay) that if we went upon a long planned buffalo hunt, the Piegans would kill some of our men; and that a woman would protect the remainder of the party. Coyote said, 'Your old men, now gone (dead) came in a dream (vision) and dropped a blanket-robe across your trail which meant, do not go, danger awaits.'

"We went, last evening camp in the mountains, old Owl flew to tree, near fire, and in old Salish words said 'Go back! Go back!' We were fools. We heeded not the ancient signs of our people.

"We were on the plains many days. We got much buffalo meat and hides. Our hearts were happy, our heads were empty of the old wisdom. We were in the evening camp. Tomorrow we go home. Our young men joke and say: 'Coyote, Blue Jay and Old Owl have become frightened old women. Their fears put lies in their tongues. Many days here, plenty meat, no Piegans.'

"When growing dark, Piegans came riding around camp. They began shooting, some of our warriors drop dead. We shoot back, some Piegans killed; but many more came riding, and shooting into our camp. More of our men and ponies died. Soon we must all die. Louis Moleman was then about 10 years old. We thought, we will save the boy anyhow. Within our circle of teepees, were two brush clumps, close together. We hid the boy among their roots and covered him with foliage. We hoped he would find a chance to slip away in the night, when we were killed.

"Our medicine man had not (would not) come with us upon this hunt, but Elizabeth, the squaw of one of our braves, was with us. She had strong medicine powers. She came out of her teepee with a strand of otter pelt. She dipped it into buffalo water bag. She walked about camp, shaking water off it. Then she sang Nez Perce medicine song. She called to us, 'Do not be frightened. I make storm medicine; no more Salish to die.' Then we heard our dead braves speak. They spoke our names. They said, 'No more Salish to die.' The sky had been very clear, but now quickly came clouds; and then rain, wind and lightning, such as we had never seen before. The Piegans knew they could not fight Salish medicine—they left.

"Many years later, when there was peace with Piegans, old men smoked pipe with me. We talked about battles, they remembered one, when Nez Perce squaw made storm medicine and saved Salish hunters."

Note

Harry Burland and Dominic Michell, interpreters.

Story of the Buffalo

Told by: **Harry H. Burland's Notes**
Writer: **Bon I. Whealdon**
Date: November 17, 1941

"A number of years ago, I was working at my carpenter trade in San Francisco, California. One very pleasant evening, I decided to go see a widely advertised western show. When I arrived at the entrance, I learned I was rather early for the show, so I whiled away the time by inspecting the bill posters. They portrayed a buffalo hunt by wild Indians upon the plains of eastern Montana. I was very much amused over the painter's work, and could not repress a chuckle. The manager, who had been watching me, came over to my side, and said: 'I trust you will pardon me, but I have been observing your very keen interest in our pictures, and I heard you laugh. Is anything wrong?'

"'Yes,' I replied. 'Everything here pictured regarding the hunt, the buffalo, the Indian is decidedly incorrect. That I know for I am an old Indian from Montana, where my ancestors were hunting buffalo, when yours were 'mooring their barques upon the wild New England shore.' (For I saw he was a 'down-east Yankee.')

"'Here, you have wild Indians, garbed in nondescript articles of ceremonial regalia, sitting in lately made saddles upon the backs of a heavy breed of horses that were never seen upon the plains, shooting arrows and jabbing spears all over the body of a buffalo bull that bears upon its grotesquely misshapen head—of all things—the horns of an old Texas range steer. Then, as if to give this beastly monstrosity a soulful touch, your artist gave it the fully open, wistful eyes of an Oregon coast seal. Brother, if this caricature of the monarch of the plains is a faithful representation, then I, a Flathead Indian, am truly the long sought for Miss Link Sitting in choir loft of St. Alban's Cathedral, divinely playing "The Lost Chord."'

"'In his preparations for the hunt, the Indian cast aside every vestige of clothing, and all equipment such as worn in battle—shield, quiver, lance and unnecessary arrows—so as to be free to use his bow and the very few arrows required for the kill. Always his horse was one of the light wiry breed that roamed the prairies in great bands. These mounts were fleet of foot, and of great endurance. The Indian had no saddle nor bridle. The horse, carefully trained for the hunt, was guided by a jawline, or rope. The small, intelligent animal seemed to sense its rider's will.

"'The hunter rode quite close to the herd. When he had selected the animal he wished to kill, he generally managed to work between it and the herd, thus giving himself opportunity to finish it off. Always he pressed his horse to the right side of his quarry, in order to shoot his arrow to the left and downward into the vulnerable heart and lung region. Instantly the well trained horse sheered off to the right to avoid impalement upon the horns of the furious buffalo, as it wheeled to face its adversaries. Sometimes, in spite of its caution and swiftness, a horse was gored to death while the rider narrowly escaped the same dreadful fate.

"'Never, my friend, did a buffalo possess eyes such as this billboard nightmare with its full seal eyes. I wish it were possible to take you to the Moiese U.S. Bison Range, which is well stocked with buffalo. I am sure you would instantly note a peculiarity in the buffalo's eye, which when once seen is never forgotten. The ball of the eye is purest white in color, and as a rule quite large, while the iris is coal black. The beast habitually rolls the eyeball forward and down, which carries the larger portion of the iris below the lower lid. The effect upon the spectator is startling. One visitor remarked: "The buffalo eye with its iris nearly hidden by its lower lid gives me the impression that the brute has knowledge of a lot of ancient wisdom, which it tantalizingly conceals from inquisitive, intruding human beings."'"

"I Will Be Meat For My Salish"

Chapter 2

Salish Buffalo Legends

The Flatheads Meet the Buffalo
Told by: **Chief Mose Michell**
Writer: **Bon I. Whealdon**
Date: September 8, 1941

"Once during the long, long ago, a terrible famine came upon our people. There were but few fish in our lakes and streams. A contagious disease spread among the elk and deer until they became unfit for food. The frosts killed the berries in the blossom stage. For many days, the hot sun baked the earth, and so the supply of edible roots became limited.

"The Flathead and Kootenai Indians assembled in a mighty council. The medicine men, who had great power over the forces of nature, brought out their sacred robes of otter and beaver. For many days and nights they made medicine, thinking to please Thunder Bird, who, in return, would send rains to the earth, more fish to the rivers, and healthy game to the mountains.

"Their invocations were fruitless, for Thunder Bird was still angry over the accidental killing of his mate by a Flathead warrior. He swore in a loud voice—and the valley trembled from the force of his anger—that all the Flatheads must starve to death. However, the spirits of the water were able to protect the fish life from his wrath.

"For many weeks, the Indians lived upon fish and the few roots they found deep in the ground. They became thin, and many sickened. Their hearts were heavy with sorrow, for the they thought that very soon they must perish.

"They held another council. Many warriors arose and spoke, but they could devise no plan whereby to save the people. Then came Elmin, the youngest and purest medicine man of the tribe. He had been fasting and praying upon Mount E-tam-a-na.[1] He said, 'My people, take heart. While I fasted, our tribal helper, Coyote, came and instructed me. Our bravest warriors must take all the strongest ponies and follow Quas-quee[2] (Blue Jay) across the high mountains into the hunting region of the Piegan. There Coyote will show the braves great plains covered with animals that are new to us. These the Piegan kill and eat, and the flesh gives them much strength.'

"They traveled many days until they arrived in the Judith Basin. Here, as Elmin had told them, they found the great brutes grazing upon the prairie. They were many in number, like the leaves on the quaking aspen tree. When they ran, the ground gave back a deep rumble like the sound when Thunder Bird speaks.

"The spectacle caused the Flathead to wonder, so Coyote explained: 'These are buffalo. They are food, clothing and shelter for my people. Now I shall teach you how to hunt and kill them, how to cure the meat, and how to make robes and teepee coverings. Famine never again shall visit the country of the Flathead. Only one rule you must follow—never needlessly slaughter our buffalo.'"

Notes
1. E-tameaves, a peak in Mission Range, fasting place of an early Salishan people.
2. Quas-quee (bluebird) with Coyote were tribal spirit helpers.

Sun Buffalo Cow Sacrificed Her Life
Told by: **Lassaw Redhorn, François Skyenna, and Dominic Michell**
Writer: **Bon I. Whealdon**
Date: December 12, 1941

"Not in the life of our grandfathers, nor during the span of their grandfathers, did this thing happen, but when the land was very young and our people were not many did it occur.

Salish Buffalo Legends

Only our oldest men told the story, for they knew it was a true tale, and not one to amuse children.

"Our people had hunted for buffalo all the summer, but the animals were very few that year. There were many Cree, Blackfoot, Piegan, Crow and Snake hunters upon the plains. There were many wars over the buffalo, for the fear was great that there would be little meat for the wintertime.

"When fall time came, many of our people returned to the mountains that they might kill elk, and thus have meat. However, a little group remained on Sun River. They thought they might be able to obtain a few buffalo robes. Early each morning, leaving a guard at the camp, the hunters sallied forth in search of a herd. The season was growing late, and still the Salish found no buffalo.

"One day, a strong band of Piegan warriors came upon the camp. The four guards and the women fought very bravely, but they were all killed, excepting two women whom the Piegans took as slaves. They also carried away all the Salish teepees and supplies.

"Late that evening, the hunters returned to find their dead scattered about. There was lamentation, intensified because they had no hope of overtaking the enemies and wrecking vengeance upon them.

"The chief man said: 'When our strong warriors come again, we will join them to kill out many Piegan. Now we must hunt to live till that time.' They hunted much but found no buffalo. The shaman made strong medicine to the buffalo spirit, asking meat that they should not starve.

"Two days, two nights, the shaman made medicine. Then came his helper (supernatural being) in shape of old Coyote. Old Coyote stood by the big rock and talked. He said: 'The Salish are to go to the bank of the other river (perhaps, the Upper Missouri). The Salish will find meat by the river.'

"Old Coyote ran to meet Sun Buffalo Cow. He said: 'Sun Buffalo Cow, there are no herds left upon the plains. The Salish camp will soon starve. You must go quickly to the great rock by the river to meet the Salish. Feed them, or they starve.'

"Sun Buffalo Cow ran to the place. The Salish came, and they saw Sun Buffalo Cow, but they saw no herd. They were very sorrowful. They said to the shaman: 'Old Coyote drips crooked words from his mouth. Here, there is not meat, as he said.'

"Sun Buffalo Cow said: 'My Salish, old Coyote drips straight words. Go on a little further to the foot of the cliff by the river. There lies a buffalo that fell from the rock. The meat is good. Take it, and camp by the river. Soon will come a herd to the plain.'

"The people said: 'Our Mother tells straight words.' They traveled toward the foot of the cliff.

"Sun Buffalo Cow ran very fast along the other trail to the top of the cliff. She said: 'I go into (change to) the form of earth buffalo. I will be meat for my Salish.' She jumped headlong from the high rock to the foot of the cliff.

"The people came and saw the dead buffalo. They said: 'Our Mother spoke true words. Here is herd buffalo fallen from the rock. It is warm meat. It is good.'"

Note

From notes given to Bon Whealdon by Lassaw Redhorn, François Skyenna, and Dominic Michell in 1926.

Buffalo Story Myths
Told by: **Harry Burland**
Writer: **Bon I. Whealdon**
Date: October 24, 1941

It appears that our Salish, in common with the other tribes, built up their folklore around the outstanding individuals, animals, and physical objects that constantly occupied their attention.

The buffalo, being the main source of food, clothing, and shelter during innumerable centuries, became the central, all important figure around which their lives and welfare revolved.

Is it to be wondered that this benefactor of the race was soon esteemed as a tribal god, or tutelary spirit being? Gradually the belief was evolved, that this god animated and controlled the herds for the sole benefit of its superior children—the Indians.

To please "Great Buffalo," and thereby obtain additional helps during the hunt, the Flathead offered prayers, sang the buffalo song, and performed ceremonial rites, such as the "Buffalo Dance." The sacred medicine bundle always contained a bone, a piece of horn, and a wisp of hair of the buffalo. The medicine man wore a buffalo tail tied around his waist. Each article was part of an elaborate buffalo ritual, used in invoking the spirit presence of god buffalo, or of the spirits of slain buffalo.

"Buffalo power," being considered supernatural, was appealed to for the healing of the sick, for protection from enemies, and for prophecies regarding the welfare of the individual petitioner and the destiny of the tribal group.

The Indians also invested the buffalo with very human characteristics. Thus their myths reveal a close intimacy between Indian and buffalo, they visit and joke each other, quarrel and conciliate.

These human qualities and capabilities imparted to the buffalo by the Salishans are portrayed in the elements of a very ancient myth. (A version of the myth was told by old Kootenai and Crow.)

"Several young braves were hunting buffalo. One grew weary and started home by a new route. While passing through a ravine, he found a buffalo cow mired down. She appealed to him in Salish for aid in extricating herself and the Indian had compassion. (Here, offensive excerpt deleted.) [Deletion by Whealdon or Montana Writers Project staff.—Bigart Note.] It was during her mating season, and she suffered because of separation from the herd, so she became his "buffalo wife." Later, she bore issue—half Indian, half buffalo. The young brave shared his teepee with both his Indian and buffalo wives, who, at times, jealously quarreled over the favors of their mutual spouse."

****

Again a Blackfoot myth from Clark Wissler and D. C. Duvall, "Mythology of the Blackfeet Indians," *Anthropological Papers of the American Museum of Natural History,* vol. 2, pt. 1 (1908), pp. 36-37, illustrates human powers ascribed to buffalo, as well as the Indian's sense of humor:

Old Man Makes Buffalo Laugh

Old Man looked from Red Deer River over to Little Bow River. He saw some buffalo. He tied up his hair in knots, and crawled along on hands and knees. The sight made the buffalo laugh. One of them laughed himself to death, and the Old Man butchered him.

In the above, we have a blending of myth and truth elements. Prior to the introduction of the horse among the western tribes, buffalo were hunted afoot. Sometimes by using a buffalo robe as a disguise, an Indian hunter was able to approach to within killing distance of a herd. He, with robe draped over him, presented an amusing spectacle, comical enough to almost make a buffalo laugh.

The Indians perpetuated their myths by word of mouth. They delighted in whiling away the long winter evenings in telling tales of the past. The young men listened, and, when they became elderly themselves, they repeated the stories to their children. Often visiting members from other tribes would be present and there was an exchange of legend with the result that today, among widely separated groups, we find versions of the same original tale as myth.

Mostly these tales concerned some unusually important incident or experience in a hunt or battle of the long ago. The main subject was always truthfully adhered to, but through ages of telling, it became enlarged upon; and embellished fragments of other experiences clustered around the central topic.

Some of these myths, so plainly related by older Indians, would prove offensive to the taste of exacting white people. Therefore so much is deleted that they are rendered incomplete.

Sun Buffalo Cow

Told by: **Dominic Michell**
Writer: **Bon I. Whealdon**
Date: November 24, 1942

"A long, long time ago, the herds upon Montana's plains became very sick. Much blood passed with their excrement.

They began to die. Soon only one small herd was left in all the country. These buffalo were very frightened. They said to one another: 'We are not very many. Soon will come the deep snow time. Then the Cree, who are always hungry like wolves, will come upon us to kill every buffalo. What shall we do? What shall we do?'

"Sun Buffalo Cow came to the herd. The buffalo all said: 'Sun Buffalo Cow, you are a very wise mother. Your children sickened and passed blood. Now many are dead. Soon comes the deep snow time. The Cree, who are hungry wolves, will hunt us out, and kill us. What shall we do? What shall we do?'

"Sun Buffalo Cow, who had very good heart for her children, cried many tears. She said: 'My children, I cannot lead you to the Sun Country, (for) you are still earth buffalo. On Flat Willow Creek is camp of my Salish. They are very good people—not hungry wolves like north Indians. They have strong shaman. My people will choose from the herd three young she buffalo who have never mated. Give to one the head-bone piece of a long dead buffalo bull, which you can tell by the horns. Give to one this other robe bundle of sweet smelling grass. Give to one this hair braid from tail of White Buffalo Bull Calf. Let them bear this medicine token to the Salish shaman in camp upon Flat Willow Creek. He will tell my buffalo people what they shall do.' Then came a whirling white cloud over Sun Buffalo Cow. When the buffalo look again, she was swallowed up (disappeared) in the fog.

"Then the buffalo talked on their mother's words. They said: 'Our mother is very wise, (best) we do what our mother told.'

"The three young cows, who had never mated, carried the medicine tokens to Salish camp. The hunters saw them. They were ready with arrows. Then the shaman said: 'It is not permitted to kill the three heifers, who had not had seed in their wombs. They came with supernatural tokens from our mother, Sun Buffalo Cow.'

"The shaman took the head-bone piece (skull). He put it upon clean ground where men had not defecated. He put the sweet smelling grass in its eyes, nose and mouth holes. He made fire in the head-bone piece. Then he stood on the otter robe and held the hair braid from the tail of White Buffalo Bull Calf.

Then his power went into the buffalo bull head-bone piece and it stood up as a live buffalo. It spoke words to the three young cows for their people and for the Salish: 'When the Salish break camp to go to their land Sinyelenin (Flathead), my buffalo people (herd) must follow them to their land. There the snow is not deep, the grass is green. My people will be safe, for my Salish are not hungry wolves like the north Indians. The Cree will say: "The buffalo are gone. We will follow them by their piles of dung heaps." Now, my buffalo people will fill their holes with buffalo grass. Then they will not drop their dung while they travel.' The buffalo filled their holes (rectums) with much dried grass. They followed the Salish across the high mountains. They came to a very good land.

"The shaman said: 'When you pull out the dried grass, much dung will come. We do not want dung all over our prairie. You must all drop it in one place.' The buffalo came to one spot to defecate. It became very high.

"The Salish all said: 'This is a place of defecation. It is a mountain.'"

White Cloud Legend: Buffalo Brings Life to Montana Hunter

Told by: **Peter Pierre, Dominic Michell, and Harry Burland**
Writer: **Bon I. Whealdon**
Date: November 6, 1941

"A long time ago, White Cloud, the Salish medicine man, went with the buffalo hunters. Now all the braves had wives but White Cloud; as no woman would sleep in his teepee, for he was big like a bull. They hunted upon the prairie near Square Butte many weeks, and killed many buffalo. Then the old chief said, 'We have much meat; now we will go back to Spetlemen, for hard winter will come early to this land.'

"The braves laughed at White Cloud, and said: 'Come, hurry, young buffalo bull; the seeds from your bag are now calves in Spetlemen. They want meat for winter.'

Salish Buffalo Legends

"White Cloud replied, '(You) go home; I will come later.'

"He went into his teepee and slept. When morning came snow was in the air. He said: 'I must get my horses, and hurry to catch up with my people.' He looked, but his ponies were gone. Then he saw many new horse tracks. He thought: 'The Piegan came by and stole my horses. Now, when the snow falls no longer, I must cross the mountains on foot.' But the snow fell many days. It was so deep he could not walk in it. He must stay there all winter. His teepee was near Arrow Creek. There was much dead willow. He said: 'I have dried meat, many robes, and wood for my teepee fire. I shall not die.'

"The snow grew deep, then much deeper. Then the nights grew cold, like White Cloud had never seen before. He sat in his teepee. He was very lonely. He made medicine to bring company. Then old Owl came to the willows at night, and he made mock at White Cloud. He called: 'Long cold—much cold. White Cloud sleep; White Cloud die.'

"White Cloud became angry and picked up the wood to throw at Owl, but Quasquee (Blue Jay) flew into the teepee and said: 'Owl wants you to throw all your wood away, so you will freeze. Then he can say, "I am a truth bird; I told (warned) White Cloud he would freeze to death."'

"White Cloud say, 'Blue Jay, you are friend.'

"Then White Cloud took his own frozen dung, and threw at Owl, saying, 'Eat that, old liar, blood-brother of the Piegan.'

"White Cloud sat by the teepee fire many days and nights. Then came the long cold, and the fire did not heat the teepee. The cold came into White Cloud's bones. He said, 'I will lie down on my pallet of robes, before I freeze.' The cold was sharp; it came through the robes and White Cloud slept like the dead. Then the teepee was cold and dark and very still. The death wind (blizzard) blew in snow and filled the teepee.

"Blue Jay came and when he saw that snow had covered his friend, he said, 'I will go and bring Sun Buffalo to White Cloud's teepee.' He flew many, many days until he came to Sun Country. It was very warm. The grass mat was full of flowers. He went into the Big Teepee, then to the hearth and sat down.

"Then Akona (Buffalo god) asked: 'What you want (you) happy little bird?'

"Blue Jay said: 'My friend in the snow country, White Cloud, sleeps in his cold teepee; I came to lead Sun Buffalo to awaken him.'

"Akona said: 'It is now that time. Bring my Sun Buffalo to White Cloud in the snow country.'

"Blue Jay flew to the grass plains in Sun Country. He went to the youngest buffalo cow in the great herd. He said: 'Come, it is now that time to go to the snow country. White Cloud sleeps. You must awaken him.'

"Blue Jay sat upon the Sun Buffalo's head. She ran fast. Her warm breath melted the snow before her. The herds followed behind. After many days, they came to White Cloud's teepee. Sun Buffalo blew into the teepee. The snow went to water and ran away. Soon they saw White Cloud lying there in his robes.

"Owl said: 'White Cloud is all dead.'

"Sun Buffalo Cow replied, 'No, liar, I can awaken him. Take the robes away.' Then she blew her warm breath over White Cloud's bare body very long time. Then his penis jerked and stood straight. Soon he opened his eyes.

"He said: 'Sun Buffalo, you have warmed and stirred life in me. Before I go to my people in Spetlemen; I will give you my medicine bag as thanks.'

"'No,' said Sun Buffalo, 'not your medicine bag, lest without it, the Piegan slay you; but when I breathed upon you, your penis stood up, and my vulva quivered for it, for my womb, without you, is empty.'

"Then White Cloud asked: 'How can this be (accomplished)? You are larger than I. I am not a bull to mount on you.' Then Sun Buffalo lay down and pressed her vulva against him, so he could enter it.

"After many months (moons) Sun Buffalo came to the Big Teepee in Sun Country. Akone said, 'Daughter cow, the calf in your womb is son of White Cloud. It will be good medicine to my people. That my people may respect it, it shall have a white robe, for its father is of the Snow Country.'"

Note

Interview with Peter Pierre, medicine man, and Dominic Michell and Henry Burland.

White Cloud Saved

Told by: **Peter Pierre**
Writer: **Bon I. Whealdon**
Date: November 12, 1941

"Long, long ago our first people came from land of spruce trees to the big lake in Sinyelemin (Flathead Lake and Valley). There was much shiny fish in the water. Then our people moved to Spetlemin (place of much bitter root) and began to cross high mountains to kill buffalo.

"Came the time of leaf falling (autumn), White Cloud say to Little Snow Wolf, 'Son take many arrows; we go.' They walked *many* days. They came to the dry grass country. White Cloud was much tired. He spread down upon the ground. He sleep.

"Little Snow Wolf say: 'My father (winter) spread over the ground, he is cold, he sleep. I must hunt alone.'

"Little Snow Wolf drew close to Sun Country. It was much warm. The Sun-fire pulled out his skin-water (sweat). He was much sick (weak). He said: 'I must go back to my father.' He walk, he fall, he sleep.

"Sun Buffalo Cow say to her child, White Buffalo Bull Calf: 'Your brother, Little Snow Wolf, sleeps from sickness (weakness); go, carry your brother to his father's teepee.'

"Then came White Buffalo Bull Calf. He ran to Little Snow Wolf. He smelled at him. He saw the tribe mark on Little Snow Wolf's moccasin. He said: 'Little Snow Wolf is member of my father's people. I must carry my brother to the teepee of my father.' He put Little Snow Wolf upon his back. He started to snow country.

"Little Snow Wolf awoke. He said: 'White Buffalo Bull Calf, where go?'

"White Buffalo Bull Calf say (to) him: 'Sun fire caused too much sweating and make you sleep. I come. Tribe mark on moccasin tell me Little Snow Wolf is man of my father's people. I must carry my brother man to teepee of his father.'

"Little Snow Wolf say: 'How can we be brothers (since) White Buffalo Calf you buffalo, (while) Little Snow Wolf is man?'

"White Buffalo Bull Calf say: 'My mother, Sun Buffalo Cow tell (me) she go to snow country; find frozen man of your mark (tribe). She blow her warm breath on man. Man come to life. For thanks he put his seed in her. I came out of her womb.'

"Little Snow Wolf say: 'Carry me to teepee of my father. We put heat on him (as) he awake. We tell him White Buffalo Bull Calf words. (If) he say words of White Buffalo Bull Calf are lies like talk of Piegan, (then) Little Snow Wolf (will) put his arrow in you!'

"Many days, they came (to, or in) teepee of White Cloud. He lay cold. He was stiff. Little Snow Wolf say: 'My father is stiff—dead; he can not melt into life.' Little Snow Wolf cried many times.

"White Buffalo Bull Calf say: 'Make teepee fire, then make little fire (altar fire in teepee). Little brother, Little Snow Wolf, drop your warm tears on your father. I blow sun breath on his life-stick (penis). We melt his stiffness (frozen condition).' (Then) new buffalo grass came on the prairie of White Cloud's belly. Green slopes came on the two mountains of his seat. From his valley ran much water. The herds came to eat.

"White Cloud stood up. He say to Little Snow Wolf: 'Son, why (came) White Buffalo Bull Calf in my teepee?' Little Snow Wolf tell the words of White Buffalo Bull Calf.

"White Cloud say: 'Son man, son calf, it is true word (you) are brother seed from my life stick.'"

Salish Buffalo Legends

"I Will Be Meat for My Salish"

Chapter 3

Buffalo Behavior

Swimming Habits of Buffalo
Told by: **Tony Barnaby, son-in-law of Michael Pablo**
Writer: **Bon I. Whealdon**
Date: September 19, 1941

"Like my deceased father-in-law, Michael Pablo, I honestly think his buffalo derived a real pleasure from a plunge into the Pend Oreille [Flathead] River. Then, too the cool water must have temporarily given them a pleasing respite from the swarms of flies that infested our plains and mountains.

"At times they would graze upon the low foothills west of the old Sloan Ranch. Perhaps, other days they would range high among the timber. When disturbed by some prowling forest animal, or irritated by the flies, they would come streaking down the long, grassy slopes. As they approached the river, the combined sounds of their deep-toned bellowing and pounding hooves created a din deafening to human ears. The sight that followed is unforgettable.

"Without any checking of speed, they sprang from the high bank into the swiftly flowing Pend Oreille [Flathead], splashing spray into the air. For a few moments, a welcome silence hovered over the scene. The bulls treaded the lead. The cows, with calves by their sides, swam in the wake of the males. Their massive, dark heads, held rather high above water, always made me think of an old painting wherein prehistoric animals were pictured, emerging from a palm fringed lake of an ancient period.

"Sometimes, without the least visible provocation, I've seen that herd stampede from prairie to river, which they would swim from bank to bank, and then either up or down stream a long distance."

Buffalo Habits
Told by: **Andrew Stinger**
Writer: **Bon I. Whealdon**
Date: October 28, 1941

"A buffalo likes, in fact must have, the almost constant company of its kind. If one becomes separated from its mates, it is restless and inclined to be sullen and dangerous until it rejoins its herd.

"I think the cows are even more attached to their calves then are the domestic cows. For the protection movement [sic]; and woe be unto an intruder. Even in swimming and wallowing, the calves were near their mothers' sides.

"Contrary to a current idea, our buffalo in the Flathead Valley did not roam in one large herd; and I presume that was because there were no mass migrations during summer and winter, as had been the habit of the Plains bison. Here, a leader bull, and possibly a younger aspirant to that station, would head a band, composed of some 20 or 25 cows and calves. This was but one of many similar size groups. In this arrangement, nature made no mistakes. A small band had a better chance to graze, there was less strife among the males, and should something happen to the older bull, the junior member became leader."

Wallowing Habits of Buffalo
Told by: **Tony Barnaby**
Writer: **Bon I. Whealdon**
Date: October 13, 1941

"During the height of the fly season, two or three bands of buffalo would gather at a common wallowing spot. Once I was fortunate enough to see just how the buffalo made a wallow. I sat unobserved upon a ridge and watched them pawing deep holes in a miry ravine. When this work was completed, they began wallowing in the muck. After they had rolled to their hearts' content, they sought higher, drier ground. At a short distance they presented a queer spectacle. They appeared like huge mud balls slowly rolling around about the prairie. Temporarily the coatings of moist clay afforded them protection from the swarms of tormenting flies."

The Buffalo Calf
Told by: **Lassaw Redhorn**
Writer: **Bon I. Whealdon**
Date: December 5, 1941

"Yes, I knew Indian Samuel very well. I've camped and visited with him many times. I've seen the calves he brought to Sinyelemin (Flathead Valley). Whether he captured them himself, or whether some other Indian gave them to him, that I do not know, as he did not tell me how he got them. Anyhow, a buffalo calf is very easily captured.

"I will tell you something about the buffalo calf. When it is young, it looks very much like a tame calf. Its robe is red, and it is a very pretty little animal. Were you to place it among tame calves in a pasture, I am sure most people today—both whites and young Indians—would pass by and say, 'This man has very nice range stuff.' During autumn, the buffalo calf changes its red coat for one of brown, which will be its permanent color, though with the seasons it will vary from very dark brown to almost black.

"When I was a boy, I went with a very strong party of Flathead and Pend Oreille hunters for the tribal hunt in the Yellowstone River country. We camped there all summer. Two times our hunters came riding back to camp with buffalo calves following close at the horses' heels. We children were very pleased. We asked the hunters how they captured them, and why the calves were so tame that they followed the horses. Indians like to joke with their children and to mystify them, so they answered: 'We have very strong buffalo medicine powers; we command the calves to follow and they obey.' Then as we grew older, the men showed us why the calves followed them.

"When a great herd of buffalo is frightened by the approach of hunters upon horses, its sweeps away over the prairie. The very young calves cannot keep up with the older buffalo. Separated from their mothers, they try to hide. They drop to their front knees, and try to conceal their heads among clumps of grass and sagebrush. They close their eyes and feel very secure. The poor frightened things look very silly on their front knees and trying to hide their heads, while they stand on their hind legs with their rumps high in the air. They will stay in this position for a very long time, or until the mother cows, who have escaped slaughter, come back for them. The little ones, who are orphans, wander about until the coyotes and wolves get them.

"Often the hunters on their return trip, would ride up to the kneeling calves and, dismounting, walk to their heads and seize them. For a brief while the calves put up a desperate struggle, but finding their efforts futile, are submissive to their captors. If an Indian wished a calf to follow him, he would place a hand over its eyes, while he breathed strongly, several times, into its quivering nose. The little calf thus became familiar with the scent of the hunter, to whom it instantly transferred its affections, following his horse like a camp dog.

"During later years, I have often done the same thing with fawns that had lost their mothers. I, after fondling their heads, have had them follow me for several miles.

"So I have found that many things that our old people believed were workings of a strange medicine power, are very natural things, and not mysterious at all."

Note
Notes from many interviews with Lassaw Redhorn, intelligent old Pend Oreille.

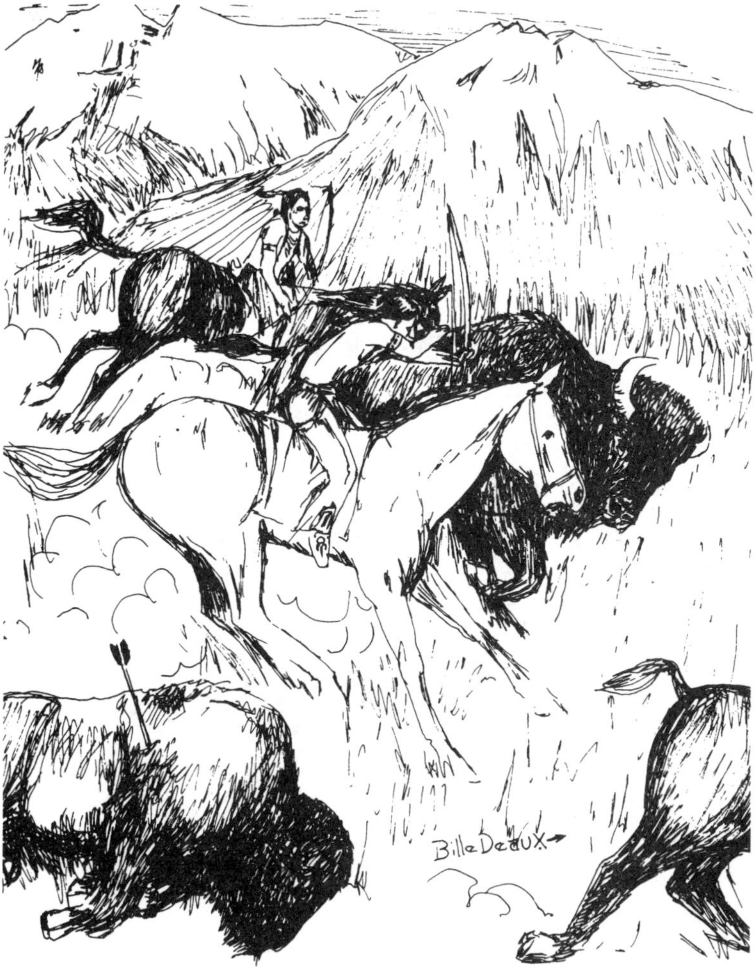

"I Will Be Meat for My Salish"

Part II

Flathead Indian Reservation Buffalo

Michel Pablo's and Charles Allard's buffalo herd on the Flathead Reservation was a critical link in preventing the extinction of the American bison. Pablo, Allard, and Samuel Walking Coyote are justly famous for their roles in North American conservation history.

Chapter 4 of this volume is an excerpt from an unfinished book-length Montana Writers Project manuscript, "The Story of the Buffalo" by W. A. Bartlett. This manuscript synthesizes the material collected by Montana Writers Project field workers about the Pablo-Allard herd in contrast to the other chapters that reproduce surviving field worker reports. No biographical information about Bartlett was located, but he was hired by the Montana Writers Project to author the project's book about the buffalo. This portion of the Bartlett manuscript is included because it summarizes the historical evidence from the interviews and other sources about the Pablo-Allard herd. The manuscript provides a context for better understanding the interviews in chapters 5 through 8, some of which Bartlett quoted from at length. Since this was a draft manuscript, all references to published sources or Montana Writers Project research reports were checked for accuracy and corrected. In addition the text was edited for typographical and grammatical errors. The footnotes were written by Robert Bigart from notes in the unfinished manuscript.

Chapter 5 presents a number of different—and at times conflicting—versions of the origins of the Pablo-Allard herd that were gathered by the Montana Writers Project. These interviews are offered as sources, and the reader will need to evaluate and decide which ones are accurate.

Chapter 6 contains interviews about the Pablo-Allard herd on the reservation. Chapter 7 includes stories about the roundup of the herd between 1907 and 1909. The forced opening of the Flathead Reservation to white settlers ended the free range on which the buffalo relied. Michel Pablo tried to sell the herd to the United States government but was turned down. Fortunately the Canadian government was interested in preserving the buffalo and purchased the herd. This meant, however, that the wild buffalo had to be rounded up and shipped to Canada by railroad. The ensuing rodeo was a big event on the reservation and resulted in extensive coverage by newspaper reporters and photographers.

Chapter 8 gives those interviews that talk about the Flathead Reservation buffalo after the sale to Canada. The publicity from the roundup and political support from Senator Joseph Dixon of Montana made possible the establishment of the National Bison Range on part of the former range of the Pablo-Allard buffalo herd. The American Bison Society raised money to purchase buffalo to start a new herd.

Chapter 4

The Pablo-Allard Herd: Origin

by W. A. Bartlett

The history of the conservation of the American bison is a story full of drama, thrills, self-sacrifice, and many unpublished interesting anecdotes. It is the history of the Pablo-Allard herd of the Flathead Indian Reservation in western Montana. From the foundation of this herd of bison in 1878 to the time it was sold in 1908 for the largest single sum ($200,000) ever paid for live bison, runs a narrative that combines Indians' traditions and love of the buffalo, their religious beliefs, clever commercial deals, national negligence, international bargaining, and the thrilling exploits of cowboys. It is a 30-year drama of western Montana in which the buffalo, staging their peculiar, unpredictable habits, play the leading role, with Indians, cowboys, and financiers appearing in the most spectacular scenes. Like the story of *Black Beauty*, which created public sentiment for better treatment of the horse; and *Uncle Tom's Cabin,* which aroused sympathy for freedom of the slaves, so the last scenes in this buffalo drama were responsible for the establishment of the first national buffalo preserve and a definite national policy for the preservation of large game animals.

In the conservation of the American bison the Pablo-Allard herd furnished the foundation stock from which the most virile bands of bison have sprung—those constantly increasing herds of the National Bison Range, the Yellowstone National Park, the Crow Indian Agency, Alaska, and thousands of plains bison in Canada. The six little buffalo calves, which a homesick Indian captured in 1878 in northern Montana near the Canadian border to appease the punishment for the violation of the religious beliefs of his tribe, can now number their descendants by the thousands in 38 different states of the union and several Canadian provinces. God works in a mysterious way, His wonders to perform.

The origin of the Pablo herd of buffalo has been the subject of various fables and half-truths which confused locations, names and dates. It has been printed that Mr. Pablo started his herd from thirty buffalo captured on Wild Horse Island in Flathead Lake, but the most reliable accounts prove that this herd was started at a much later date.[1] Several reliable authors credit the catching of four buffalo calves which started the herd to a Pend d'Oreille Indian named Walking Coyote, commonly known among his people on the reservation as Samuel. He was also known as Hunting Dog, and Charles Aubrey reported that he was known among the Blackfeet as Short Coyote.[2] Joe MacDonald, a brother of the well known fur trader of the Flathead Valley, says he knew Indian Samuel, or Sam Wells, very well; but he never heard him called Walking Coyote.[3] He says Samuel had four buffalo calves, two bulls and two heifers, which he kept confined in a small pasture, and later let them feed about his home: "I saw them many times, grazing near the Post. I saw them during their mating season and remember the local excitement when the two buffalo cows gave birth to calves. Charles Allard, Sr., and Michael Pablo bought Sam's herd when it numbered 12 or 13 head. I have heard that they purchased a few others through different sources. They increased rapidly."[4]

Charles Aubrey gives an interesting account of the family and religious incidents that induced Indian Samuel to capture these bison calves. Aubrey had an Indian trading post on the Marias River, a winter range for the bison, and a favorite hunting ground of the Indians:

> Among the Pend d'Oreille Indians who made up the hunting party from across the mountains, was an ambitious, bright, middle-aged man—of the warrior class, not a chief—whose Christian name was Sam. He was known to the Blackfeet as Short Coyote. He was a typical Pend d'Oreille, with the economical turn of those Indians as gathered from their early Christian instructors, Fathers De Smet and Ravalli. I often met Sam in the way of trade, and

he indicated more than ordinary friendship for me, caused perhaps by my fairness in trade. My interpreter for the Blackfeet was a three-quarter blood Blackfoot, Baptiste Champaigne. His father was the noted Michel Champaigne, trader and interpreter for the American Fur Company.

Baptiste's wife was a sister of Yellow Wolf, a Blackfoot warrior, still living here. She had a niece whose name was Mi-sum-mi-mo-na, and who being rather a comely girl, had attracted the attention of Sam. The Pend d'Oreille Sam made propositions to her kinsfolk, Yellow Wolf, Champaigne and his wife that he be permitted to marry Mis-sum-mi-mo-na, and offered for her sixteen head of good horses. The offer being very tempting, she became his wife. A short time afterward Baptiste gave me the story of the affair. I told him very frankly that he had made a mistake. He asked my reasons. I said to him: "You are a strong Catholic and your Church does not permit polygamous marriages."

By the rules and laws regulating marriage among the Pend d'Oreilles, Sam was punishable by both fine and flogging. The punishment is carried out by the soldier band of the Pend d'Oreilles. Baptiste was worried over my view of the marriage. Sam's Pend d'Oreille wife was very much opposed to his second marriage, and appealed to me to talk with him and tell him that he must not go crazy, that the Pend d'Oreilles were taught to have but one wife, while the Blackfeet could have any number they could buy and support.

In course of time Sam's first wife made so many objections, and so continually quarreled with him over his second marriage, that there was no peace in the family. By early spring (1878) feeling had risen to such a condition that Sam shot and wounded his first wife. It was a flesh wound in the shoulder. She was still asserting the rights of Christian marriage. She showed great love and affection for Sam, which he did not appreciate or reciprocate. Conditions were such that the Blackfoot wife, though fond of excitement and war, could not endure the continual strife, and found life in Sam's lodge unbearable.

When Baptiste spoke to me about his niece's troubles, I informed him that from an Indian point of view she was simply a piece of merchandise, sold for value received, and his interference would not be permitted. To Baptiste affairs now assumed a serious turn, as he feared for the life of his niece.

In the course of a few days, Sam, whom I had not seen for some time, called on me. I found him in the condition called by the Indians, "my heart is bad." He had his gun out of its cover and his blanket off. This in an Indian means war. I noted at once that there was a crisis in his affairs, and I signed him to sit down. I sat down beside him, knowing that if he wanted to make a gun play, which I apprehended from his actions, I would be close to him, and could close with him and give him an even showdown for the gun. I reasoned with him in the sign language, reminding him that he was alone among the Blackfeet, his people all having gone back home across the mountains. I told him he had made a mistake, but there was time yet for him to make it right, and advised him to come back in two days and I would tell him what I thought best. What I wanted was time, for a wild Indian in his war paint, mad and wanting to kill some one, is a bad customer to argue with. Sam departed without ceremony. He was faithful to my request and returned in two days' time.

In the meantime I had a talk with my interpreter, Champaigne. I found he had counseled with his wife and had advocated a separation of his niece and Sam. This fact had been communicated to Sam, and led him, in his now desperate frame of mind, to desire to kill Champaigne, and this was the object of his visit to my store.

When Sam returned I found him in a somewhat better frame of mind. I said to him, "When do you cross the mountains to your people?" He informed me that he was lonesome, and wanted to go, but he feared he would be punished by the fathers of St. Ignatius Mission. He had been married at this mission in the Flathead Valley. I carefully went over his affairs and impressed on him the fact that he had violated the law of his people. Now he must be careful and keep out of further trouble. I thought there was still a chance to make peace with the soldier band of his tribe by getting a pardon through the fathers. To that end I would assist him by giving him a letter to Father Ravalli, stating that he (Sam) was not a drunken or lazy Indian. I also suggested that in connection with my letter he make a peace offering to the fathers, in the hope it would lighten the punishment for marrying the Blackfoot woman. He told me he had nothing to give, and he could not stop the punishment, which I found he dreaded very much. I then suggested that as he was a good hunter, and expert horseman, and could handle a lasso well, he rope some buffalo calves—now nearly a year old—hobble them and keep them with my milch cows. He could use my corrals until they were gentle, he could then drive them across the mountains by the Cadotte Pass, and give them as a peace offering to the fathers at the mission. He looked at me in surprise and doubt. I then showed him that as there were no buffalo in the Flathead country, I thought the fathers would appreciate the gift. He at once said he would try my plan. I encouraged him to go to work at once, and soon saw him arranging for a hunting trip.

Next day I made a visit to his lodge and found him and his Pend d'Oreille wife hard at work, and both in a very pleasant humor. I asked in the sign language of the wife, "Where is the Blackfoot woman?" She informed me in a very serious manner that when the Blackfeet had broken camp, her people had taken her away. I then asked her to help Sam all she could. She smiled and said she would. I asked Sam, "When will you be ready for your trip?" He answered "In two sleeps."

In answer to my inquiries as to how he proposed to handle the buffalo, he told me he would catch the young buffalo; he would then picket each by one leg at the place where he caught it. He would then take a blanket, peg it down at the ground at the outer limit of the picket line. I asked him why he did this. He replied it would attract the buffalo's attention and keep him quiet; by smelling the blanket it would become accustomed to the smell of man, and would not be alarmed at his approach. He would catch and handle two at one time on the prairie. They would then be driven in and kept with the milch cows.

Sam was successful on his first hunt and soon drove in two fine calves, then, April, 1878, nearly yearling buffalo—a heifer and a bull. The heifer was loose, the bull side-hobbled. The milch cows did not take kindly to the buffalo, but the buffalo persisted in being friendly. They finally made friends, for after a while the cows ceased to regard them as a curiosity, and seemed to enjoy their presence. Sam rested a few days after his first trip, his wife joining him in telling me the story of the wild chase and the fierce struggles with their captives. The hunt was far away, as the buffalo were already working to the summer range on the Saskatchewan. This would now cause some change in his plans. Being alone, he was afraid of the enemy—the Indians of the North. He would only risk one more hunt, and informed me I could look for him in eight sleeps. If he did not return then, he had been attacked by some war party. In that event he hoped I would make some effort to look him up. When I got up the next morning Sam was gone.

True to his promise, he returned at the end of eight days with five young buffalo—two bulls and three heifers. Each buffalo was head and foot hobbled; the head and front foot tied together, with a skin strap two feet long. Each bull was dragging a long lariat, so as to be easily caught for night picketing. Sam was well pleased to find the first two buffalo so contented with the domestic cows. The milch cows objected as before, but the new arrivals took kindly to their new-found friends. Sam told me they had met with no accident. He had worked hard—like a white man, as he expressed it—the rope skinning his hands many times. One could never tell when a buffalo would jump for liberty. He told me of killing one heifer, which he would have liked to save. She had a very fine, bright coat. In a hard chase along the side of a steep coulee, he singled her out of a bunch of cows. He threw his rope, and the noose settled on her neck. His horse, a powerful roan, settled for the shock. In snubbing, he gave her too much rope, and in the fall, which came an instant later, this fine heifer's neck was broken.

His wife advised him to quit now. They already had five on the last hunt, and she did not like the signs brought out by the death of this fine animal. She said to him, "This means we must stop."

Sam herded his buffalo with the milk stock for five days, resting and making arrangements for his trip across the mountains. He was feeling satisfied with his work, and hopeful that his peace offering would be accepted. He told me of his route of travel, and that he would be fifteen sleeps on the way home. Taking a small memorandum book from a parfleche, he showed me where he had six straight marks and then a cross for Sunday. He told me he did not want to start on his trip home on Sunday, and wished to know the day of the week, as he had lost his reckoning. I put him right, and he said he would start on the following Monday.

His buffalo were doing well, and were becoming quite docile. All preparations were made for his departure, and he talked hopefully of getting safely across the mountains. He always impressed me as being an Indian of marked determination, and at no time did it occur to me that he would not succeed in his effort.

On Monday he bade me a cordial good-bye, passing out, his wife and pack horses in the lead. They had discarded the travois with which they usually traveled, saying they could handle the buffalo better with her as a rider. Sam brought up the rear, the buffalo following the pack horses. The three bulls were head and foot hobbled, the four heifers loose; seven head in all is my recollection of the bunch.

Of the trip to the Teton River, to the Sun River, to the Dearborn and up that stream to the Cadotte Pass I have heard no word; of the crossing of these streams at this season, of the trip over the main range, down the Blackfoot River, all trace is probably forever lost. Through Indian sources I afterward learned that on the way over by some accident one bull became disabled and died. Sam arrived safely in the Flathead without further accident to the other buffalo. I also afterward learned, through Indian sources, that immediately upon his arrival upon the reservation he was arrested and severely flogged, by order of the soldier band of his own tribe of Indians. As I understand the story, Sam had no time or opportunity to meet the fathers and tender his peace offering.

In course of time I heard of Sam's death, not in battle as a warrior, but passing away peacefully in his lodge or cabin. His wife followed him some time after.[5]

E. Douglas Branch in his volume, *The Hunting of the Buffalo*, credited Walking Coyote with driving 30 buffalo from Alberta to the Flathead Valley in 1880.[6] But Aubrey's account appears to be more authentic: that the Indian started from his trading post with seven buffalo calves in 1878, and after losing one, arrived on the other side of the mountains with six head. Other residents of the Flathead Mission at that time reported from four to six head of buffalo calves in Sam's herd. It is quite possible that some of Sam's seven calves were captured in Canada, as he was gone for eight days from Aubrey's post on his last hunt, and may have wandered into Alberta, but the most of them were undoubtedly caught in Montana. Sam ranged his calves ten miles below the St. Ignatius Mission, between Crow and Post Creeks, until 1882 or 1883, at which time they had increased to 12 or 13 head, when he sold them to Michael Pablo and Charles Allard, part-blood Indians who had stock ranches on the reservation.[7] They are reported to have paid Sam $250 a head, and moved them to the open range on the western side of the valley.

When his buffalo were gone, residents of the district lost interest in Sam. He is reported to have lived there with his first wife until his death in 1886, and left little except a small herd of horses. Tom Jones, in his history of this herd, wrote that Sam didn't enjoy his prosperity very long; that he went on a spree to Missoula, and was there found dead under a bridge.[8] J. B. Monroe, a rancher of the Sweet Grass Hills, stated that Sam lived on Crow Creek until his death in 1886, which would be several years after he sold his buffalo, and that his widow afterwards married Alex Finlay, a mixed-blood Indian.[9] At any rate Indian Samuel's second and unfortunate marriage to a Blackfoot squaw and the resultant family troubles, brought about the foundation of the most valuable bison herd in the country, and proved to be a good investment for the time and energy he had spent in their capture.

The detailed account of the origin of the Pablo herd as given by Charles Aubrey is substantiated by other evidence. Chief Mose Michell, of the Flatheads, said he knew Indian Samuel well, and remembered when he brought four calves from the other side of the mountains, and went to see them several times. He said,

> Our old Pen d'Oreille and Flathead Indians were much pleased that we had buffalo in our country, as the herds across the mountains had been killed. I heard some old Indians tell, that once, our tribesmen had been very angry

with Samuel because he took as wife, a woman not of our nation. And that Samuel then left us, and went to Sun River. He was there several years, and became lonely and unhappy because he could not come home. His wife told him, "Samuel, the buffalo, which your people love, will soon be all gone. They are sad because of that. You capture what calves you can, and take them to your people. When they see them they will be very glad, and they will forgive you that you married not one of their women." So Samuel did as his wife told him.

When the Indians heard that Samuel and his woman had brought back buffalo calves, they were happy and made a feast for the Samuels. My father, Chief Charley Michell, of the Pen d'Oreilles, arose and talked to the people, saying, "Our brother is back with a gift for us. Now we shall bring gifts to his teepee."[10]

The late Andrew Stinger, one of Michael Pablo's partner's in the buffalo and cattle business, said he often heard Mr. Pablo refer to buffalo he obtained from Indian Samuel, and again alluded to the same band as "the Walking Coyote buffalo." Samuel Wells and Walking Coyote were one and the same Indian, according to Mr. Stinger. He said it was common for an Indian to be known by several different names given him by different tribes or groups with whom he associated.[11] Tony Barnaby, son-in-law of Michael Pablo, gave Indian Samuel credit for starting the herd, and bringing them over the mountains. He added an interesting bit of information about this journey; that just before starting a Piegan Indian gave him a very young, half-famished buffalo bull calf. Its mother had been killed and it was too young to feed on grass. At first Sam did not think he would be able to save this feeble addition to his precious band. In desperation he tried an experiment. In his pack-string was a mare whose recently born colt had died. To Sam's delighted surprise, this gentle, low-built mare permitted the orphan calf to suckle. He made frequent stops to take the bull calf from off its foster-mother's back, and then let it feed upon her warm milk.[12]

Tom Jones, in his history of the buffalo herd of the Flathead Valley, wrote that when Walking Coyote's buffalo increased to such an extent that they became a burden, Duncan

MacDonald, the Hudson Bay fur trader, made negotiations to buy them in 1884, but that C. A. Allard, a reservation ranchman and shrewd, capable businessman, realized the value of the bison as a financial investment, and outbid MacDonald for their possession. Allard succeeded in interesting his fellow ranchman and friend of his boyhood days, Michael Pablo, and the two entered into a partnership and bought ten of Walking Coyote's thirteen buffalo as a speculation, paying $2,500 for them.[13]

Old-time residents of the Flathead Valley, in reporting Walking Coyote's capture and sale of the bison calves from memory, differ somewhat as to dates, prices paid for them, and the number of calves he started with, and the number of buffalo he sold to Allard and Pablo. Dave Couture, of Camas Prairie, recalls that a Flathead Indian named Feenon Finley and his wife brought in the first buffalo calves in 1882 or 1883. This date is five years later than that reported by Aubrey.[14] The four calves were placed on the Finley ranch at the mouth of Mission Creek, near the present town of Dixon, and that later when the herd had increased to 25 or 30, they were sold to Allard and Pablo. Although the names and dates differ, these were probably the Walking Coyote calves, as other old-timers have reported that Samuel "ranged his calves on the Finlay Ranch part of the time," and his widow afterward married Alex Finlay.[15]

Two descriptions of the sale of the buffalo to Pablo and Allard carry an incident that makes the Finley sale and the Walking Coyote sale identical. Zephyr (Swift) Courville recollects that the old-timers reported the amount agreed upon was $1,600 (not $2,500) and that the cash was spread out on a blanket in an open space in the Finley pasture; Finley like most Indians, demanded the money in cold cash. Hearing a noise in the brush while the deal was being consummated, the participants hastily fled, fearing a holdup, but forgot to take the money with them. However, it turned out to be a false alarm, and the deal was completed to the satisfaction of all the parties concerned.[16] Another version of the same incident was that after the money was spread on a blanket in bills to pay Indian Samuel, a rabbit ran by, and the buffalo deal was delayed while the participants went in pursuit of the small animal. The money was not disturbed during their absence. As stated above, as

Indians were known by several different names by different groups, it is reasonable to believe that Courville remembered him as Finley, his Indian friends called him Walking Coyote, and the white men knew him as Indian Samuel.

Antoine Morigeau, an Indian who moved into the Flathead Valley as a boy with his parents from Fort Colville, Washington, in 1859, in an interview (Sept. 3, 1941) recalled Indian Samuel's trip over the mountains with four buffalo calves in 1873, and the sale of the small herd to Michael Pablo in 1884. He said, "Indian Samuel succeeded in capturing four calves. He brought them back upon pack-ponies. Now, some of my friends say 'two calves,' but I counted them, there were four—two heifers and two bulls. Samuel kept a close guard over his young buffalo. Every Indian in the valley, believing these to be the last ones, aided in their protection. They were permitted to roam wherever fancy led them, but always there was an Indian rider in their vicinity. It seemed but a few years until Samuel's buffalo had increased to 12 head. Thrifty Michael Pablo, during his rides through the valley, often noticed the animals. Once in my hearing, he remarked to Samuel, 'We have thousands of acres covered with native grasses, steams of pure water, high mountains shielding the valley against severe winters. Above all else, Indians who love the shaggy brutes. Yes, our valley will be the safe home for the buffalo.' Inspired by this vision, he quickly persuaded Samuel to sell him the 12 head. Later Charles Allard, who had acquired a herd, put his with Pablo's. So, for a while, the two friends were partners."

This old Indian made Pablo the prime mover in acquiring the small herd, while other authorities assert that Charles Allard made the deal, and took Pablo in as a partner. His statement that Allard had previously acquired a few buffalo, is interesting. There were other rumors that Sam's herd was increased from other sources. One of these is reported by Joseph Ford, who said that Pablo and Allard had a start in raising buffalo before Walking Coyote arrived with his calves. He said that in 1874, Jock Miller, who had a ranch on the Teton River, below the Old Agency, now Choteau in Teton County, captured three buffalo calves in the Teton Basin, near Freezeout and took them to his ranch. They were very young and he fed them on cow's milk until they were old enough to live on grass. His brother-in-law Jacob Smith, had a ranch on Smith Creek, a tributary of the South Fork of Sun River. His range was between Smith Creek and Ford Creek, and here the buffalo were ranged with the cattle until they were three years old. About this time Jacob Smith tried to sell the two buffalo cows and one bull to Samuel Ford for $300.

Samuel Ford had a herd of several hundred cattle and thought the buffalo would not be a good investment and would be a detriment to his plans. Charley Allard was quite a speculator and dealer in livestock at that time, and on one of his trips saw the buffalo and dealt for them. As Jock Miller was about ready to drive a bunch of cattle to the Flathead country, through the Lewis and Clark or Cadotte Pass, Allard threw the buffalo in with Miller's herd of cattle, and they were driven into the Flathead country by Jock Miller, Samuel Ford and others in 1877. The buffalo were offered for sale to Alex Matt and others, who did not care to take the risk of keeping them as they were unbranded and might be considered as public property. Michael Pablo, a part Mexican and Blackfoot Indian, had stock on the Mud Creek range, so Charley Allard made some kind of a deal with him to take the buffalo. Joseph Ford claims that these three buffalo became the nucleus of the Pablo herd.[17] As Aubrey reported that Samuel Wells, or Walking Coyote, brought his calves over the mountains in April 1878, it is quite possible that the bison which Antoine Morigeau reported were added to the herd which Pablo purchased from Wells, were the same bison that Allard, Smith and Miller brought into the Flathead Valley in 1877.

Another version of the origin of the Pablo-Allard herd comes from Frank Nelson, a carpenter employed by the government on the Crow Indian Reservation. He reports that during the late seventies, two full-blood Indians of the Flathead tribe (names forgotten) were hired to take a bunch of cows to the North Bend country at the extreme upper part of the reservation for delivery to a white man who had settled there. The Indian men with their families started on the trip, taking their time, and before they reached their destination, they encountered a very heavy snowstorm, which turned into a blizzard.

Both the cattle and the Indian families suffered much from cold and hardship, and finally decided to make camp until the storm blew over. The camp was close to where a small bunch of buffalo also were found, having escaped the buffalo hunters who were making a clean sweep of the bison at that time. Some cattle calves were born and died, adding to their difficulties. The Indian men took it upon themselves to substitute the dead calves with buffalo calves from bison cows that they had killed for food. This was done, no doubt, to relieve the full udders of the living milk cows.

They were on the road for forty days, and when they at last arrived at their destination, there were only twelve buffalo calves and eight cows left of the thirty head they had started with. In time the buffalo calves grew and increased in number, but the owners found that they were difficult to tame like cattle. The herd was then sold to two Flathead Indians, Michael Pablo and Charles Allard.[18]

All these records as to the origin of the Pablo-Allard herd agree on the main fact that these two bison conservationists were constantly on the search for live buffalo, and never passed up an opportunity to buy any of these rare animals.

Walking Coyote's trip over the mountains with his buffalo calves was described by Charles Aubrey and others as being one of great difficulty as he had to cross many streams that were then swollen by spring flood waters. His route was recorded as being over Cadotte Pass, and down the Blackfoot River, which would have taken him by the present sites of Ovando and Missoula. Joseph Ford said they drove a bunch of cattle and buffalo over the "Lewis and Clark or Cadotte Pass," which was in the seventies the main pass over the mountains. This pass is located northwest of Wolf Creek, and connects with the head waters of the Blackfoot. Five miles southeast of this pass is the Rogers Pass, through which a proposed highway may connect Lincoln with Augusta and Simms, Montana.

Martin S. Garretson, in his book, *The American Bison*, wrote that Walking Coyote caught his four calves "on the Milk River near where the town of Buffalo, Montana, now stands."[19] This must be an error, as the town of Buffalo is located in central Montana, a hundred and fifty miles from the Milk River, on the headwaters of the Judith River. The reference was probably meant as "Buffalo Lake," in Glacier County near the Canadian boundary, which would coincide with the district where Charles Aubrey reported Walking Coyote went in search of the calves. Aubrey's camp was on the Marias River which heads in the southern part of Glacier County, and the Indian went north in search of the calves.

Andrew Garcia, an old time buffalo hunter, who married a Nez Perce woman and hunted with the Indians, furnishes another report as to the origin of the Pablo-Allard herd of buffalo. He says that when the Indians of the Flathead Valley went with their families over the mountains to hunt buffalo, they often killed the cows and left the young calves motherless and stranded. The squaws, feeling sorry for the little calves, caught them and put them with their horse herds, where they suckled the mares until they could eat grass. They followed the horses back to the Flathead and started tame bison herds, which were later sold to Pablo and Allard. He said that the Kootenays, who lived on the west side of the divide, had more bison calves than any other of the Flathead tribes.[20]

"Many-Tail-Feathers," a Blackfoot Indian, has laid claim to the honor of catching the buffalo calves which started the Pablo bison herd, although he furnished no dates to prove that his captures predated those of Walking Coyote. In an interview printed in *The Plains Plainsman* (April 29, 1920) he said it was customary for the Indians of the Flathead Valley to bring buffalo calves alive back from their hunts, and rear them in their camps. He said he raised several and afterwards sold them to Michael Pablo.[21]

The Pablo-Allard Herd: Care and Growth

Little has been written about the growth and care of the Pablo-Allard herd of bison from the time it was started with ten or twelve buffalo in 1884 up to the time in 1896 when it was divided by the death of Charles A. Allard, one of the co-partners. Then Michael Pablo retained his half of the 300 buffalo, which in ten years increased to more than 700, when they were sold to the Canadian government. As long as they were safe in the Indians' care nobody worried about them, but when they were taken to a friendly, but foreign, country a general protest was aroused. They never missed their sweet-voiced songs until the birds had flown. Then they received plenty of publicity. Unlike the weather, everybody began to talk about buffalo, and some even did something about it, with the result that a national policy was established for saving the remaining herds under government control.

The history of this herd cannot be written without some knowledge of the men who nourished it and guarded it for so many years. Michael Pablo and Charles Allard were both of mixed white and Indian blood. They were both frugal and industrious ranchmen and cattle owners. They inherited business acumen and tireless activity from their white ancestors, and an instinctive knowledge of nature and wildlife from their Indian forebearers. Their love for the buffalo came from their Indian heritage.

Tony Barnaby, Pablo's son-in-law, gives us a good picture of Michael Pablo's character, and the motives that led to his ownership of the largest American bison herd and made him the only man who reaped a fortune from saving rather than destroying the big beasts.[22] Mr. Barnaby, in describing Michael Pablo, said:

> Many people today, while appreciating the fact that Indian Samuel, Michael Pablo, Charles Allard, Sr., and Andrew Stinger were the ones who saved the buffalo from extermination, question their motives. Some say that the plan was to build up a vast herd, that later could be sold at a great profit. Perhaps that is a very natural view; but we, who were associates of these four men, know it is erroneous. The acquisition of money meant little to men of their type, but the preservation of the bison was their duty, privilege and pleasure.
>
> Pablo, for instance, did not consider a buffalo as just a great, shaggy beast of the plains; but rather as symbolic of the real soul of the Indians' past. It was something grand that, with the culture of his own race, had somehow managed to survive the undesirable features in the whiteman's system. In years gone by, the buffalo had always been the greatest benefactor of the Indians, often saving entire tribal groups from starvation; now Pablo, a red man,

would repay the race's Karmic debt. He would protect the mighty monarch and provide the remnant a secure paradise in Valley Sin-yel-e-min.

Only a soul patterned on a large scale was capable of such magnificent visions, and Michael Pablo was large in every respect. A deep thinker, philosophical, efficient planner, lavishly generous person to friend and foe, lover of both races, fond of all animals, of innate spirituality, with faith in his own destiny, Michael Pablo was bound to succeed where folks of lesser caliber would have failed. With a keen sight to his animals' welfare, he knew at all times just about where his buffalo were grazing. He soon realized that they were increasing at a rapid rate; and after he returned from each daily ride on the range, he would remark, "It is well."

Only upon one occasion was Pablo really discouraged. When he was positively assured that the reservation was to be opened to white settlers, he knew that free, open range was ending, and that his beloved herd must go. He vainly sought to sell them to our government in hopes that they would find a haven in some refuge set aside for that purpose. We knew that when Pablo heard that our Congress could not be induced to appropriate a purchasing fund, he was moved to manly tears. Only as a last resort did he sell them to the Canadian officials.[23]

J. B. Monroe described Michael Pablo as a half Blackfoot, half Spaniard who was born on the great plains, and when quite young moved to Colville, Washington. His early life was one of hardship and rustle, and he seems to be a man who knows every phase of Western life.[24] About six feet two inches tall and weighing 240 pounds without any spare flesh, active and pushing, he seems to be a man thoroughly awake and alive to all business ventures.

Monroe gives us a good picture of Pablo's home and ranch as he saw it in 1902:

....His ranch is run like clockwork; a skilled Chinese chef runs the kitchen; two businesslike men, a French-Canadian and a German, attend to the ranch and farm work; meals are had on time, horses curried night and morning, stables swept out, wagons, buggies and farm machinery under cover, fences and all buildings in good repair.

Everything denotes push and progress. He has an elk park, and two cows, two bulls, and one last year's calf occupy a well-fenced, twenty-acre tract. I saw some wild geese, and some queer looking geese around the house. During our talk he told me he had some cross geese, between wild and tame. I forgot to examine them in my haste to catch the boat.

He told me of having had a white mountain goat which would get upon an ordinary rail fence and walk the top rail for a quarter of a mile. Some hounds one day caught it away from home and killed it. He is now negotiating with parties in the Northwest Territories for some antelope.

Large fine work horses are used on his ranch, and lighter horses for cow and driving purposes. In winter he runs a private school close to his ranch and pays the teacher. He has tried the mission schools, but they were too slow and worshipped the past. He wants his children to progress and look to the future. His wife is a full blood Flathead.

There were three children at home; a good-looking girl of about 16, who keeps books for her father and keeps account of all his many business transactions; a boy of about 12, who seemed to have his father's rustle and go. There was a younger boy: all could answer almost any kind of a business question.

The ranch contains some 450 acres of good farming and grass land. It is situated on the east side of the valley close to the belt of timber. He has large irrigating ditches. He has a barn that will shelter 100 head of stock. All kinds of improved harvesting and haying machinery are carefully housed. The broad level prairie rolls away to the west. Here is all a western man wants, plenty of fine timber, water and grass. His house is large and commodious, suitable for his business, and he is building an addition.

The cowboys or herders of the ranch are living about ten miles west, on the Pend d'Oreille [Flathead] River. They have a good ferry and a good house and stable.[25]

Range of the Pablo Herd

Pablo grazed his buffalo on the open range on the Flathead Indian reserve about ten miles south of Flathead Lake. Here the valley is about 20 miles wide; the range about ten miles west of his home. The Flathead River (formerly called the Pend d'Oreille) flows through the western part of the valley with fine grazing lands, small lakes, and a few round-topped buttes on both sides of the river. In winter they fed around the hills on the west side, and in the summer swam across to the eastern side. The snow frequently covered the ground several feet deep, and temperatures dropped to thirty degrees or more below zero, but the bison weather the cold, and when necessary dug the snow away with their noses, and rarely required hay for feed. Pablo employed several riders, or "buffalo herders" as they were known, to keep an eye on the animals to see that none traveled far from their home range. These riders, apparently, had little to do except to watch them, as there is no record that the buffalo every attempted to leave the valley.[26]

The memory of Michael Pablo as a buffalo conservationist, reputable citizen and successful businessman will not be forgotten in the Flathead Valley for generations to come, as the town nearest to his home and bison range bears his name, as well as the Pablo Reservoir, and the Pablo Bird Refuge, located where his bison formerly grazed and watered.

Charles Allard was an ideal partner for the home-loving Michael Pablo. Allard was described by Tom Jones as being "a very shrewd, farseeing, capable business man, quick to grasp an opportunity as this afforded."[27] He was a successful ranchman and cattleman, and a neighbor and friend of Pablo. At times he handled from 5,000 to 10,000 head of cattle, and he made large shipments to the eastern markets. He rode through the cattle country on both sides of the Continental Divide, buying and selling stock. He was more aggressive than his partner, and was credited with initiating most of the purchases of buffalo for the partners. It was Allard who brought a large band of buffalo to Butte for exhibition in wild west riding sports, and in 1893 planned to take 100 to the World's Fair in Chicago for exhibition on the Midway.[28] While Pablo was taking care of them on the ranch, Allard wanted to show them to the world. Many sales, some small, and some large, were made from the partnership herd, but there is no record as to which of the two men negotiated them; but from the known characteristics of the two partners, it is generally believed that Allard started the sales and Pablo delivered the stock. There is no evidence to prove that Pablo ever tried to sell any bison until he was forced to by the loss of the animals' grazing lands.

Allard's death at the age of 70 years in 1896, broke up the partnership. In the settlement of his estate Allard's half of the buffalo were sold to different owners and scattered. Pablo held on to his share of 150 head and nourished them for ten years until they increased to more than 700. Mr. Allard's demise robbed him of much of the credit for saving the buffalo, which during the partnership of the two was shared equally by both. However, the division of the herd at that time was later declared to have been a fortunate incident in the preservation of the bison species, for it was divided into five parts, each of which went to vitalize new herds, and one fifth provided the foundation for the famous National Bison Range herd in 1909.

At the time of Mr. Allard's death the herd numbered about 300 head. The 150 head belonging to the Allard Estate were subdivided equally between his widow, daughters, and two sons, one of whom was destined to play an important part later in the Pablo roundup.[29] Mrs. Allard sold her share to Charles E. Conrad of Kalispell, Montana, who chose 28 [38?] of the best animals, basing his selection on his earlier experience as a buffalo hunter.[30] Howard Eaton bought the shares of the Misses Allard and their brother Charles; and Judge Woodrow, of Missoula, purchased those owned by Joseph Allard. He later sold them to the 101 Ranch. An equal division of 150 buffalo into five parts would have given each a share of 30, so Mr. Conrad must have secured a lion's share, or purchased eight additional buffalo from Mr. Pablo. Howard Eaton afterward sold some of those he obtained to the Street Railway Company of Winnipeg, Canada; two bulls were shipped to Texas in 1902[31]; and a portion of the same herd was purchased by Sir Donald A. Smith, Lord Strathcona, and were presented by him to the Canadian government, before the Dominion secured the Pablo herd. Thus the descendants of Walking Coyote's calves were widely scattered over the American continent and closely allied with the leading herds in existence at that time.[32]

The Conrad Herd

Mr. Conrad moved his buffalo to his pasture, which is now a golf course, near Kalispell. The *Jordan Gazette* reported that the purchase was made in 1902, six years after Mr. Allard's death, which may have accounted for the addition of eight animals by natural increase to Mrs. Allard's share of 30.[33] The investment proved to be a good one financially. They were well cared for and multiplied rapidly. Thirty-six were sold to the American Bison Society in 1909 for more than $10,000 and moved to the National Bison Range at Moise [Moiese]. The Conrad herd went out of existence in December 1921, when 90 head were sold to Gibson Brothers of Yakima, Washington, and shipped to a range at Wenatchee. The Biological Survey reports this herd as numbering 39 in 1939, owned by O. D. Gibson.[34] The animals remaining were slaughtered for the holiday trade and the meat shipped to various parts of the country. Mrs. Alicia D. Conrad, executrix of the C. E. Conrad estate, said that Mr. Conrad's original motive in purchasing the herd was prompted by a realization of the likelihood of the extinction of the species unless individuals carried on the work of propagation and perpetuation. She said that she felt that the Conrad interests had done their share in carrying on the work of preserving the buffalo for posterity, although expressing regret in parting with the animals. She had been compelled to give a great deal of time and thought to the work, and felt that as the Conrad estate was nearing settlement, a disposal of the buffalo was necessary, as none of the heirs were in a position to carry on the work. In discussing the financial side, she said that while they had not shown a large profit, they had always shown a fair return of profit on the capital invested.[35]

The growth and care of the Pablo-Allard herd has been cited as an example of what can be accomplished in the propagation of large game animals under proper conditions. Tom Jones in his Scenic Souvenir publication stated that in 23 years this herd increased from 36 head to over 30 times the original number.[36] And that estimate is probably too low, for during that period many sales were made from the herd for exhibition, propagation and slaughter before 709 were sold to the Canadian government. Single animals were also butchered on the Pablo and Allard ranches, and for the benefit of Indians on the reservation. Of these no records were kept. Jones estimated that from 250 to 300 were sold. J. B. Monroe recorded 17 small sales from 1898 to 1902 of 64 head, 34 of which went to privately owned parks for exhibition and propagation, and 30 to the butcher's block.[37] The meat was shipped to Idaho, Washington, and to Horse Plains, Helena, Kalispell, and other towns in Montana. The exhibition animals were scattered pretty well over the country, some going as far as Massachusetts. In addition to the above, Montana newspapers reported four larger shipments aggregating 115 head; 30 went to New York, 20 to the Yellowstone National Park, 35 to Oklahoma, and 30 were butchered at Plains, Montana.[38] A few animals purchased from the herd were kept on exhibition at the Columbia Gardens in Butte, and in the City Park at Helena. Undoubtedly many sales were made of which no record was kept or reported to the newspapers. That the owners were able to dispose of so many animals and still show such a large increase, is ample proof of their careful and practical management of their buffalo herds.

In 1893 Charles Allard and his cowboys drove 34 head of buffalo to Butte where they were exhibited for a week at the race track south of that city. Here a new kind of rodeo was put on for the entertainment of the Butte residents. Cowboys rode the shaggy beasts, some of which were saddled and others were ridden bareback. The crowds of spectators got a thrill watching the cowboys rope and saddle the bison even before the riding started. Reports differ as to the antics of the bison when ridden in this exhibition. Some describe their bucking as worse than broncos, and others reported that some of them just trotted around and did not try to dislodge their riders.[39]

Purchase of the Jones' Herd

It was in Butte at this time that Charles Allard purchased a herd of 46 buffalo from Colonel C. J. "Buffalo" Jones. He had shipped them from his Nebraska ranch and unloaded them at Silver Bow. When the two herds were joined there were some spirited battles between the bulls who were rivals for the herd leadership. This addition increased the Allard herd to 119, which the newspapers at that time reported to be the largest herd in the world and valued at more than $100,000.[40] Allard received a contract to ship 15 two-year-old calves to England in the spring of 1894 at a price of $1,000 each.

It is interesting to note that the bison sold to Mr. Allard were the ones which Buffalo Jones had previously purchased from Colonel Bedson, of Stony Mountain, Canada, where they originated from some calves captured by an Indian in the Dominion, duplicating the origin of the Pablo-Allard herd; and that some of these same animals or their progeny were later to be returned to the Dominion of Canada.[41]

Joseph Clark Financed the Purchase

An interesting incident occurred during the purchase of the Jones' herd. Jones had contracted to deliver them to Butte, where they arrived on a Sunday afternoon, and Mr. Allard found that he did not have sufficient money with him to accept the shipment. In his predicament he went to Jos. A. Clark [Joseph K. Clark], a brother of Senator W. A. Clark, the millionaire copper-mine owner. Before Clark had amassed a fortune from the Butte mines, Jos. A. Clark [Joseph K. Clark] had been engaged as a cook on the Allard and Pablo ranch on the reservation, when W. A. Clark was driving the mail wagon there. The servants at Clark's mansion did not extend a very cordial reception to Mr. Allard when he appeared in his picturesque ranchman's attire, seeking a personal interview with the millionaire on Sunday, but the latter was delighted to be in a position to accommodate his former employer, and Mr. Allard's financial difficulties were speedily removed.[42]

In 1905 it was announced that much of the Flathead Indian Reservation would be thrown open to settlement by white homesteaders. As this had been the pasture of Michael Pablo's buffalo herd for 21 years, he realized at once that he would have to dispose of his "Indian cattle" which numbered between 700 and 800 head.[43] Since the government was taking away his free pasture, he first turned to that source for relief, and offered to sell the whole herd to Uncle Sam. He secured the help of President Theodore Roosevelt and the interest of some Congressman to secure a federal appropriation for the purchase of the buffalo, but Congress failed to provide the money.[44]

Canada Bought American Bison

The Canadian government, however, had a greater appreciation of buffalo values and grasped an opportunity to make a profitable deal in bison livestock after the United States had turned it down. In 1906 through the office of the Hon. Frank Oliver, Minister of the Interior at Ottawa, the Dominion obtained an option on the largest herd of purebred buffalo in the world, a deal involving the sum of $200,000. The transaction was negotiated through the office of the Canadian National Park, at Banff, Alberta, of which Mr. Howard Douglas was the superintendent, and Mr. Alex. Ayotte, of the department of immigration in the State of Montana. These two gentlemen, by their untiring efforts, brought the deal to a satisfactory consummation, and made arrangements for shipping the entire herd into the central part of Alberta from Montana, a distance of 1,200 miles over five railways. The loss in transportation amounted to less than half of one-percent of the animals.[45] Mr. Pablo is reported to have received $250 a head for each buffalo delivered at the railroad at Ravalli, Montana. The deal was larger than the Dominion had anticipated, for Mr. Pablo delivered 709 buffalo, which at the above price cost Canada $177,250 and transportation charges.[46] Mr. Pablo still had a number of bison left which were too wild to drive and load into the railroad cars.

Laments over the loss of the Pablo herd were many. Charles Russell, the famous painter, who was camped at Allen Sloan's ranch, said to him, "My friend, the buffalo now follows the Indian—into oblivion. Two fine types of early Americans exterminated by the damned greed of the whites. Here, while it is possible, I shall picture them both in their natural colors." And he did.[47]

The Pablo Bison Roundup

The most spectacular and dramatic part of the history of the Pablo bison herd was the famous roundup. The owners thought they could round up and load these semi-wild bison into railroad cards within a few weeks; but it took nearly three years, and then they didn't catch them all. It started in the spring of 1906 and toward the end of June 1909 they had loaded

709 bison into railroad cars at Ravalli, Montana.[48] Before starting the roundup, Michael Pablo carefully selected 75 of the most expert cowboys in the valley, both Indians and white men, and picked the swiftest horses available. The animals were ranging over a large area, making it necessary to drive them many miles across one large river and many smaller streams, into corrals, and from corrals into lanes and loading chutes. It was a lively, colorful spectacle, with gaily attired Indians upon splendid, spirited horses, with many visitors intermingled with groups of Indian women and children dressed richly in barbaric colors of beaded skins and blankets. They dotted the sides of the runways to loudly cheer the symbolic cavalcade of their early primitive life—braves, ponies, and buffalo.[49]

A strong corral, nine feet high, was made from two-inch planks spiked to posts set eight feet apart with loading chutes at the railroad at Ravalli. But to get the buffalo into this corral was no easy task. Every morning the cowboys started out to drive the bison toward the shipping pens, and almost every day, the buffalo wheeled and charged the encircling riders, broke away and scattered in every direction. Only three times during the first month was it possible to get a few buffalo into the corrals and loaded on the cars. Mr. Pablo then began building a bison-proof fence to help hold the animals from scattering. A large crew went to work digging post-holes and setting posts. After several weeks he had a fence 26 miles long and reaching from the loading pens to far out on the range. Again the riders rounded up the buffalo, gradually driving them along this fence. Some charged and managed to get away, but many were finally corralled.[50]

In 1907, according to Robert A. McCrea, who was an eyewitness at the roundup, Mr. Pablo built more buffalo corrals, just south of where the town of Pablo now stands. From these he had a wing fence extending westward over the prairie and low hills for a distance of three miles.[51] When enough had been corralled for loading, they were driven through a long, fenced-in lane, and driven to the loading corrals. In an interview Zephyr Courville, brother-in-law of the late Charles Allard, Sr., and one of the riders in the roundup, stated that Michael Pablo made a contract with Charles Allard, Jr., to round up and corral the buffalo at $10 a head. He had his difficulties also. After driving a large band for more than 15 miles and getting them within three-fourths of a mile from the corrals, fifty of them broke away and escaped. On another occasion, after they had trailed a good-sized herd and had them, as they hoped, safely in the stockyards, they got scared during the night, tore down one side of the heavy fence and scattered to the four winds.[52]

It was found that the animals couldn't be gathered in large herds, from which small bands were constantly breaking away. From one of the largest gatherings, only thirty were finally corralled. The more the buffalo were herded up and driven, the more unmanageable and agitated they became.[53] And it sometimes took several days to again round up some of these escaped bands.

The riders and their horses were in constant danger from the sudden attacks of the buffalo bulls. While two cow punchers were trying to drive an old bull into the corral, he suddenly whirled and charged them at full speed. Sinking both horns into the side of a horse, he lifted it and the rider clear of the ground and carried them a hundred yards. When they fell to the ground, the rider escaped while the buffalo finished goring the injured horse to death. Five horses were killed during the roundup, alert cowboys were injured, and many fine horses were ridden so hard that they were thereafter useless.[54] It was a constant battle between fine horses and expert riders on one side and huge, liberty-loving beasts on the other.

After two years of such discouraging efforts nearly two hundred buffalo were still required to fill the Canadian contract. They were the wildest and most unmanageable animals that frequented the hills some 30 miles from Ravalli. To control and tame these animals, it was found necessary to build a strong corral costing $3,700, 32 miles from Ravalli. Booms were built across the Flathead River, which at that point was 520 feet wide and 19 feet deep. The buffalo were driven in small numbers into this corral, fed during the winter, and cowboys rode among them to tame and accustom them to the smell of horses and riders. They were then hauled by thirty four-horse teams in racks carrying one bull or two cows for a distance of 35 miles to the loading chutes at the railroad.

One incident nearly brought on international disagreements. Many regrets had been made that the buffalo were leaving Montana for Canada. Two hundred and fifty of them had been corralled in an enclosure, one side of which was a precipice, which it was believed that no animal could climb. One morning it was found that all had escaped. It was reported in a news dispatch in Canada that men from Missoula had released them to save them for this state. The Canadian Commissioner, Howard Douglas, was quoted as saying that he would make a protest to the authorities in Montana. Later Mr. Douglas stated that he had made no such statements, and it was afterwards discovered that the entire herd had climbed a cliff and escaped. That such a feat could be accomplished, one of the cowboys discovered when chasing a buffalo cow, which climbed up 40 feet on a precipitous cliff, fell back and raced off without injury.[55]

In the interval of thirty years the names of most of these daredevil riders have been forgotten, but the names of a few of them are still recalled by the older residents of the Flathead Valley. At that time they were called "Buffalo Boys" to distinguish them from the ordinary cowboy. Among the riders were Tony Barnaby (Pablo's son-in-law), Zephyr Courville (Allard's brother-in-law), Frank McCloed [McLeod], Malcolm McCloed [McLeod], Joseph Houle, James Peone, Jim Grinder, Antoine Morigeau, Bill Lewis, Billy Ervine [Irvine], Billy Archibald, Tom "Butch" O'Connell, and Mrs. Emily Ervine [Irvine]. Alvin Peone, then too young to ride, with Mose Delaware, and Henry Moss were attending the loading chutes leading to the railroad cars. The riders were paid $5.00 a day and they probably earned it, as they were usually in the saddle from dawn to dark. It has since been said of them that they rode not for the money but for the excitement and glory of the chase.

In an interview, Mrs. Mary Blood, told of Michael Pablo's pleasure when her sister-in-law, Mrs. Emily Ervine [Irvine], offered her services as a rider in the roundup. Billy Ervine [Irvine], her husband, was one of Pablo's friends. She was an expert horse rider, had ridden broncos, and bad ones, over much of the Flathead Valley. As she was part Indian, she understood buffalo, their habits, and how to handle them. Her fellow-riders said she was an equal of any two ordinary riders. She was a graceful and beautiful woman, and was always mounted on a splendid appearing horse; a sight which Charley Russell said, "was enough to stir any he-man's blood." She demonstrated her efficiency one hot day, when after continuous riding of about 100 miles, she, unaided, was successful in steering the herd and thus preventing what would have been a most disastrous stampede. Her husband also participated in the roundup, and Mr. Pablo was so well pleased with their work, that he presented them with the best buffalo cow in the herd. This was an Indian's appreciation, aside from the wages they had earned. They treasured the hide of that cow and were proud in telling their visitors its history.[56]

Frank McCloed [McLeod] remembered how one old bull smashed his way out of the corral, and before a fine saddle horse could be gotten out of the way, it was gored in the bowels so badly that it had to be shot. At another time when they were hauling buffalo in wagons to Ravalli, a cow, which had been placed in a wagon crate made of heavy material, became furious when she heard her calf bawling from its cage further back in the wagon train. In her struggles she gained considerable freedom of action for her head. She was so determined to get to the side of her calf, that she rammed the side of her prison wall, driving the points of her horns through a two inch plank. She broke her neck and was butchered. The Canadian purchasing agent took a hind quarter to his camp for his partner and Charley Russell, saying he was going to feed them enough of this meat to make them paw the ground, snort and bellow.—"They were so damnably strong on buffalo atmosphere."[57]

Charley Russell camped for some time during the roundup with the Canadian agents on the bank of the Flathead River, and sometimes helped by riding with the cowboys. He probably spent more time with his paints and brushes than he did in the saddle. He drew one picture of a maddened buffalo cow that stampeded thorough their camp, as the cook was going for water. The view showed the bison climbing the riverbank while the cook, Howard Douglas, and Mr. Alex Ayotte were hot-footing it for protection to nearby trees. This picture was presented to Mr. Ayotte.[58] Another picture of the incident of the roundup was painted by Tony Barnaby, who was present when a large bull separated from the herd, stationed himself on a brush covered knoll and refused to move. One of the riders thought he would dismount, go up and grab him by the whiskers and pull him down, but he didn't do it. They couldn't make him move for the best part of a day, and finally gave it up as a bad job. The next morning he was back with the bunch.[59]

Loading buffalo into the railroad cars was no small job. Alvin Peone, whose duty it was to snub the bison back as they entered the car doors to keep them from jumping through the far side of the car, told of methods used to control the big animals. The snubbing was done with a rope about the buffalo's neck. This rope also was used to tie each animal to the side of the car to restrain their movements and prevent plunging through the car's sides. Each car held from 10 to 12 head, and five or six were tied to the sides of each car. One big bull did butt through and got half way out, and it took all hands with ropes and prods to get him back where he belonged.[60]

In this snubbing process one of the men suffered what he afterwards decided was a lucky accident. It was James Peone. He had been suffering for some time from several ulcerated teeth and was unable to go to a dentist. He was in great pain from his teeth one day, while attending the hoist gates at the back end of the wagon crates. He was manipulating the levers which lifted the gates and gave the animals an opening into the chutes. One of the levers jammed when the gate was only partly raised, and an impatient bull, seeing the opening, crowded under the opening so quickly that the levers released and struck Peone squarely in the mouth. He was not killed, but the blow knocked out every front tooth and loosened some others. That ended his toothache. After that his Indian friends called him, "Teeth Pulled by Bull."[61]

The roundup was not without its humorous incidents. Frank McLoed [McLeod] relates how, among many news correspondents, amateur and professional photographers and curiosity seekers, was an old, gray-haired photographer with a long flowing beard, and the appearance of a biblical patriarch. Mr. Pablo was sorry for the old fellow, and for his safety had a small platform built among the limbs of a dead pine tree. This elevation provided an excellent and apparently safe view of the buffalo being driven in from the prairie. But one of the bison unexpectedly swung against the base of the tree with such force that the platform and patriarch came down across the buffalo's back. The old man found himself astride a bewildered buffalo cow. As the animals were crowded closely together, he couldn't be tossed off and trodden to death. There he sat at the rear end of a moving sea of broad backs, with his long beard fluttering in the breeze, a very serene lord of the thundering herd. After traveling nearly a hundred yards, the herd split and the old man fell off to a safe landing. He said he was lucky in getting a back seat in that ride.[62]

The adventure of another photographer, N. A. Forsyth—or perhaps it was the same incident as previously related by different narrators—recounts how Forsyth fell upon the back of a stampeding buffalo, as the herd passed his stand, and saved himself by grasping the branch of an overhanging tree, as the herd sped onward. This incident was painted by Charles Russell, and was displayed in the windows of the Missoula Mercantile Company in December 1908. The picture was presented to Mr. Forsyth, and shows him clinging to the branch, which saved him from being trampled to death. His large camera was trampled into bits by the bison, but in his struggles he touched the spring of a small camera he had swung over his shoulder, which accidentally focused on the stampeding herd, and left a very realistic snapshot of his thrilling experience.[63]

James Peone related a similar experience suffered by a very persistent newspaper man, who repeatedly climbed the corral fences, and was requested to get down as it was dangerous. Finally to get a better view to take a snapshot, he perched himself upon the top pole with his feet hanging over. One big bull was trying to get out where the reporter was roosting. This bull made a determined lunge, got his horns under the top rail where the man sat, and loosened the rail from the posts. The rail fell across the buffalo's neck and he carried it with the reporter half way around the corral, before dropping both to the ground. The poor fellow, yelling like a Comanche Indian, scrambled to safety, just in time to avert a fatal goring. He presented a most ludicrous sight. He had hit the ground in a pile of soft dung. His fiery red hair was plastered with it, and his suit and white shirt were well discolored. With so much buffalo "atmosphere" he was thus enabled to write a real story about the beasts.[64]

Footnotes

1. The Story of the Buffalo, 3,850 words, various bibliographies. [The editor has been unable to identify the manuscript referred to in this footnote. The word count suggests a manuscript about thirteen typed pages long. It could be a shorter version of the manuscript from which this chapter has been excerpted.]
2. Chas. Aubrey, "Montana's Buffalo: The Pablo Allard Herd: The Origin of the Herd," *Forest and Stream*, vol. 59, no. 1 (July 5, 1902), p. 6.
3. Buffalo Research Report 300.055, Works Progress Administration Papers, boxes 128-29, collection 2336, Burlingame Special Collections, Renne Library, Montana State University, Bozeman, MT (hereafter WPA Papers).
4. Ibid.
5. Aubrey, "Montana's Buffalo," p. 6.
6. E. Douglas Branch, *The Hunting of the Buffalo* (New York: D. Appleton and Company, 1929), p. 228.
7. According to J. B. Monroe. See Charles Aubrey, "The Edmonton Buffalo Herd," *Forest and Stream*, vol. 69, no. 1 (July 6, 1907), pp. 11-13.
8. Tom Jones, *The Last of the Buffalo* (Cincinnati, OH: Tom Jones Publisher Scenic Souvenirs, 1909), no page numbers.
9. Aubrey, "The Edmonton Buffalo Herd," pp. 11-13.
10. Buffalo Research Report 300.020, WPA Papers.
11. Buffalo Research Report 300.094, WPA Papers.
12. Buffalo Research Report 300.095b, WPA Papers.
13. Jones, *The Last of the Buffalo*.
14. Aubrey, "The Edmonton Buffalo Herd," pp. 11-13.
15. Buffalo Research Report 300.081, WPA Papers.
16. Ibid.
17. Buffalo Research Report 300.099, WPA Papers.
18. Buffalo Research Report 300.198. [This particular research report could not be located in the WPA Papers.]
19. Martin S. Garretson, *The American Bison* (New York: New York Zoological Society, 1938), p. 215.
20. Interview with Andrew Garcia, Rivulette, Montana. Missoula County—Biography, WPA Papers.
21. Stuart I. Hazlett, "Many Tail Feathers, Famous Red Warrior...," *The Plains Plainsman* (Plains, MT), Apr. 29, 1920, p. 5.
22. Buffalo Research Report 300.092, WPA Papers.
23. Ibid.
24. J. B. Monroe, "Montana's Buffalo: The Pablo-Allard Herd," *Forest and Stream*, vol. 59, no. 2 (July 12, 1902), pp. 24-26.
25. Ibid.
26. Ibid.
27. Jones, *The Last of the Buffalo*.
28. [no headline], *Stock Growers' Journal* (Miles City, MT), May 6, 1893, p. 3.

29. Jones, *The Last of the Buffalo*.
30. "Conrad Buffalo Herd Marketed," *The Plains Plainsman*, Dec. 29, 1921, p. 2.
31. Buffalo Research Report 300.093. [This citation in Bartlett's manuscript must be in error as Buffalo Research Report 300.093, WPA Papers, is not about the Conrad herd.]
32. Jones, *The Last of the Buffalo*.
33. "Conrad Buffalo Herd Marketed," *Jordan Gazette* (Jordan, MT), Dec. 29. 1921, p. 6.
34. Research Report 120.105. [This Research Report could not be found in either the Montana State University's WPA Papers or Colorado Historical Society's Montana Writers' Project Papers.]
35. "Conrad Buffalo Herd Marketed," *Jordan Gazette*.
36. Jones, *The Last of the Buffalo*.
37. Monroe, "Montana's Buffalo," pp. 24-26. [The list of sixty-four head sold from the Allard-Pablo herd includes two animals killed in a roundup in 1901 and one animal killed in 1900 by Michel Pablo for food for his home.]
38. Monroe, "Montana's Buffalo," pp. 24-26. [The editor could not find references to sales of 30 buffalo to New York or 20 to the Yellowstone National Park in the Monroe article.]; "Two Carloads of Buffalo Sold," *Daily Missoulian* (Missoula, MT) [hereafter *DM*], Apr. 25, 1905, p. 8; Buffalo Research Report 300.115, WPA Papers.
39. "A Fortune in Buffalo," *Evening Missoulian* (Missoula, MT), Sept. 26, 1893, p. 4.
40. Ibid.
41. Jones, *The Last of the Buffalo*.
42. Ibid.
43. "Two Carloads of Buffalo Sold."
44. Buffalo Research Report 300.010, WPA Papers.
45. Jones, *The Last of the Buffalo*.
46. Buffalo Research Report 300.010, WPA Papers; Garretson, *The American Bison*, p. 216.
47. Buffalo Research Report 300.010, WPA Papers.
48. Ibid.
49. Buffalo Research Report 300.148, WPA Papers.
50. Jones, *The Last of the Buffalo;* Buffalo Research Report 300.185, WPA Papers.
51. Buffalo Research Report 300.148, WPA Papers.
52. Buffalo Research Report 300.118, WPA Papers.
53. Buffalo Research Report 300.019, WPA Papers.
54. Buffalo Research Report 300.185, WPA Papers; Jones, *The Last of the Buffalo*.
55. "Charges by Canadian Commissioner Are Ridiculed," *DM*, Nov. 26, 1908, p. 5; "Caught on the Run About Town," *DM*, Nov. 28, 1908, p. 8; "Canadian Official Says He Never Said It," *DM*, Dec. 6, 1908, p. 1.
56. Buffalo Research Report 300.162, WPA Papers.
57. Buffalo Research Report 300.163, WPA Papers.

58. Painting now in Buffalo Research Report 300.025. [The file in the WPA Papers referred to by Bartlett contains a "rough copy of the original sketch by C. M. Russell," not the original. The original Russell sketch has been reproduced in Brian W. Dippie, compiler, *Charles M. Russell, Word Painter: Letters 1887-1926* (Fort Worth TX: Amon Carter Museum, 1993), p. 164.]

59. This sketch in Buffalo Research Report 300.091. [No drawing or sketch was found with the transcript of the interview with Tony Barnaby in Buffalo Research Report 300.091, WPA Papers.]

60. Buffalo Research Report 300.189. [This particular research report could not be located in the WPA Papers.]

61. Buffalo Research Report 300.181, WPA Papers.

62. Buffalo Research Report 300.022, WPA Papers.

63. "Bison Riding," *DM*, Dec. 12, 1908, p. 12.

64. Buffalo Research Report 300.180, WPA Papers.

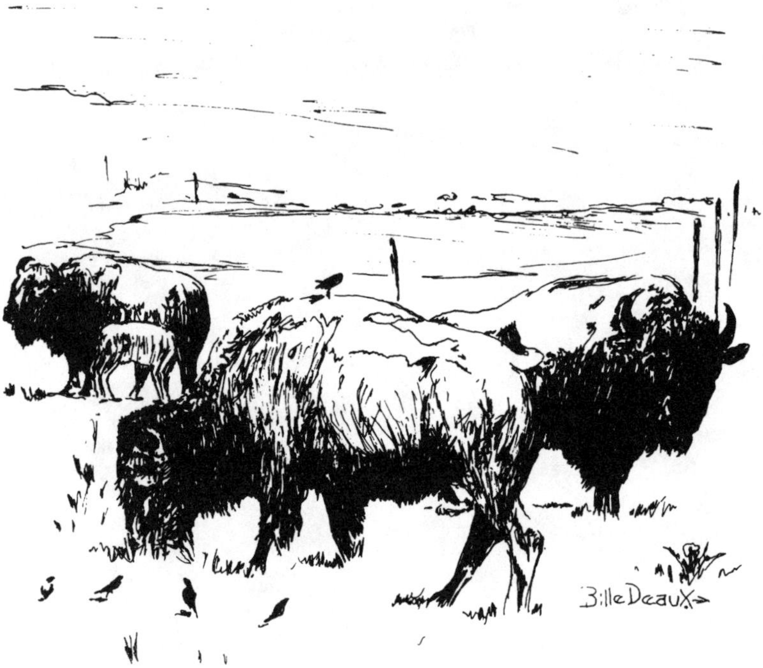
BilleDeaux

Chapter 5

Origins of the Flathead Reservation Buffalo Herd

Joe McDonald Recalls Samuel's Buffalo Calves
Told by: **Joseph McDonald**
Writer: **Bon I. Whealdon**
Date: September 29, 1941

"My father, Angus McDonald, came from Scotland when he was a very young man. Whether he came around Cape Horn and then up the Columbia River to the Ft. Vancouver Hudson Bay Post, or to eastern Canada, and thence overland from post to post until he reached the West Slope, we do not know. However, he was at Fort Hall early in the [18]40's.

"In 1846, he was sent to the Flathead Valley, then called by the Salish name Sinyelemin (Surrounded), to see if the possibilities of the region would warrant the founding of a Hudson Bay Company trading post. In all probability, Angus was the second (?) white man to make a thorough investigation of the territory. [Question mark by Whealdon or Montana Writers Project staff.—Bigart Note.] He found a beautiful valley with grass-covered prairies, ranged only by deer and elk. There were friendly groups of Indians from the Flathead, Pend Oreille, and lower Kootenai tribes occupying the region. These men were engaged in trapping the valuable fur bearing animals, and in buffalo hunting in the eastern portion. To quote his words, 'The whole damn place was running over with mink, beaver, otter; and with loads of buffalo robes being fetched in from across the mountains.'

"He was greatly impressed by the scenic features. He told me that the deep yearning he felt for his far away Scotland was satisfied when he saw this land with its towering peaks, waterfalls, lakes and sparkling streams. He turned to MacPherson, another Scot, and said, 'By Christ's grace man, a feast for our famished souls! Here is where I'll abide—braes, cloughs, rock-peaks and rills. Unhunted stags on every hill. Take these greasy savages, don them in plaids, kilts and tams; give yon frowzy chieftain a bagpipe. Man, use your eye (presumably, use your imagination) and here we have a larger, wilder, bonnier Scotland than the old.'

"His report proved most satisfactory to the chief trader at Fort Hall, so in 1847 he was instructed to conduct a crew of Hudson Bay employees and a loaded pack train to Sinyelemin.

"When they arrived, Angus McDonald's old Indian friend, Quee-teelt, aided him in selecting a site for the three log buildings that comprised the post. They chose the location in the Post Creek vicinity, because it was well protected from the severity of winter storms by the range, now called Mission. Quee-teelt advised them to build at a little distance west from Narrow Gate Creek, now named Post Creek. He sensibly pointed out that buildings too near the creek would not be safe, in case of an attack by invading enemy Indians. The banks of the stream were covered by a dense growth of brush and timber and that would have enabled the enemy to approach unseen.

"My mother was classified as a Nez Perce squaw, though her father was an Iroquois Indian. His given name was Babtiste [Baptiste ?]. I have heard that my father and mother were first married by tribal custom, and that, after father became a convert to the church (R. C.), they were remarried by the fathers. That, also, was the matrimonial procedure in the case of my brother, the deceased Duncan McDonald.

"The post did a thriving business with the Indian hunters returning from the east side with their heavy pack train loads of buffalo robes and cured meats. The storehouse was jammed with tall piles of these tanned robes, and other pelts. In spring, a long train of ponies would carry the furs to Victoria and other Hudson Bay trading centers. There supplies for our local post were obtained. Precious salt was brought in from Utah.

"I knew Indian Samuel, or Sam Wells very, very well. He had four buffalo calves, 2 bulls, and 2 heifers. These he had captured, or acquired through trading with other Indians, while upon hunting trips. At first, he kept the calves confined to a small pasture. Later they were permitted to roam the unfenced prairies, for as yet the right side of Montana had not been turned under by hordes of eastern farmers, nor had the great open plains been checkerboarded by fences. Indians, buffalo herds, cattle and bands of wild horses were free to go anywhere. Sam started his herd with four head. I saw them many times, grazing near the post. I saw them during their mating season and remember the local excitement when the two buffalo cows gave birth to calves.

"I have never heard of Walking Coyote. He must have belonged to some other Indian country, for I am sure, since I lived at the post, where all Indians came at frequent intervals, that I knew most of them, their names, business, etc.

"My father and others had seen a small size herd of buffalo, owned by an Indian in the Big Bitter Root Valley, but that was long before Sam's herd. When that Indian died, his buffalo were all slain for a 'death feast.'

"My brother Duncan and I were of the opinion that during past ages, buffalo had roamed this part of Montana. Some of the old tales of our Indians support this belief. Years ago, while I was helping Duncan clear stumps and roots off his Ravalli ranch, we uncovered an ancient appearing buffalo head and other bones. Similar evidences have been found in other parts of our region.

"Chas. Allard, Sr., and Michael Pablo bought Sam's herd when it numbered 12 or 13 head. I have heard that they purchased a few others through different sources. They increased rapidly.

"My son, John McDonald, and I aided Pablo's other riders in the roundup, and in driving some to Ravalli. Mr. Ayotte hired me to go with the first trainload of buffalo to Canada. It was a long, tiresome journey for the animals, and some sickened and died before we reached our destination.

Note

From an interview (under difficulties) with Joseph McDonald, Sept. 23rd, 1941.

Chief Mose Michell's Account of the Origin of the Allard-Pablo Herd

Told by: **Chief Mose Michell**
Writer: **Bon I. Whealdon**
Date: September 16, 1941

"I know that Samuel Wells, whom the whites called, 'Indian Samuel,' brought four buffalo calves, two heifers and two bulls, from the other side of the mountains. Several times I went to see the calves. Sometimes, Samuel had them in a pasture, near St. Ignatius town; but at other times, they were upon his homeplace on the bank of the Pend Oreille [Flathead] river.

"They were strong, lively calves. One was very young, and it took milk from a domestic cow. Samuel watched his calves very closely, as he was anxious to get a herd of buffalo.

"Our old Pend Oreille and Flathead Indians were very pleased that we had buffalo in our country, as the herds across the mountains had been killed.

"I heard some old Indians tell that once our tribesmen had been angry with Samuel because he took as wife a woman not of our nation. Samuel then left us and went to Sun River. He was there several years. Then he became lonely and unhappy because he could not come home. His wife told him, 'Samuel, the buffalo, your people love will soon be all gone. They are sad because of that. You capture what calves you can, and take them to your people. When they see them, they will be very glad, and they will forgive you that you married not one of their women.'

"Now Samuel's woman was smart like that other Nez Perce woman, Elizabeth, who had saved a party of our old warriors when the Piegans had surrounded their encampment, so Samuel did as his wife told him.

"When the Pend Oreilles and Flatheads heard that Samuel and his woman had brought back buffalo calves, they were happy and made a feast for the Samuels. My father, Chief Charley Michell of the Pend Oreilles, arose and talked to the people, saying, 'Our brother is back with a gift for us. Now, we shall bring gifts to his teepee.'"

Note

Interview with Chief Mose Michell of the Pend Oreilles, with Mrs. Mose Michell as interpreter.

Samuel's Buffalo Calves

Told by: **Que-que-sah**
Writer: **Bon I. Whealdon**
Date: January 7, 1942

"Yes, I remember Samuel Welles whom the white people called 'Indian Sam' and 'Indian Samuel.' I have heard him called by other names. He was a middle aged man when I was a young fellow. He owned a ranch along the Pend Oreille [Flathead] River, not very far from Dixon, Montana.

"I was in the village of St. Ignatius that day in 1873, when Welles rode in with his pack string (ponies). He had come in from the east side of the Continental Divide. He had four buffalo calves on pack ponies. I recall that they were rather small. One, in particular, was very young and weak. It was a bull calf. As we gathered about Sam while he was unloading, he told us how he acquired the calves. He had traded with other Indians (I believe he said Piegans) for the three older ones. The youngest had been given to him by a Piegan. Its mother had been killed, and it was too young to eat grass. Sam had managed to save it by feeding it with milk from a pack mare that had lost her colt. I heard that he taught the bull calf to suckle the mare, but I do not know if that story is true.

"Buffalo hunting had ended owing to the fact that the herds had all been killed. We were all greatly interested in the welfare of Samuel's calves. I think that every Indian upon the reservation looked upon this little herd as the last connecting link with the happier past of his people. I know we all protected them, wherever they were grazing.

"For a while they were confined to a small pasture near the Mission town. Each Sunday, after attending Mass, many hundred Indians would ride over to see the buffalo.

"They increased slowly. When they numbered twelve or thirteen, Allard and Michell Pablo paid Samuel a good price for them. Mr. Allard occasionally acquired a few buffalo through other sources, and I recall that a Piegan Indian sold Pablo several more head. Later Pablo bought Mr. Allard's share of the herd.

"Michell Pablo was very generous to his friends. Often he would tell our Indians to butcher a fat buffalo. We all liked and respected Mr. Pablo, and no Indian would steal any of his herd.

"I remember that Pablo had the buffalo and some cattalo over on Wild Horse Island in Flathead Lake for a while. About that period, we experienced several very severe winters, and many horses, range cattle, and buffalo perished."

A Pack-mare Saves One of Samuel's Calves

Told by: **Tony Barnaby, son-in-law of Michel Pablo**
Writer: **Bon I. Whealdon**
Date: October 15, 1941

"In connection with the four buffalo calves, Michel Pablo often related a story, told him by Indian Sam Wellew [Wells]. It appears that after Sam had either captured or purchased 3 calves—two heifers and a bull—all old enough to live without their mother's milk, he prepared to come back to the Flathead region. As he was leaving his east side camp, a Piegan Indian gave him a very young, half famished bull calf. Its mother had been killed and it was too immature to feed upon grass.

"At first Sam did not think he would be able to save this feeble addition to his precious band. In desperation he tried an experiment. In his pack-string was a mare whose recently born colt had died. To Sam's delighted surprise, this gentle, low built mare permitted the orphan calf to suckle.

"From then on, our Indian made frequent stops, in order to take the bull calf from off its foster mother's back, and then let it feed upon her warm milk."

Indians Have Several Names: Indian Samuel and Walking Coyote
Told by: **Andrew Stinger**
Writer: **Bon I. Whealdon**
Date: October 14, 1941

"I realize there is a confusion resulting from the difference of names of the Indian, or Indians, who first brought the buffalo calves to this region. Some say it was 'Indian Samuel Wells,' others an Indian named 'Walking Coyote.'

"When I first heard these accounts, I thought them two different persons; but after my long association with Michel Pablo in both the buffalo and cattle industries, I have changed my mind. I remember that Pablo referred to some of our bison herd as originating from the 'Indian Samuel' band; and then, again he alluded to the same band as 'Walking Coyote buffalo.'

"I've decided to my own satisfaction that 'Indian Samuel Wells' and 'Walking Coyote' were one and the same Indian to whom we should accord credit for the first step in preservation of the buffalo.

"A deeper knowledge of the names of an Indian, strengthens my contention. If you will recall your history, there were Indians from many tribes upon this reservation—Flatheads, Pend Oreilles, Kootenais, Nez Perces, Iroquois, a few Delawares, Crees, Colvilles, Spokanes, etc.

"For an example, we will take a Pend Oreille named 'Mescal Michel.' He marries a Flathead squaw, and mingles with her people, who call him 'Many Bears.' He joins a party of Nez Perce buffalo hunters, who dub him 'Shot His Horse in the Head.' He is baptized with the name 'Joseph Peter Michel.' The pioneer settlers call him 'Michel Joe.'

Here we have the same individual known to five different groups by five different names.

'Mescal Michel, Many Bears, Shot His Horse in the Head, Joseph Peter Michel, Michel Joe' passes away. Years elapse, then the few remaining survivors from each tribe tell their story of the same man, each group calling him by the name he was known to that division."

Note

Excerpt from interview with late Andrew Stinger, one of Michel Pablo's partners in buffalo and cattle business.

Finley Brings in Calves
Told by: **Dave Couture and Zephyr (Swift) Courville**
Writer: **Griffith A. Williams**
Date: August 22, 1941

Dave Couture[1] of Camas Prairie asserts that a Flathead Indian named Feenom Finley, and his wife, brought over the first buffalo calves from east of the Continental Divide into this section of the state about 60 years ago.

He is not sure as to the exact date, but to the best of his recollection it was just prior to the advent of the Northern Pacific Railroad in 1882–83.

This small herd consisted of two bull calves and four heifer calves. They were probably hauled in from the Sun River country and were placed on the Finley ranch at the mouth of Mission Creek, near the present town of Dixon.

As the years passed this small band grew into a herd of about 25 or 30 head of strong, healthy, hardy animals and were eventually sold to Pablo and Allard, who were starting in the business of raising buffalo which later were sold to the Canadian government.

Zephyr (Swift) Courville[2] recollects hearing some of the old-timers describing this sale by Finley to Pablo. The amount agreed upon was in the neighborhood of $1600 cash. The cash was spread out on a blanket in an open space in the middle of Finley's pasture. Finley, like most of the Indians, demanded the cold cash. Hearing a noise in the brush while the deal was being consummated, the participants hastily fled, fearing a holdup, but forgot in their hurry to take the money along with them. However, it turned out to be a false alarm, and the deal was finally concluded to the satisfaction of all the parties concerned.

Notes
 1. Interview with Dave Couture at Perma, Montana, on August 19, 1941.
 2. Interview with Zephyr Courville at Plains, Montana, on August 19, 1941.

Diminishing Herds in Judith Basin
Told by: **Antoine Morigeau**
Writer: **Bon I. Whealdon**
Date: September 8, 1941

"My father, who had been a Hudson Bay employee at old Fort Colville, Washington Territory, came to the Flathead Valley in 1859. My mother was an Indian woman. Here I was born in 1866.

"During my boyhood period, I lived much the same life as did the other Indian children in our community. I devoted my days to hunting game in the beautiful Mission Range, fishing in Flathead Lake, and riding my father's ponies.

"Many of our people were still going east of the Continental Divide upon their annual hunts for buffalo. I recall the many preparations for the long trip. The essential thing was an abundance of ammunition. This was obtained through bartering beaver pelts and other valuable furs at the traders' camps. My father often provided trusted hunters with necessary equipment. He knew that when they returned from the hunt, he would be amply repaid in piles of cured buffalo meat and warm robes.

"They left here with their long strings of pack ponies. Some of these horses were always traded to the friendly Indians who were in the buffalo country.

"Each year they came back with smaller amounts of meat. They complained that hunters from the Sioux, Crow, Cheyenne and Piegan tribes, driven to desperation by the extermination policy of traders, government contractors, and white settlers, were killing entire herds.

"In 1872, our people reported that there were only a few remnant bands in that vast region, where once had roamed countless thousands of 'The Monarchs.'

"The following season, Indian Samuel succeeded in capturing four calves. He brought them back upon pack ponies. Now, some of my friends say 'two calves,' but I counted four—two heifers and two bulls.

"Samuel kept a close guard over his young buffalo. Every Indian in the valley, believing these to be the last ones, aided in their protection. They were permitted to roam wherever fancy led them, but always there was an Indian rider in their vicinity. It seemed but a few years until Samuel's buffalo had increased to twelve head.

"Thrifty Michael Pablo, during his rides through the valley, often noticed the animals. He became enthusiastic over Samuel's plan for a large herd. Once in my hearing, he remarked: 'We have thousands of acres covered with native grasses, streams of pure water, high mountains shielding the valley against severe winters. Above all else, Indians who love the shaggy brutes. Yes, our valley will be the safe home for the buffalo.'

"Inspired by this vision, he quickly persuaded Samuel to sell him the twelve head in 1884. Later Charles Allard, who had acquired a herd, put his with Pablo's. So, for a while, the two old friends were partners. Then Pablo purchased Allards' interest.

"If my memory doesn't fail me, Pablo moved the buffalo to Wild Horse Island in Flathead Lake some time in the early part of the eighties.

"He had crossed some with range cattle when I next saw the herd in 1892. These hybrids, a cross between native bulls and buffalo cows, were called 'cattaloes.' They made me think of the undesirable Indians I had known—too much of a different blood to improve them any way. Our old buffalo was, and is, a noble appearing brute.

"In 1905, I counted three hundred buffalo, ranging the banks of Flathead River. Pablo did not know how many he did own.

"About this time, several white families drifted into the valley. Soon we heard rumors that the reservation was to be opened to an influx of waiting home seekers.

"Then Pablo was assured by a man in authority, that the whites were actually coming. He realized that the days of free, open range for his buffalo were ending. He was heartbroken.

"After some consideration, he decided to sell the herd to the U.S. Government. Influential persons, including Theodore Roosevelt, advised Congress to appropriate a purchasing fund, but they were unsuccessful in arousing public opinion to buy the herd and place them in a permanent refuge.

"Sadly disappointed, Pablo sold them to agents of the Canadian government. He received $250 for each of the 709 head. That was in 1907.

"I was busy with other work, so did not join Pablo's crew of roundup riders."

Charles Russell's Comments During Pablo's Buffalo Roundup

"However I do recall the many miles of fences, and the big corrals, near the river. Joseph Houle is one of the several riders still living. Charles Russell had his camp near Sloan's Ranch, and frequently he took part in the riding.

"Russell became a great friend of old Allen Sloan, pioneer settler at Sloan's Ferry. Sloan often told me that Russell was deeply moved over the removal of the buffalo. In one conversation, he remarked to Allen—'My friend, the buffalo now follows the Indian—into oblivion. Two fine types of early Americans exterminated by the damned greed of the whites. Here, while 'tis possible, I shall picture them both in their true colors.'"

Note

Interview with Antoine Morigeau, September 3, 1941.

"I Will Be Meat for My Salish"

Chapter 6

Management of the Flathead Reservation Buffalo Herd

Buffalo in the Flathead
Told by: **Mrs. Camille McGowan**
Writer: **Mabel C. Olson**
Date: December 29, 1941

"After Camille McGowan and I were married in 1891, we lived in Demersville. Two or three years later, the buildings of that place were moved to form the town of Kalispell. The Great Northern track was laid there on a snowy Christmas Day, and to celebrate the occasion a barbecue was given the public. I cannot now remember whether a buffalo or a steer furnished the meat. The buffalo on the Flathead Reservation were then tamer than the cattle that shared the range with them, and had to be driven off the road to make way for the covered wagons and ox teams that were the common means of transportation in that day.

"When Pablo and Allard butchered of their buffalo herd, they often sold the hides of the animals. These the purchasers made into robes, which had many uses. One purpose they served that is not known to many in this day, was in lieu of sheets, which the housewife did not always own. I used them often, and very snug bedding they made.

"Charley Allard, Sr., and Michel Pablo raised many cattalo, as well as buffalo. If Allard, Sr., had lived two or three years longer, he would have become a millionaire.

"Mrs. Bill Irvine, nee Emily Brown daughter of Louis Brown 'No. 1,' a pioneer hunter, trapper and Hudson's Bay trader, worked as housekeeper for Charley Allard, Sr., for a long time. In 1908, when Pablo and Charley Allard, Jr., gathered up their buffalo herd to sell them to the Canadian government, she and her husband helped in the roundup. She was an expert horsewoman, and on the drive sometimes rode 100 miles a day. On one occasion when not a man could head off the buffalo, she checked a stampede of the herd.

"She lived on the reservation when few white women were there; she herself was a breed. Nothing would keep her home if she took a notion to be elsewhere, for she could ride or drive a horse as well as any man."

Note

Mrs. Camille McGowan, 516$^{1}/_{2}$ Spruce Street West, Missoula, has lived in Western Montana all her 71 years.

Malcolm McCloed [McLeod] First to Ride a Buffalo

Told by: **Alex McCloed [McLeod] and Robert McCrea, nephews of Malcolm McCloed [McLeod]**
Writer: **Bon I. Whealdon**
Date: December 10, 1941

"Malcolm McCloed [McLeod], a young Indian boy of the Flathead Indian Reservation, was the first to have ridden a buffalo. It is said that he began riding broncs when he was a little boy. As he grew older, his services as a bronc-buster, cowhand and buffalo-boy where constantly demanded by the stockmen of the valley.

"When Charles Allard, Sr., exhibited a little band of his buffalo at the Butte racetracks in 1893, it took but little persuasion to induce young Malcolm to be present.

"As an original, sensational feature, he was billed to ride a buffalo. This attraction drew a mighty crowd of spectators. Many old-timers said that this could not be done; and, as a result, some stiff bets were placed.

"Young Malcolm, confident daredevil that he was, chose the most vicious young bull in the herd. The maddened creature was roped, thrown and saddled by other 'buffalo boys' from the Flathead range.

"Malcolm, clutching the saddle horn with one hand, and with the other waving his tattered sombrero at the cheering crowd, circled the track at top speed. A thrilling ride it was, but Malcolm, son of warrior stock, gave attention to the old Salish battle cry of victory, as he brought his strange mount to a stop."

Buffalo Cow Steals Pablo's Prize Calf
Told by: **Andrew Stinger, one of Pablo's partners**
Writer: **Bon I. Whealdon**
Date: November 25, 1941

"When the buffalo calves are quite young and might easily become the prey of prowling wolves and coyotes, the bulls share with the dams a mutual protection of their young. During this period the males seem always near the sides of their cows; and woe be unto any foe of the herd, for this is one of the rare occasions when buffalo combine efforts and turn upon the intruder.

"A buffalo cow's maternal nature will often lead her to do the most unusual thing, as was evidenced at the old Pablo Ranch in 1898. Mr. Pablo, a lover of fine breeds of cattle, had purchased a very valuable heifer calf. He kept it in a pen pasture near one of his barns. The hired men tried to make a 'bucket fed calf' of it. However, it never seemed reconciled to its tin pail mother and made the nights hideous with its incessant bawling.

"Upon several successive mornings a buffalo cow was seen as it stood quite near the pasture. Mr. Pablo surmised that she had recently lost a young calf, and hearing the tame one's plaintive calls, her motherly love kept her in the vicinity.

"Such was the case, for going out to feed the calf one morning, he discovered it was gone. The buffalo cow had broken through a parcel of fence, permitted the calf to suckle and then led it out across the prairie.

"That afternoon Mr. Pablo and I rode out on the range about eight miles from the ranch. We entered a ravine, where a small band of buffalo were grazing. There among them were the buffalo cow with the tame calf. Mr. Pablo said, 'That old she has surely adopted my calf. It appears well satisfied, so I'll just let her rear it.'

"Three years later, this same tame critter with a cattalo calf at her side was frequently seen with the buffalo."

Cattalo

Told by: **Andrew Stinger and Robert McCrea**
Writer: **Bon I. Whealdon**
Date: October 20, 1941

"I have seen many of the cattalo, both calves and the mature ones. I will say that they were beautifully formed, and looked promising for beef creatures.

"I was told by Mr. Pablo, and other stock raisers, who were then experimenting with breeding to produce these hybrids, that they resulted from either of two manner of breeding—the domestic bull and the buffalo cow or the buffalo bull and range cow. The crossing of the tame bull and buffalo cow proved the more desirable method, as there was no danger of injury to the buffalo cow in the birth of her hybrid. Often the average domestic cow had some difficulty in delivering a calf from a buffalo bull. However, Mr. Pablo possessed so many range cattle, that the loss of a few did not trouble him any. His preference in hybrids was the cross between short horn bull and buffalo cow.

"Mr. Pablo told me, that at one time he had between 150 and 200 head of cattalo. The hybrid first made its appearance as a result of a range cow mating with a buffalo bull. For awhile, Mr. Pablo was enthused over the new creature, and envisioned a profitable future for its kind. Other cattlemen were of like opinion, and carefully planned efforts to raise cattalo were made.

"The cattalo were large of frame and had deep meated rumps. The flesh was firm, and while I liked it as well as I did range beef, others thought it was inferior.

"Its hide made a fairly good robe, but as the cattalo was several decades removed from the prosperous period of hides and robes, there was little market for that product.

"Andrew Stinger, one of Mr. Pablo's partners dismissed cattalo raising with the remarks: 'We know range cattle and buffalo. They are legitimate things of the range, raised with little effort upon our part; so why in hell waste time producing these bastardly creatures that no one wants?'"

Pablo Loved His Herd

Told by: **Tony Barnaby, Pablo's son-in-law**
Writer: **Bon I. Whealdon**
Date: October 14, 1941

"Many people today, while appreciating the fact that Indian Samuel, Michel Pablo, Chas. Allard, Sr., and Andrew Stinger were the ones who saved the buffalo from extermination, question their motive. Some say that the plan was to build up a vast herd which later could be sold at great profit. Perhaps that is a very natural view; but we, who were associates of these four men, know it is erroneous. The acquisition of money meant little to men of their type, but the preservation of the bison they believed was their duty, privilege and pleasure.

"Pablo, for instance, did not consider a buffalo to be just a great shaggy beast of the plains; but rather a symbol of the real soul of the Indians' past. It was something grand, that, with the culture of his own race, had somehow managed to survive the undesirable features in the white man's system.

"In ages gone by, the buffalo had always been the greatest benefactor of the Indians, often saving entire tribal groups from starvation; now Pablo, a red man, would repay the race's Karmic debt. He would protect the mighty monarch, and provide the remnant a secure paradise in valley Sin-yel-e-min.

"Only a soul patterned on a large scale was capable of such magnificent vision and Michel Pablo was large in every respect.

A deep thinker, an efficient planner, a lavish benefactor of friend and foe; lover of both man and beast; possessor of lofty spirituality; and a believer in his own destiny, Michel Pablo was sure to succeed, where folks of lesser caliber would have failed.

"With a keen eye to his animals' welfare, he knew at all times just about where his buffalo were grazing. He soon realized that they were increasing at a rapid rate; and after he returned from each daily ride on the range, he remarked, 'It is well!'

"Only upon one occasion was Pablo really discouraged. When he was positively assured that the reservation was to be opened to white settlers, he knew that free open range was ending and that his beloved herd must go. He vainly sought to sell them to our own government, in hopes that they would find a haven in some refuge set aside for that purpose. We know that when Pablo heard that our Congress could not be induced to appropriate a purchasing fund, he was moved to manly tears. Only as a last resort did he sell them to the Canadian officials."

Buffalo Solve a Love Problem
Told by: **Que-que-sah**
Writer: **Bon I. Whealdon**
Date: December 29, 1941

"Early in the spring of 1889, a young Coeur d'Alene Indian, whom we called John, came into the Flathead Valley. He established his camp near my property. He was a friendly, splendid appearing chap, and we became very intimate friends. In reply to my inquiry regarding his presence here, he related his story and requested my advice.

"He was in love with a young lady of his tribe. He wished to marry her, but her father was opposed to a marriage upon the grounds that John, being a Christian, would not consent to the ancient tribal rite of matrimony. Then John, with his improved farm lands and civilized manner of life, was too much like a white man to be pleasing to the old brave, who was a blanket Indian!

"When the young fellow persisted in his intention to marry the girl, according to the rite of our Holy Faith, the old man grudgingly consented, provided John would first take bow and arrow, travel into Montana, kill four buffalo, and bring him the robes. Evidently the old warrior thought he had imposed requirements impossible of achievement, and so it appeared to all of us. The buffalo had practically disappeared from Montana's plains, therefore there had been no hunting parties from our region for nearly eighteen years. Then, had there been buffalo, John was of that generation of our people who had never used bows and arrows.

"When he had finished his tale, I told the boy that the quest was hopeless. That he was wasting time to go to the east side, so he would do well to forget that particular Coeur d'Alene maiden and take unto himself one of our Flathead girls, who were much more charming in manners, and shapelier of form than are the squatty Coeur d'Alene females. However, John continued downhearted. He moped around like a forlorn male coyote unable to find a bitch during mating season. We felt very sorry for him. Our prettiest girls went to his teepee to make talk with him, but he would not look at them. He became like another son to my old Mother, who lived with us. Now, my Mother was fully of years, and with a deep knowledge of things. One day she said: 'It is not good for John that his soul carries a weight from week to week because he cannot kill four buffalo, and take that old fool Coeur d'Alene robes fresh from the carcasses. We have more sense than that man. We can help John. What say?'

"Mother, you are crazy like the old Coeur d'Alene. There are no buffalo for us, for John, for anyone.'

"Then my Mother told us: 'Michel Pablo is Indian. He is man of good heart. He has many buffalo. I have many range-steers and ponies. To Pablo I shall give some cattle, some horses. To him I shall talk. Que-que-sah, my son, shall kill four buffalo with his bow and arrows. John shall take the robes to the Coeur d'Alene fool. He shall say the words: "Here old man, are four fresh robes from Montana buffalo killed with the bow and arrow. Now, I take the girl to Holy Church."'

"The old mother talked to Michel Pablo very long time. At last he said: 'Down by the bank of Pend Oreille [Flathead] River is one herd of my buffalo. Que-que-sah shall kill four with his bow and arrows. We shall all have fresh meat to eat. John shall take the robes.' This we did. In three years, John and his wife came to visit us. The old Coeur d'Alene was very happy to get the robes."

Management of the Flathead Reservation Buffalo

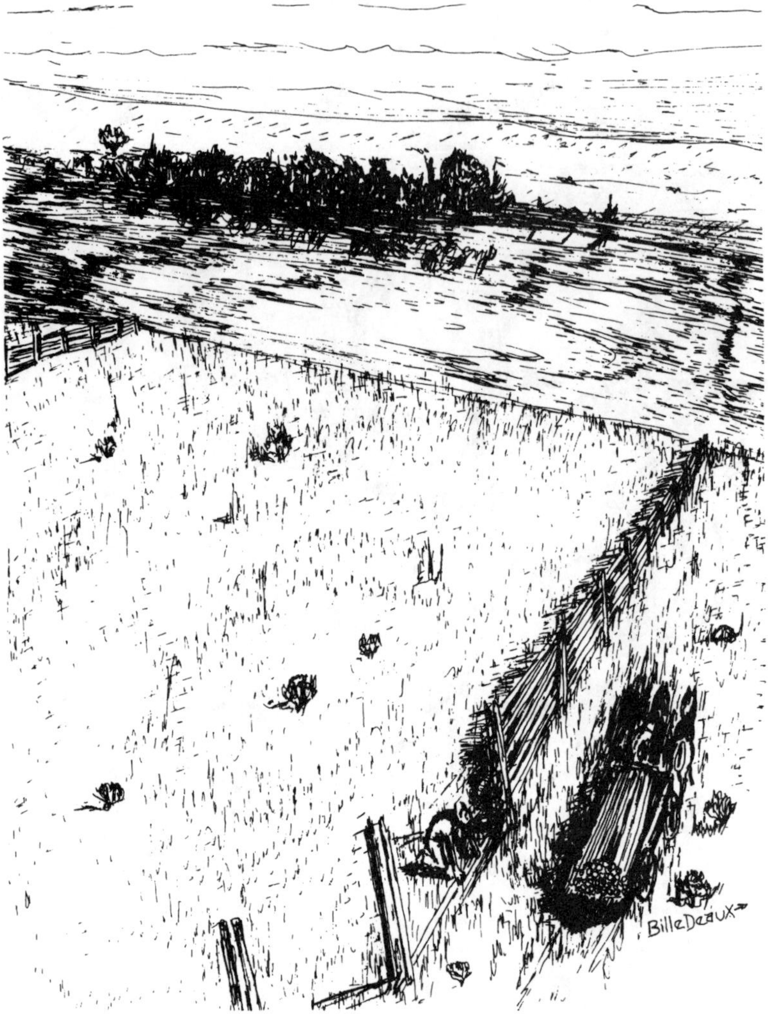
BilleDeaux

Chapter 7

The Buffalo Roundup, 1907-1909

Buffalo in the Flathead Valley
Told by: **Allen Sloan**
Writer: **Bon I. Whealdon**
Date: September 11, 1942

"When I first came to the Flathead Valley, there was a fair size herd of buffalo roaming the prairies. I wondered over their presence here, since from my reading, I had the impression that the region west of the divide was not the native range of the bison.

"A natural curiosity caused me to make some inquiries. I was told that they belonged to two men, Chas. Allard and Michael Pablo. The original herd, consisting of a few calves had been brought from the east side by Sam, a St. Ignatius Indian in 1873. Allard, also, had picked up a number of head through deals with the Indians.

"After I was allotted out at the river, the buffalo occasionally annoyed me by either rubbing and rubbing against my posts until they toppled over, or by completely tearing away sections of fence in their wild stampedes from the hills to the river. Other than that, I scarcely paid attention to them.

"During the roundup, I rode over to the corrals one day. The riders were bringing in a small, terrified band. They were having a tough time doing it, too. I honestly believe I heard more yelling and real western range swearing that short day than in all the years since.

"After a short chat with Arthur Ray, Joe Houle and Michael Pablo, I climbed the corral fence and sat beside Chas. Russell, who was perched there sketching pictures of the buffalo.

"I shall never forget his remark as he pointed to Pablo on his pony, the buffalo, the Indians, the riders and their horses, the prairie, and then toward the snow-capped peaks of Mission Range glistening in the brilliant sunshine—'Here, we have it, Sloan, a last glorious touch of the Old West in the grandest setting Nature ever arranged.'"

Note

From an interview with Allen Sloan, honored pioneer of the Flathead, granted his daughter Della Sloan Culligan and Bon Whealdon, August, 1934.

Buffalo History

Told by: **Robert A. McCrea, an eyewitness**
Writer: **Bon I. Whealdon**
Date: October 23, 1941

"In 1907, Michel Pablo's buffalo corrals were situated directly south of where the village, Pablo, Montana, now stands. These corrals were monstrous, strongly constructed affairs. Mr. Pablo had a wing-fence erected, leading from the corrals westward across the prairie and low, rolling hills. I believe it was nearly three miles in length.

"During the first part of the roundup season, the bison, east of the Pend Oreille [Flathead] River were fairly gentle, and without much difficulty were driven against the wing-fence, and thence into the corrals. I presume this ease in handling them at first was due to the fact that, as yet, they had not been agitated by many days of strenuous driving.

"Mr. Pablo, personally acquainted with the Indian riders upon the entire reservation, employed 25 of the very best broncriders. These 'buffalo boys,' as they were called, were busy from dawn until dark, driving in the buffalo. Mr. Pablo, efficient general that he was, rode here, there and everywhere, supervising all preparations for the big drive to the Ravalli stockyards.

"When he deemed that a sufficient number had been collected, he ordered the corral gates into a long, fenced-in lane to be thrown open. Buffalo, in a charging stream of huge, dark bodies literally poured southward along the lane. Where the fences terminated, open plains invited the ruminants to make panicked attempts to escape toward the river. Mr. Pablo had guarded against that by having his buffalo boys stationed along that side.

"After they had traveled 7 or 8 miles, the buffalo ceased their desperate efforts to get away, although they kept on a swift run all the way to Ravalli.

"It was all a lively, colorful spectacle. Gaily attired Indian riders rode upon splendid, spirited horses. Groups of Indian women and children rich in barbaric colors of beaded garbs and blankets, dotted the sides of the old stage road, to madly cheer as the symbolic buffalo swept by.

"Michel Pablo, descendant of the first American and proud Spanish Dons, savior of the buffalo, and humanitarian, paused long enough to hand a representative of a charitable institution for an alien race a generous sum of money: Magnificent, unequaled Michel Pablo!"

Attempt to Drive Pablo's Buffalo to Ravalli Not Successful

Told by: **Joseph Houle**
Writer: **Bon I. Whealdon**
Date: September 19, 1941

"After the Canadian government had purchased Mr. Pablo's herd, there arose the question of the cheapest and quickest way of getting the animals to Ravalli, Montana, the shipping point. Someone suggested that they be rounded up in corrals and then driven in small bands to Ravalli. This appeared to be the perfect solution.

"Mr. Pablo immediately hired a large crew of expert riders with their horses to undertake the task. After hours of hard labor, they succeeded in rounding up a fair size herd. Mr. Pablo and the boys then decided that instead of taking small bands upon successive days, that this entire herd be driven at once. That decision marked the beginning of troubles.

"The animals were already agitated as a result of the roundup. The mad chase upon a hot day had made them thirsty. Some cows had become separated from their calves. It was their rutting season, when buffalo are unruliest. There were too many jealous, quarrelsome bulls thrown together in one herd.

"In spite of our constant watchfulness and every precaution, a bull with a little band of cows would make a break. This would require many of the riders, in perhaps what was an unsuccessful effort to get them back into the main herd. Possibly, at the same time, another group would try to escape. So it was, all the way to Ravalli. They kept getting away, until when we had reached the Ravalli yards, we had only 30 head remaining of what had been a large herd at the start."

Note

Interview with Joseph Houle, one of Pablo's best riders, Ronan, September 16, 1941.

History of Buffalo
Told by: **Zephyr Courville**
Writer: **Griffith A. Williams**
Date: October 21, 1941

Among the skilled cowboys of the Flathead country who were gathered together in the fall of 1908 by Charley Allard, Jr., to round up the buffalo "outlaws," was Zephyr Courville, better known as "Swift" Courville, whose biography was included in that of his father, Louis Courville, written under date of November 11, 1940.

Before he was 20 years old "Swift" was a range rider and top cowhand for Charley Allard, the younger, whose father had married "Swift's" sister.

Since that biography was written, "Swift" has become the town marshal of Plains, a position he holds at this writing.

In this roundup, according to "Swift," Charley Allard, Jr., had taken a contract from Pablo to round up and corral the buffalo sold to the Canadian government. Allard was to receive $10 a head for each buffalo delivered to the Pablo corral.

Among his fellow riders, of whom there were over a score, he remembers Malcolm McLeod, Jim Grinder, both breeds, and a cow puncher named Bill Lewis, a white, who hailed from the State of Washington, and who was one of Allard's most capable men—a hard riding, tough and capable horseman, much older than "Swift."

Most of the riders were breeds and all were mounted on fast, durable cow horses.

Mr. Courville says: "After rounding up a bunch of the buffalo, maybe 40 or 50 head, we had to keep them moving at a pretty fast clip (so different from cattle) for they stretched out in a long line, with plenty of space between each other, flanked by cowboys on both sides. If allowed to go along slowly, we never knew when an old cow or bull would take a notion to plunge out of line, like a football player going wide of scrimmage, and then the others would immediately follow suit and the whole herd would have to be rounded up again, which sometimes took days.

"One time we had driven about 50 head of buffalo from down on the Flathead River, 15 or 16 miles away, and had gotten them to within about three-quarters of a mile of the Pablo corral, when the whole bunch stampeded, and we lost every one of them.

"On another occasion, in the fall of 1908 I believe, after we had trailed a good-sized herd to Ravalli for shipment to various points outside of the state, and had them, as we fondly hoped, safely in the stockyards, they got scared during the night and tore down one whole side of the heavy fence and scattered to the four winds. It was an exasperating experience, but we riders were young and full of life and rather enjoyed the work of rounding them up again, although it took days of the hardest kind of riding.

"Pablo and Allard took about 40 head of the famous herd to Butte one time in the early 1900s—I don't recall the exact year—and placed them on exhibition there. There the hard-riding cowboys and bronco busters exhibited their skill, riding the bulls bareback and roping and tying the calves. These buffalo, when off their accustomed range, were a good deal easier to handle when surrounded by thousands of gaping spectators, and were inclined to keep close together for safety.

"Many of the spectators had never seen a buffalo and they were thrilled by the clever stunts of the cowboys.

"Pablo was eager to have the government or some national organization take over his herd in the interest of conservation and preservation and tried in many ways to interest the general public in the conservation of this, our largest and most important wild animal. He sold a few head at various times to private parties and to zoological organizations as far west as California and east as far as Maine. These, usually in pairs of the opposite sex, were transported in wagon crates to the railroad at Ravalli for shipment and did not entail much trouble, for they were usually young and easily handled.

"The larger herds, like the one sent to Canada, were trailed north by the cowboys.

"It was while exhibiting the buffalo in Butte that Allard met the famous 'Buffalo' Jones of Omaha and purchased 45 head of mixed buffalo and cattle breeds, or cattalo. These were shipped to Ronan and slaughtered for the butcher trade.

"'Buffalo' Jones, who was an ardent conservationist, was one of the original members of the National Bison Society. He had evidently had some success in his efforts to cross the buffalo and cattle breeds.

"When the big Pablo herd was being dispersed, part of it went to my sister, Mrs. Allard, or rather Mrs. Andrew Stinger, for she had married again after the death of Allard, Sr. To the number of about 30 head, they were later sold to C. E. Conrad, a prominent banker of Kalispell, who later sold his holdings to the government to be placed on the National Bison Range near Ravalli."

Mr. Courville says that the buffalo belonging to the smaller, privately-owned herds were kept close to the home ranches in winter, but, when spring came, they seemed to know that they were soon to be allowed to go out on the open range to feed and would huddle by the corral gates for days, waiting for them to open. They were just like a bunch of children breaking classes for the long summer vacation and anxious and eager to be away.

"Close herd was maintained on these bands on the range, in order to keep them from interfering with domestic cattle," said Mr. Courville, "but, of course, occasionally two or three would turn up missing and be later sighted by ranchers in such sections as the Plains Valley and the Lower Flathead, where the ranchers quickly got rid of them."

Mr. Courville says they did not injure the domestic stock in a vindictive manner, but they were very playful animals and, being much larger than the cattle, they caused injury to the ranchers' stock.

Inquiring as to the characteristics of these mountain buffalo, Mr. Courville, like James A. Cruzan, whom we interviewed recently, is emphatic in his statement that there was a distinct difference between them and the plains buffalo, the former being darker, smaller, wilder and considerably more agile and alert while on the range.

"This is entirely the result of the environment," he says. "Their darker color conformed to the darker background of their shaded mountain recesses, as if to camouflage them from their enemies: the wolves, the coyotes, the mountain lions and, most deadly of all, the white man killer.

"Their sight and sense of smell were very keen and their tapered legs and sharp hooves were made for speed and agility and the important and necessary duty of digging through the crusted snow in search of forage."

Asked concerning the size of their humps in comparison with those of the plains buffalo, he made this very interesting observation: "Their humps were certainly larger, or at least they stood out more prominently than those of the plains variety. The animals themselves were smaller and thinner than the sleek, lazy, well-fed creatures of the plains, and the size of the hump was thus emphasized.

"There may have been little differences in the actual size of the humps of these two animals, but, taking into consideration their different sizes and weights, they certainly were larger on the mountain buffalo.

"Lack of winter feed in its higher and more difficult environment may have had something to do with the size of the hump, and nature, as if to compensate for this lack, may have provided the smaller animal with more space in which to store its fat gathered in the summer. At least, that is my firm belief, for nature has a way of maintaining a balance in all things."

Note
 Interview with Zephyr Courville at Plains, Montana, October 20, 1941.

Pablo Roundup
Told by: **Mrs. Clara Poene [Peone] Reed**
Writer: **Bon I. Whealdon**
Date: November 3, 1941

"My father, James Peione [Peone], was one of Michel Pablo's buffalo boys; as his riders during the 1908 roundup were called. I was old enough to go with him to the corrals, where I would wait until the day's work was ended. Often Mr. Pablo, who was a very kind man, and especially fond of children, would put me on a gentle pony and allow me to ride around with him.

"Many very prominent people from all over the United States came to see the buffalo in the big corrals near Pend Oreille [Flathead] River. They were also interested in talking to Mr. Pablo, the Indian whose vision had saved the great monarchs from extermination. Michel Pablo was a very courteous gentleman, and possessed a remarkable degree of patience in answering the visitor's questions regarding the buffalo, the Indians, horses and range cattle. He was thoughtful of their comfort, too, in conducting them to safe spots, from which to obtain excellent views of the animals.

"I remember a newspaper man, whom Mr. Pablo repeatedly requested to keep off the corral fences, lest he be hurt by the enraged buffalo. The man would climb down, but the moment Pablo turned away, up the fence he would go. He was eager to obtain a feature story for his paper and this he eventually got in a totally unexpected way. He sat upon the top pole with feet dangling in the pen. Occasionally he would stop writing long enough to snap a picture of the infuriated beasts below.

"One ferocious old bull persisted in attempts to break out of the enclosure. I noticed it seemed to concentrate its attention on the side where the writer was sitting, as though that poor literary fly on the fence had caused all his ignominious humiliation of chase and confinement. Finally it made a determined upward lunge, hooking its horns under the top pole, where sat the man. The pole, loosened from the posts, fell across the neck of the buffalo who bore it and its frightened occupant half way around the corral, before heaving both to the ground. The poor fellow, yelling like a Comanche Indian on the warpath, scrambled to safety, just in time to avert a fatal goring. He surely presented a ludicrous sight. He had hit the ground in a pile of soft dung. His fiery red hair was plastered down with it, while green streamlets of the stinking stuff oozed down across what had been a snow white shirt. I have always hoped that with so much buffalo atmosphere clinging to him, he was enabled to write a real story about the beasts."

Note
    Interview with Mrs. Clara Poene [Peone] Reed, daughter of one of Michael Pablo's Buffalo boys.

Ride of the Old Photographer
Told by: **Frank McCloed [McLeod]**
Writer: **Bon I. Whealdon**
Date: September 19, 1941

"The roundup brought many photographers, amateurs and professionals, to the corrals. Among them was an elderly gentleman, whose long flowing gray beard imparted almost the appearance of one of the biblical patriarchs. He was rather feeble physically, and we were all fearful lest he be trampled under foot.

"Mr. Pablo felt sorry for the man, and for his safety had a small platform built among the limbs of a dead pine tree. This elevation provided an excellent and, apparently, safe view of the buffalo.

"All went well, until a band of buffalo, being driven in from the prairie, unexpectedly swung against the base of the tree. The force toppled pine, platform, and patriarch down across the backs of the animals. The old man found himself astride a bewildered buffalo cow. Due to the fact that the animals were pressed together so closely, he couldn't be tossed off and so trodden to death. There he sat near the rear end of the moving sea of broad backs, his long beard fluttering in the breeze, a very serene lord of the 'thundering herd.'

"The herd travelled nearly a hundred yards, before it split, and the old man found a safe opening to fall off. As we picked him up, he said, 'Boys, I was lucky to get a back seat for that ride.'"

Buffalo's Horns, Defensive Weapons
Told by: Frank McCloed [McLeod] and Andrew Stinger
Writer: Bon I. Whealdon
Date: October 28, 1941

"When enraged, they were ready to do battle with man, prowling animals, or horses.

"Their stout, sharply pointed horns made dangerous weapons. While we were hauling them in wagons to Ravalli in 1907 and 1908, one cow, who had been placed in a wagon crate made of heavy material, became furious when she heard her calf bawling from its cage, further back in the long wagon train. In her struggles, she gained considerable freedom of action for her head. She was determined she was going to get to the side of her calf. She rammed the side of her prison wall, driving the points of her horns through a two inch pine plank.

"However, she broke her neck, so we had to stop and butcher her. Mr. Ayotte, the Canadian purchasing agent, took a hind quarter to camp saying: 'Douglas (his partner) and Chuck Russell (C. M. Russell) are so damnably strong on buffalo atmosphere, that I'm going to feed them enough of this meat to make 'em paw the ground, snort and beller.'

"One unusually hot day at the corral, an old bull smashed his way out; and before a fine saddle horse could be gotten out of the way, it was gored in the bowels so badly by the Monarch Bull, it had to be shot."

Buffalo Gal Prevents a Stampede
Told by: **Mrs. Mary Blood, sister of Billy Ervine [Irvine]**
Writer: **Bon I. Whealdon**
Date: October 27, 1941

"Michel Pablo was very happy when Emily Ervine [Irvine], wife of his old friend Billy Ervine [Irvine], offered her services as a rider on his buffalo roundup.

"He knew her ability as a top hand, as she had ably assisted at many a roundup of cattle. She had ridden broncs—bad ones at that—over every mile of the Flathead rangeland. Then, too, she knew buffalo, their habits and how to handle them, since her part Indian girlhood days.

"Her fellow-riders said she was the equal to any two of them. A beautiful, graceful type of woman, always mounted upon a splendid appearing horse; C. M. Russell said, 'The sight was enough to stir any he-man's admiration.'

"She demonstrated her efficiency one hot day, when after continuous riding amounting to 100 miles, she was successful in sheering the herd unaided and thus preventing what would have been a most disastrous stampede.

"Billy Ervine [Irvine], also participated in the 1908 roundup. Mr. Pablo was so pleased over the work performed by Billy and Emily Ervine [Irvine], that when the season was ended, he presented them with the best buffalo cow in the herd. That act was an Indian's token of appreciation—quite aside from the big wages paid them. Until the day of his death, Billy Ervine [Irvine] treasured the hide of that creature; and delighted in telling his visitors its history."

Teeth Knocked Out: Buffalo Bull Plays Role as Dentist in Extracting Indian's Aching Teeth

Told by: **Clara Poene [Peone] Reed and Alvin Poene [Peone]**
Writer: **Bon I. Whealdon**
Date: November 4, 1941

"Our father, James Poene [Peone], assisted Michel Pablo during the roundup of buffalo sold to the Canadian Park Service. Later his services were engaged in transporting the animals to the Ravalli stockyards. Often he assisted in getting the buffalo into the cattle cars.

"Father had suffered from a number of ulcerated teeth all that summer, but appeared unable to contact the agency dentist, and have them either treated or extracted. At one time he, and another Indian, were assigned as a crew to unload buffalo from the wagon into the corral chutes.

"They attended the hoist gates at the back end of the wagon crates. When the wagons were backed into position at the chutes, father and his partner manipulated the levers, which lifted the gate and gave the animals an opening into the chutes.

"One day, while unloading a wagon, the levers jammed, when the gate was only partly raised. Father's teeth were dealing him indescribable agony right then, and with every bodily strain to lift the gate, he would groan, and mutter: 'Blessed Virgin, my god damn teeth are giving me hell!' An impatient old bull, seeing the opening, crowded under the gate so quickly that the levers released striking father squarely in the mouth with its upper board edge. Fortunately he was not killed, but the blow knocked out every front tooth and loosened the others. After that father's Indian friends dubbed him: 'Teeth Pulled by Bull.'"

Buffalo History

Told by: **Bias Stinger, son of Andrew Stinger, Michel Pablo's partner**
Writer: **Bon I. Whealdon**
Date: October 13, 1941

"Andrew Stinger, a pioneer buffalo raiser in the Flathead Valley, was born in Ontario, Canada, 1871.

"He came to this region in 1884 at the age of 17 years, [and] he went to work for Fred Rouillier [Roullier], driving stage and freight from Polson to Kalispell, Montana. Then for a while, he was a cowboy upon the Flathead range. After his marriage to Louise Courville Allard, widow of Chas. Allard, Sr., he acquired his wife's interest in the Allard herd. Michel Pablo, taking a liking to young Stinger, immediately formed a partnership in both the buffalo and cattle business. Pablo and Stinger had large herds of buffalo and range cattle all over Flathead Valley.

"At one time, these partners had better than 5,000 head of choice cattle, marked with Stinger's brand

$$\overline{11}$$

(Bar eleven). Each year they made large shipments to the Chicago markets. One season they sent an entire train load of 3,000 head.

"When the Allard-Stinger-Pablo herd of buffalo was sold to the Canadian government in 1907, to Mr. Stinger fell the task of transporting the animals to Ravalli.

"He hired every available teamster, team and wagon in the sparsely settled region. They built a stout crate to hold two or more buffalo, according to sizes, upon each wagon. At one time, Mr. Stinger had 31 wagons on the road between the corrals upon the east bank of the Pend Oreille [Flathead] River and Ravalli. He received $10.00 for each head delivered to Ravalli, Montana.

"Mr. Stinger opened Ronan's Pioneer Meat Market with Antoine Morigeau as partner in 1909. They did a profitable business, as they owned their own buffalo and range cattle.

"Andrew Stinger's favorite rope-horse was called 'Babe.' This animal was known and admired by every Indian and cowboy upon the reservation."

Buffalo on the Prod

Told by: **Tony Barnaby**
Writer: **Bon I. Whealdon**
Date: October 15, 1941

"This buffalo left the bunch—went up on this pinnacle slope and turned around—refused to budge. One of the boys made a remark that he had a good notion to get off his horse, walk up there, grab him by the whiskers and pull him down. That sounds like a hard problem. Anyone who knows a buffalo, would tell you that it would be as good as any. They worked biggest part of the day, but could not move him out of there. One of the old heads finally said he knew a very good way what to do with him. (So what) they asked? Leave him alone. They did, (and) the next day he was back with the bunch.

"The buffalo looks very clumsy. The buffalo boys when driving a bunch will bet you $5.00 against a chew of tobacco you can't ride up to any one of them and quirk him."

Note

Source: Tony Barnaby, Michel Pablo's son-in-law, eyewitness sketch and account of roundup incident.

These are Mr. Barnaby's words; and as Mr. Barnaby is an elderly Indian, and so generous in helping, I did not deem it quite fair to correct his language. Then, too, being an Indian myself, I like the Indian manner of expression. Bon I. Whealdon.

The Buffalo Roundup, 1907-1909

"*I Will Be Meat for My Salish*"

Chapter 8

After the Roundup

Pablo's Remnant Herd
Told by: **Fred Beaulieu, a pioneer settler**
Writer: **Bon I. Whealdon**
Date: November 4, 1941

"I did not know how the story originated that all of Pablo's buffalo, excepting 10 head, were rounded up. It surely cannot be from any account given by our old-timers, who were, and are, truthful people.

"As the total of shipments to Canada revealed, Mr. Pablo owned several hundred more buffalo than he had figured on. The riders all knew that a number of buffalo had eluded the roundup and found temporary refuge among the hills west of the Pend Oreille [Flathead] River. The current attitude was that the Canadian government had already gotten many more than it bargained for. Further attempts to get these few would prove quite expensive to our friend Pablo, so why kill our horses trying to corral the scattered remnant?

"In April, 1911, an Indian and I crossed the river at Buffalo Ferry, rode across the flats, and into the open foothills. Our search for a valuable team of stray horses included a thorough inspection of all the gulches and bench lands. In one canyon we ran into a small band of Pablo's buffalo. We had with us a foolhardy pooch that we were afraid could be trampled to death, should he startle the little herd into a stampede down the narrow defile. Therefore we very quietly retraced our route in order to take a trail following the canyon ridge. From the height we counted the animals—31 cows, a few bulls, several calves, and 3 cattalo.

"What became of this remnant band? Well, there are several elderly Indians and white settlers who can, if they so desire, inform you that several buffalo hunts—the very last in the United States—were conducted during 1912."

Buffalo Story

Told by: **Henry Burland, grandson of August Finley, buffalo hunter**
Writer: **Bon I. Whealdon**
Date: November 21, 1941

"I was reared in the teepee of my grandfather. His place at the head of Spring Creek, near Ronan, Montana, was the meeting place for all the old Indians in the vicinity. Here they came to visit and relive the experiences of the earlier days. It seems that since I was a small babe, strapped to the 'papoose board,' my environment has been distinctly Indian.

"When I was about ten years of age, Michel Pablo hired my grandfather, his brother Dave Finley, and some of the older Matt families to hunt out, and butcher the buffalo still roaming at large in the Magpie Springs district. These animals had escaped the roundup of Pablo's herd when it was sold to the Canadian government.

"The party also included Mrs. August Finley and Mrs. Matt and the children of the respective families. We set up our teepees in a pine grove near the river. While the men hunted and butchered the buffalo, the two women did the cooking for the crowd, and we youngsters entertained ourselves in juvenile games known to children of every race and clime.

"The men were very successful in their hunt, and soon had all the small band of buffalo, excepting one cow, who had eluded the riders so often that we began to think she was under the devil's care and protection.

"August arose one morning and informed the crowd it would be the last day to hunt the 'devil cow.' He stationed a few men at points along the river bank. Then he gave the women and us children instructions that should the cow come toward camp, we were to make a lot of noise that might scare her toward the river.

"August with a small crew rode to the foothills, where they hoped to rout the old girl from her hiding place.

"Of course we completely forgot the orders left with us. The women began preparing dinner for the crew. They had several large pots of camp grub bubbling over the fire. As they worked, they gossiped, as all Indian women love to do. Dear old ladies, they were both very fat. So heavy on their feet, they waddled about just like Xmas geese.

"Finally one of the boys looked up the long slope and saw the buffalo cow making a bee line for our camp. Like so many pine squirrels we children climbed up among the branches of the trees. The ladies, at last seeing the reason for our commotion, managed to hoist and pull at each other until they got into a buggy, where they filled the seat to overflowing. Mrs. Matt in her excitement had carried with her a pot of hot beans. This utensil she waved in the air, while she and her companion fairly shouted the prayers for the faithful dead.

"Apparently the old cow neither saw nor heard any of us, as she charged between campfire and buggy on her way to the river. However as she swept by the old ladies, Mrs. Matt hurled the pot of scalding beans at her, yelling: 'More heat to you daughter of hell!'

"Soon August rode into camp. I'll never forget his look of disgust nor his scornful words, as he viewed the ladies on the buggy seat, the steaming beans scattered over the ground, and us kids perched like jabbering magpies upon the pine limbs: 'I have very goddamn soft Indians today. So damn soft, I could poke a cat's tail through them at any spot and not ruffle a hair on it. We are all soft, fat old squaws. We go to Ronan now, and live in wood house like whites.'

"Years later, I understand, that another party captured the buffalo cow and turned her in on the Bison Range."

Indian Ward Aids Dr. Morton J. Elrod in Selecting Site for Buffalo Park

Told by: **Andrew Stinger and Sander's** *A History of Montana*
Writer: **Bon I. Whealdon**
Date: November 26, 1941

Dr. Elrod, influential member of the American Bison Society and head of the biological department at the University of Montana, was delegated to find a suitable site for the buffalo park. His search included the northern part of Idaho as well as Western Montana.

When he arrived in the Flathead Valley, the home of the last free herd of buffalo in the United States, it was appropriate that he contacted Duncan MacDonald, intelligent and well-informed native of the Flathead Indian Reservation.

Mr. MacDonald, oldest son of Angus MacDonald, first pioneer in the region, knew the topography of that portion of Montana better than any other human being—Indian or white. In addition to this useful knowledge, Duncan was very familiar with buffalo, their habits, and their range requirements.

Mr. Elrod could not have chosen a more delightful helper and companion, for Duncan knew the history of the valley, the Indians, the flora and animals of the country. He was well versed in the white man's way of life, possessed an analytical mind, and was a gracious, charming conversationalist.

In Mr. MacDonald's words: "Professor Elrod and I saddled our horses and began a thorough inspection of the entire countryside. As we rode along, we discussed the advantages and disadvantages of each locality. I know we both kept eying the possibilities of the slopes around Quilseeh Peak, which is near the confluence of the Pend Oreille [Flathead] and Jocko Rivers. After we had satisfied ourselves that the Flathead Valley proper would very soon be utilized for agricultural purposes, we again turned to the Quilseeh Peak region. We rode to that highest elevation, which commands an excellent view of the adjacent country. On the south the ridges dip and flatten toward the

Jocko; to the east is beautiful Mission Valley; to the north the slopes terminate near meandering Mission Creek; and to the west they halt at the Pend Oreille [Flathead] River bank.

"Here, at last, we had discovered a vast, ideally situated natural park, that, because of its topography of ridges, gullies and steep slopes, could never be converted into profitable farming lands. The numerous gullies were knee deep in luxuriant growth of wild grasses. Besides this forage, these depressions would give animals ample shelter from the wintry blasts. There was an abundance of fattening bunch grass upon every slope. The ridges to the south and west were always fairly free of deep snow; and upon these exposures grew the very first green grasses of springtime. There were spacious woodland stretches of fir and pine, where big game could find protection from severe storms, and find cooling shade during the extreme heat of summer. Equally important, the ravines, as I knew from childhood days, were well watered the year round, by countless springs and small creeks."

Note

Source: Notes on interviews with Mr. Andrew Stinger; also Helen Fitzgerald Sanders, *A History of Montana* (Chicago: The Lewis Publishing Co., 1913), vol. 1, pp. 690-94.

"I Will Be Meat for My Salish"

Part III

Biographies and Other Subjects

A few of Bon Whealdon's interviews of Salish elders in the 1920s to 1940s were published in the *Hot Springs Sentinel* (Hot Springs, MT) in 1954–56. The newspaper refers to sixty-eight articles but only fifteen were published. These interviews covered a number of topics such as Salish legends, religious beliefs, and crafts. Chapter 9 includes the Montana Writers Project interviews that made it into print in the *Hot Springs Sentinel*. These interviews had been edited for an unpublished book-length manuscript of Flathead or Salish stories called "Sunlight and Shadow: The Story of the Flathead Indians."

Also in Chapter 9 is "Myth of the 'Sheep's Head,'" a chapter of "Sunlight and Storm" that was not published in the *Hot Springs Sentinel*. A copy of this chapter was preserved by the Whealdon family and made available by Jack Whealdon and Wallace Evans.

Chapter 10 includes the Montana Writers Project interviews that discuss various aspects of horse raising and cattle ranching on the Flathead Reservation.

The final chapter, number eleven, reproduces the biographical information gathered by the Montana Writers Project about Salish and Kootenai tribal members and white people who married into the tribes. Most of these biographical sketches were found in the files relating to the livestock and grazing history of the western United States, and consequently mainly cattlemen were included.

Chapter 9

Other Aspects of Salish Culture and History

The Bitterroot
Told by: **Lassaw Redhorn and Alex Beaverhead**
Writer: **Bon I. Whealdon**
Date: Not given

In those olden days before the coming of the white man, the Indian inhabitants of the land occasionally experienced seasons of near famine.

During one of these periods of privations, the people eked out their scanty diet by adding the edible roots of the region. It is told that during one of these times of suffering that an aged Salish woman discovered that the roots of the bitterroot (*Lewisia rediviva*) possessed satisfying nutritious value.

A beautiful myth regarding its origins was told by several elderly Salish Indians:

An aged woman, wife of a shaman, saw her children slowly starving to death because they had neither meat nor fish. The sunflower shoots that the people had been eating had grown old and woody. "My sons have not food," she murmured. "They will all die. I will go to the Little Bitterroot, where I will weep, and sing the song of death." She went to that place. There she sat. She bent until her face touched the ground causing her silvery hair to spread out upon the earth. The spot where she sat became wet with her bitter tears.

The Sun god, coming up over the mountains of Sinyelemin (Mission Range) heard the music of her death song. He said to the woman's supernatural helper: "Your child sorrows for her people. Go and comfort her with beauty out of dead things and with food!" The helper assumed the form of a red bird. It flew to the suppliant upon the ground. It nestled in the silver of her hair and whispered:

"The tears of your sorrow have gone into the soil; your bitterness has become roots of a strange plant. The plant shall send up leaves. It shall have as flower, the silver of your hair, the rose of my wing feathers. The people will come to dig and eat the roots of the plant. They will find it bitter with your sorrow, but it will be food to them. They will see the flower and will say: 'Here is the silver of our mother's hair upon the ground and the rose from the wings of the spirit bird. Our mother's tears of bitterness have given us food.'"

Amot Kan, Highest Mystery, Was God of Old Flathead Indians
Told by: **Lassaw Redhorn, Que-que-sah, and Dominic Michell**
Writer: **Bon I. Whealdon**
Date: Not given

Flathead Theology

The Supreme One of our older beliefs was given several names: "Amot Kan," "Big Spirit Above," "Sky Chief," and "Highest Mystery." However, Amot Kan and Highest Mystery were the names most generally used in praying to, and praise of, the Deity. In connection with the subject of Amot Kan, it is well to always bear in mind that He was ever present in our older Indians' thoughts, and that they were a very religious people, and as faithful in their prayers to Amot Kan, the Highest Mystery, as their Christian descendants are in their churchly devotions.

Some have imagined that the old Flathead worshipped the sun, and believed it to be God, but that is not true. Often the Indians, knowing that the sun was necessary to their physical existence, looked toward that orb and gave thanks for, but not to, it. Amot Kan, creator of sun, earth, and all forms of life, was the One to whom thanks was offered. The sun was the symbol of Amot Kan (Life Giver), the sole object of their adoration, in somewhat the same way as the cross is an emblem of the Christian faith. Thus, the Flathead were never worshippers of the sun, as were some other western tribes.

When an old Indian was asked if the sun was Amot Kan, he said: "No, no, the sun is Amot Kan's child who helps us. We look at the sun, and thank Amot Kan for it. The sun is our very good friend."

Amot Kan, ruler of the upper world, master of the unseen, helper of mankind. He created Coyote, a tutelary being, to be his special helper, and to him entrusted the welfare of all Indians. It was Coyote's mission to neutralize the evil work of Amteep, the wicked chief of the lower world. Thus, when Amteep sought to bring famine upon the earth by blighting the berries, fruits, and vegetables, Coyote prevented its accomplishment by inducing salmon and trout to seek places of spawning in the freshwater streams. Then he taught the Indians how to catch and prepare fish for food. When Amteep, the author of all sickness, emptied his parfleche of diseases upon the Flathead, Coyote brought healing plants and herbs from the upper world, and after they had begun growing upon the earth, he taught their medicinal values to the shamans. Acting under Amot Kan's instructions, Coyote brought the bison to the plains of Montana, and then taught all Indians how to make bows and arrows to slay the great beasts, and so obtain supplies of meat and tallow. When Amteep blew his icy breath over the land to freeze the practically nude Indians, Coyote taught the people to use the warm robes from the buffalo in making teepees, clothing, and bedding.

However, during the early days of the race, and before the creation of Coyote, Amot Kan would often appear in person in order to live as a man so that he might teach his people how to live better. Amot Kan always came in the body of an elderly man, and strange to relate, this body was that of a white man. During Amot Kan's sojourns upon earth, there were no afflictions, deaths, or misfortunes of any kind among the Indians. Winter did not come, and the harvests of berries, fruits, and roots were bountiful. During these Eden-like periods, Amteep and the evil spirits were unable to come up into the earth world.

There is an old myth to the effect that Amot Kan, during his last visit in the flesh, promised the Indians a future period when Amteep and his works would be eternally banished from the earth, and man would be restored to a state of spiritual innocence. However, it is possible that this belief is the result of some infusion of Christian doctrine.

Excepting during incarnations in human form, Amot Kan was always alluded to, and addressed as an incorporeal, all-pervading Spirit. Even in the underworld, the wicked ones at time sensed his presence, and it was believed that in the fullness of time, ages hence, those hapless ones would be liberated into a newness of life. Thus, eventually the entire universe would know and respond to the goodness and mercy of Amot Kan. An Indian student, who insists that the older beliefs of the race have great spiritual significance, interprets this ultimate universal redemption of all creatures as follows: There are in the universe visible and invisible laws and forces, that we, in ignorance of their nature and operation, call evil but which, if properly controlled and directed, are in reality good and constructive. Some time, somewhere, man fully developed according to the Divine Image within his being, shall have understanding of, and dominion over, all things now deemed evil. Then potential good will have become reality.

It was Amot Kan's will, expressed through shamans and direct revelations, that all Indians dwell in a state of peace. The thought of the Amot Kan message was that all men are brothers and that good will soon banish strife. Thus ages before the whites with their Jewish-Christian message, set foot upon the North American continent, the fatherhood of God, and the brotherhood of Man was taught and practiced by the Indians.

The Red and White Races: A Flathead Legend

Told by: Not given
Writer: **Bon I. Whealdon**
Date: Not given

According to Flathead legends Old Man Coyote was the figure of good, while Mountain Sheep was the symbol of evil.

Old-Man-In-The-Sky had just drained off the earth which he had made. When he had it all crowded down into the "big salt holes" (seas), the land became dry.

About the [that?] time Old Coyote became lonely. He went up into the Sky Land to talk to Old Man. Old Man questioned him.

"Why are you unhappy and crying? Have I not made you much land to run about on? Are not Chiefs Beaver, Otter, Bear, and Buffalo on the land to keep you company? Why do you not like Mountain Sheep? Did I not place him up in the hill parts, so that you need not fight? Why do you come up to talk so often?"

Old Coyote sat down and cried many more tears. Old Man became very cross and he began to scold. "Foolish Old Coyote, you must not be dropping so much water upon the land. Have I not worked many days to dry it? Soon you will have it all covered with water again. What is the trouble with you? What more do you want to make you happy?"

"I am very lonely, because I have no one to talk to. Chiefs Beaver, Otter, Bear, and Buffalo are busy with their families. They do not have time to visit with me. I want a people of my own that I may watch over them," Old Coyote replied.

Old Man said: "If you will stop this shedding of water, and cease annoying me with your visits, I will make you a people. Take this parfleche (a case made of rawhide) and take it to the mountain where there is red earth. Fill it full and bring it back to me. Hasten!"

Old Coyote took the bag made from the skin of an animal, and traveled many days and nights. Finally he came to a mountain where there was much red soil. He was very weary after such a long journey, but he managed to fill the parfleche. Then he was sleepy.

"I will lie down to sleep for a while. When I awaken I will run swiftly back to Old-Man-In-The-Sky." He slept very soundly.

Mountain Sheep came along. He looked at the red soil in the bag.

"The poor fool has come a long distance to get such a load of red soil. I do not know what he wants it for, but I will have fun with him," he said to himself.

Mountain Sheep dumped the red soil all out upon the Mountain. He filled the lower half of the parfleche with white earth, and the top with red soil. Then, laughing very heartily, he ran away to his hiding place.

Old Coyote awakened. He tied the top of the parfleche and hurried with it to Old-Man-In-The-Sky. When he arrived the sun was going to sleep. It was so dark, they could scarcely see the soil in the parfleche.

Old-Man-In-The-Sky took the dirt and said, "I will make the soil into the forms of two men and two women."

He did not see that half of the soil was red, and other part was white.

"Take them to the dry land below. They are your people.— You can talk with them, so do not come to trouble me," he said to Old Coyote, when he had finished shaping them.

Old Coyote put them in the parfleche, and carried them to dry land. In the morning he took them out, and put breath into them. He was very surprised that one pair was red, and the other white.

"Now, I see Mountain Sheep came while I slept. I can not keep these two colors together," he said.

He carried the white ones to the land by the big salt hole. The red ones he kept in his own land, so he could visit with them, and that is how Indians and white men came on the earth.

The Mystery People of the Lake Taught Local Indians Many Things

Told by: **Alex Beaverhead, Eneas Conko, Charley Michell, Lassaw Redhorn, and Joseph MacDonald**
Writer: **Bon I. Whealdon**
Date: Not given

Speaking in awed tones, Alex Beaverhead, Eneas Conko, Charley Michell, and Lassaw Redhorn related the following tradition to Bon Whealdon in 1923. Harry Burland, who had grown up with the elderly Salish, translated slowly so that he could record it as it was told. The following year Joseph MacDonald told him the same tradition and also the story of Burning Star. MacDonald called Whealdon's attention to two distinct types in stature and in head formation and features among the old Salish and Kalispel on the reservation. Su-appi is the Salish term for white man.

You are old friends and are not here to laugh at our tales. Soon we shall all go to the Spirit Land. Our sons care not for the old ways and the old stories of the Indians. We tell what our grandfathers' grandfathers passed on about the strange people of long, long ago. Put our words into the Su-appi language, so that our sons' sons and their sons may know them.

Then when they come to us in Spirit Land, they will say, "The old men spoke true words."

Then we and the Mystery People will reply, "Yes, the words came from whole tongues, not from forked tongues."

Where did the Salish first come from? We know only the story our old men told our old men down from the beginning: the first Salish were driven down from the country of big ice mountains, where there were strange animals. Fierce people who were not Salish drove them south. So in our stories, our people have said, "The river of life, for us, heads in the north."

After many generations, the Salish held the grounds from way west, eastward, and past the red paint caves near Helena. Then our warriors were so many that the three enemy tribes of the Dakotas dare not fight us. The west tribes by the Great Salt Water Mystery were our friends. With them we traded.

After a long, long time men in strong canoes came up the rivers from the great river which flows into the Great Salt Mystery. The men were not Su-appi and not true Indians. They brought with them the women who were Coast Indians, and their children. The children's heads had been pressed flat with boards when they were babies.

There were not many of these people, and they troubled no tribes. They lived on fish, small game, berries, and roots. They made their homes on the islands in the lake, and they did not hunt far from water. Our people liked them. Sometimes they would paddle west and be gone a long time, all the summer moons. When they returned, they brought with them much dried red salmon which they traded to our fathers for buffalo pemmican, bitterroot, carrots and camas.

They were skilled in curing sick people and knew how to make good medicines from roots, seeds, and leaves of plants. They showed our old men how to make good healing salve by mixing deer tallow and balsam pitch, boiling it over low fire, and then putting it into hide bags until used. This salve cured cuts and deep wounds quickly.

They taught our old people, whose eyes were weak and sore from much tepee fire smoke, to wash their eyes with clean water and then to put in them a little clean bear oil. They made tea from the bark of the chittim tree and drank it when they wanted to clean out their insides. They told our people not to throw filth near the water they drank and to keep their bodies clean.

At that time our people got their fire-starters in two ways: by rubbing two sticks together and by taking embers from trees hit by lightning. Both were slow, slow ways. The Mystery People taught all the river tribes the right rocks to strike together in order to throw sparks into dry leaves, pitch wood, and moss for quick fires. They told our women to dry or bake or roast fish and meat. Raw and frozen fish, they said, cause sickness.

Where did the Mystery People come from and what became of them?

We know only what their old men told our old men. "Our fathers," said the Mystery People, "came from a land beyond the Great Salt Mystery. The winds blew on the sails of their big salt canoe, and carried them far. They were lost. In many sleeps they came to the mouth of the great river and toward land. Another storm broke their big canoe. The Indians along the shore treated them kindly.

"Soon a bad sickness came to all the Indians along the rivers. Many, many people went to the Spirit Land. Our fathers told the Indians not to use sweat baths for this sickness, and not to plunge into cold water, or they would all die. They stopped their sweat baths, and many got well. All the Indians were happy to have our first men as friends and gave them wives, canoes, paddles, bows, arrows, and spears. Afterwards, our fathers thought that perhaps they might find people of their own kind inland, so they went eastward up the rivers and on to Flathead Lake."

That is all we know about the Mystery People. They were smaller than the Salish and the Nez Perce and the Coast Indians. Their features were finer, but their color was the color of Indians. They were kind people, good to women and children, and they liked to laugh and to play. They knew many things which they taught our people.

Long ago all this happened, long before the Su-appi came. The First Mystery Men died. Their sons' sons and daughters married Salish people. Soon no Mystery People were left on Flathead Lake.

When the first Su-appi came, they saw with the Salish a few old Mystery Men with flat heads. So they called us Flatheads. They thought that all Salish had flat heads, but that is not true.

Myth of the "Sheep's Head"
Told by: Louise Finley, Chief Mose Michel, Mrs. Allen Sloan, and Joseph McDonald
Writer: Bon I. Whealdon
Date: Not given

High in that picturesque cluster of snow-capped peaks, jagged ridges, waterfalls, and shining glaciers, known as the Mission Range, is a mountain brow called the "Sheep's Head." This odd formation of granite rock bears a most striking resemblance to the face, head, neck, and front shoulders of a colossal sheep quietly lying down, but keeping a watchful eye on the northeastern hills.

A drive on the highway, southward from Ronan, Montana, affords one the best view of the "Sheep's Head."

The early white settlers soon discovered this rock, and for many years it has been pointed out to visitors as one of the unforgettable natural attractions of the Mission Range. At one time the Ronan State Bank drew considerable attention to the similitude by issuing a series of checks, each having on its face, a likeness of "Sheep's Head."

That the keen-eyed Indians of the past detected the resemblance is evidenced by the name, Sheep Face Mountain, that they gave the same slope of rocks. A myth, accounting for the phenomenon, was passed down to later generations.

>When the country was young, old Mountain Sheep showed his brutality towards the animal, bird, and fish tribes, and before long they all came to hate him very much. He spent most of his time devising methods of tormenting the other peoples of the mountains and valleys.
>
>When he saw the birds flying down to drink or bathe at the edge of the streams, he rushed up to frighten them away. If he saw the fish on their way up the little creeks, he diverted the water into new channels, so that the fish perished in the shallow pools along the old creek courses. He frequently loosened stones in the precipice trail, so that deer, elk, and goats, attempting to pass that way, dislodged sections of the path, which carried the poor creatures to death at the foot of the cliff.
>
>He particularly detested the young of all species. When he found bear cubs playing upon some high mountain ledge, he watched until the mother had unsuspectedly withdrawn to a distance, whereupon he would rush in and butt them into the deep canyon. Many a litter of playful skunk kittens were trampled under his sharp, death-dealing hooves.
>
>By striking trees with his head, he was able to jostle eggs and young birds from their nests to the rocks below.
>
>Nor was his cruelty restricted to animals, fish and birds, for the Indians were also subjected to his brutality. Were he to see hunters down at the bottom of a ravine, or

climbing a mountainside, he would, if possible, start an avalanche of boulders tumbling from the peak to bury the hapless men.

When during his constant rambling about the hillside he found a patch of ripe huckleberries that might be visited by the pickers, he delighted in running between the clumps of bushes, brushing them violently with his head, until the ripest berries were all shaken off.

Among all animals, birds, fishes, and Indians he had not even one friend. Only two did he fear—Chief Old Man Coyote, who was very wise and good, and Chief Eagle of the Mountains whose beak and talons were sharp and tearing. These two he always sought to avoid.

At last all the animal tribes, birds, and fish became so desperate that they gathered for a council at that creek called Narrow Creek (Post Creek).

"One thing," they said, "we must do. We must kill Mountain Sheep, the old enemy, who delights in maiming and destroying our people. We are not wise enough to devise plans to protect ourselves, or destroy this evil that harasses us all the span of our lives. Will our two great friends, who are wise, good and powerful lead us?"

Now Chief Eagle of the Mountains had flown down for the conference, and Chief Old Man Coyote was also present. They knew the plea of the tribes was for them.

Old Man Coyote spoke: "Chief Eagle and I have talked. We know what must be done, and how. We must hunt out, and restrain this enemy of all living things, but we have not the power to destroy this evil creature, for he was with us when life came to all. Chief Eagle, whose vision is clear, and I have chosen the place where he shall be forced down—alive, but powerless to hurt the peoples.

"Mountain Sheep now takes his sleep in the sunshine on the rocks, west of the ice-spread (McDonald Glacier). East Wind will come quickly bringing the stiffening of the ice-spread. The men of the valley, the birds, and the animals must go swiftly to the mountain where lies that enemy. All will carry the good rocks, both large and small. These they will place upon the back and hind quarters of the abominable creature, but the head of it shall be left uncovered, so that all the peoples when they see it, will say: 'This is our enemy.' We shall weight him to earth with the burden of all our good rocks, so he cannot move about to destroy us."

All this, the tribes quickly attended to, and the peoples of the valley and mountains were very happy, and they said: "This thing that is evil is now kept down by our good rocks, that we carried against it."

How Ancient Tom-Toms Were Made
Told by: **Lassaw Redhorn**
Writer: **Bon I. Whealdon**
Date: Not given

Before the advent of the white men with their saws and wood chisels, the making of a tom-tom or Indian drum, was a slow task. The ones used by Indians today are mostly factory built, and are obtained at those curio stores and mail-order houses that cater to Indian patronage. It was not so during the days of my elders, who had only the crudest of tools to fashion desired articles.

Sometimes the craftsmen were fortunate in finding a log which had been hollowed out by forest fires. In lieu of a tree so prepared, a cottonwood was felled by burning at its base. If decay had already eaten away or pulped the heart region of the trunk, the work was greatly simplified. Then followed the exacting job of burning off a trunk section of desired length. The shell between the two rings of fire was kept moist, so the flames would not spread, and so spoil the exterior of what was to be the tom-tom shell. The rotten center was the starting place for the hollowing out process, which was done with either fire or a primitive stone gouging tool. When the exterior was one-half to three-fourths of an inch in thickness, the gouging work was deemed completed. The tom-toms were usually the hides of elk or buffalo, cut into two round pieces, each a trifle larger than the end of the shell it was to cover. Before being placed over the ends, the two pieces of hide were thoroughly soaked in water. When in position, the hides were laced together with very strong thongs. Then the tom-tom was set out in the sunlight to dry. As the tom-tom heads dried, they shrunk until they were tightly stretched, but with always the required resiliency for proper tone effect.

If the maker were artistically inclined, and wished to adorn his handiwork, he might paint the sides, using a vermilion obtained in a cave near Helena.

The First Tom-Tom—A Gift from Father Sun (Myth)

Sun looked upon his children. He saw that they were very quiet people. He said: "I have given them many things, but their hearts are heavy." He sent for Coyote and asked him: "Why are my people so quiet and their hearts sad? I have given them many gifts yet they are silent.

Coyote replied: "True are thy words, Father Sun. They have been given many things to eat, and to wear but their hearts you forgot to make light. They hear the strong voice of Thunderbird; the water talking at the falls; the yellow birds singing from the swaying thistles; the night birds calling; the wolves on the ridges; the buffaloes pounding the earth when they run, and the north wind whistling on their teepee poles. They have all these sounds in their hearts, but they cannot tell them out and so lighten their hearts."

Then Sun asked: "What shall I do to make them express themselves? Go, Coyote, and call out the sounds from their hearts, that my people may be happy, as are my other children." (Presumably, the birds and animals.)

Coyote went down to earth again. He met old Beaver on the trail. They talked about the peoples' sadness. Old Beaver told Coyote his thought: "We will go to the teepee of the young hunter. From it, we will steal all his elk hides and buffalo robes. He will want more, but it is the wrong season for him to go kill buffalo so he will go elk hunting. Then he will work our plan. It is very good, brother Coyote."

The young hunter was very angry when he found that all his hides and robes had been stolen from the teepee. He asked Blue Jay: "Who stole my hides while I was away?"

Blue Jay replied: "Two wise old men carried them away. Get a wife to live in your teepee. If she is lazy, she will sleep on the robes, while you are gone. Then the old men cannot take them away."

The young hunter and his people went to the mountains to hunt more elk, and killed a bull. He carried it to his camp. The fire flame jumped out and burned off the hair. The young hunter was disgusted when he saw the hair burned off, so he threw the green hide over a burned out pine stump. In the morning, he went to the mountain. He was gone many days. When he came back to camp, the people said: "We have been waiting for you a very long time. Now, we must go to our homes in the valley." They started down the mountainside. The young hunter was very slow putting his things together.

He went to get his elk hide but the sun dried it fast over the hollow stump. He pulled at the hide, but it did not come away from the stump. He pulled again but he fell back upon a stone. He was very angry at the hide. He picked up a club and struck it. It gave a great noise like Thunderbird. He beat it fast many times and he heard buffalo feet pounding on the prairie.

His people down the mountain heard the Thunderbird and the buffalo feet. They came running back to the young man crying: "We heard the voice of Thunderbird, and the sound of many buffalo running on the plains. How does this come from your camp? Have you made such strong medicine, you can call buffalo to the mountains? Where are the bird and buffalo? We do not see them."

The young hunter told them: "The voices are hidden in the stump-hollow, under the dried hide. When I beat upon it, their voices answer me. See!" Then the hearts of the people were very light. They made the voices under the hide speak for them. They danced around the stump. They found that the quiet voices in their hearts, and the ones from the stump, were the same. Then songs came out of their mouths.

Blue Jay Brings the Chinook Wind

Told by: **Eneas Conko, Alex Beaverhead, Lassaw Redhorn, and Phillip Pierre**
Writer: **Bon I. Whealdon**
Date: Not given

When the world was very young, Amotkan, the Creative High Mystery, gave a little part of the Salish country to Thunderbird. This was the North Crow Creek Canyon of the Mission Range. Thunderbird was happy to have an area of her own and to know that her longtime enemy, Coyote, could not enter it. There had always been much jealousy between the two. Now she was free to lay her eggs and to hatch her young without being troubled. There in North Crow Creek Canyon she gave birth to her three daughters: Blue Jay, Crow, and Magpie.

Thunderbird was kind to the people when they came from the valley to hunt, to fish, and to gather huckleberries in her canyon. If a storm was coming through the East Pass, she would warn the people to leave. Her deep thunder noises were her warning to them.

All went well for a long, long time. Then a careless hunter failed to put out his camp fire, and a great fire spread through Thunderbird's canyon. The forest on the canyon floor was destroyed; the flowers and the berries were burned; the deer, elk, birds left the canyon. Worst of all, the creek dwindled away and then dried up.

Thunderbird was very angry at the destruction of her canyon country. Angrily she beat her huge wings against her breasts and thundered out punishment against the people of the valley.

To the cold Northeast Wind she said, "Stand in the pass. Blow hard. Blow your chill breath down my canyon and out on the valley. Drive away the people who have destroyed my country."

So at each darkness, Northeast Wind came and blew his cold breath into the valley. Soon the grasses and the plants died, and ice came upon the big lake in the Salish country (Flathead Lake). Shivering with the cold, the people went into the

Bitterroot country. Animals and birds took refuge there also, as did Blue Jay, Crow, and Magpie, the daughters of Thunderbird. Nothing with life remained in the valley.

Many, many snows passed, and Thunderbird's anger softened. Then she became lonely and longed to see her daughters, the Indians, the animals, and the little birds. Again she spoke to Northwest Wind. "Cease blowing your icy breath, and go. Too long you have punished the valley. If you will go, perhaps my daughters, at least, will come to see me."

Almost at once a great stillness came over the land. A scout felt the silence and reported to the Salish chief who was living at the place where the warm waters flow.

"The ice wind blows no longer in the valley," the scout told his chief. "And Thunderbird in the canyon is making a noise like sobbing."

Then the head chief said to his people, "When the land becomes warm again, we shall go back to our old homes in the valley. Will Coyote tell us how we can please Thunderbird so that she will hasten the warming of our country?"

But Coyote, not liking Thunderbird, replied, "Let the big bird with the big noise sit forever in the region she has made desolate. I shall not help."

Then Blue Jay, who loved the Salish people, offered her help. "Coyote is old and lazy," she said. "He thinks of nothing but of filling his stomach with salmon. So he has become a deceitful boaster like my noisy sisters, Crow and Magpie. I myself will help the Salish and make glad the heart of my mother, Thunderbird."

So at the right time, Blue Jay flew west to ask Chinook Wind to warm the valley and help her friends. Chinook Wind's heart was warm and kind.

"Gay and good little bird," he said to Blue Jay. "I will hasten to the relief of your friends if you will show me the way."

So Blue Jay flew before the Wind until they came to the valley below the Mission Range. There he blew his warm, moist breath a long, long time across the land. The ice melted, grass and flowers grew, trees came to the Mission Range, deer and elk returned to the canyon.

Thunderbird was happy. "How can I repay you, little daughter?" she asked.

Blue Jay answered, "Keep your temper down, my mother, so that the innocent will not suffer with the careless ones."

Note

The above myth was told to Bon Whealdon, in 1922 by Eneas Conko, Alex Beaverhead, Lassaw Redhorn, and Phillip Pierre.

Bon Whealdon Gets Scalp Dance Story in Interview with Old Indian
Told by: **John La Rose**
Writer: **Bon I. Whealdon**
Date: Not given

I will tell you what I can recall regarding the scalp dance. Although I am a very old man, I do not think any enemy scalps have ever been taken during my lifetime. There were four among the possessions I inherited from my grandfather but I did not think they were proper things for Christians to keep, so I buried them.

When I was a boy, I saw the old warriors bring out the scalps and other war trophies, and reenact the scalp dance in a manner that was considered very true to form.

The warriors mounted their ponies and rode away from camp. After a little while a runner came riding in. He carried a bundle of arrows, their number corresponding to the scalps that the party had taken. The women and children ran out to meet the victorious, homecoming band. The warriors had painted their faces black and their hands red. Each fighter carried a lance to which he had fastened the scalps he had taken. He held it aloft, so that the admiring people could see what he had achieved. There was much excited yelling and shouting. Immediately the war chief announced a scalp dance. This was always a joyful celebration with a twofold purpose—gratitude to the unseen helpers for their aid in slaying the enemy and the rendering of homage to heroes by the home folks.

The dance was usually held in the central opening of the teepee encampment. The warriors conducted the first dance, during which by gestures they cleverly imitated all the battle experiences they had undergone.

This was always followed by the story telling period. The chief, or leader, of the war party had the honor of being first to describe the battle. Then each warrior who had taken a scalp exhibited it to the cheering crowd, and related his particular exploits and experiences. During the intermission between speakers, the drums were beaten, and the people wildly applauded each thrilling event in the recitals.

The women performed the last half of the dance. They donned the garbs of their heroes, painted their faces, and carried bows, arrows and lances. The wives, mothers, and sisters of the warriors took possession of the scalps. They bore the gory locks on poles and lances, and headed the long procession. After much shouting, they formed a dance circle. The four bravest warriors sat down at the drums, outside the circle. They beat the drums and chanted the scalp song. The women danced toward the east in a swaying circle. Sometimes the dance lasted several hours, and repeated the next day. When it was all over, each warrior claimed the scalp he had obtained in battle.

The Blue Jay Ceremonial Dance
Told by: **Chief Mose Michell, Alex Beaverhead, John Delaware, Thomas Eulopsen, Tom MacDonald, Joseph MacDonald, Antoine Morigeau, and Harry Burland**
Writer: **Bon I. Whealdon**
Date: Not given

"The Dance of the Bluejay is probably the principal expression of the hopes and woes of the Montana Salish," stated H. H. Turney-High in 1933, in his description of this annual ceremonial dance. "When the time for the ceremonial has arrived, all members of the tribe who have some ailment to be cured, some ambition to be fulfilled, as well as those who are merely interested, assemble in the sumesh lodge." Led by the shamans, the dancing begins, it consists of regular hops in the same rhythm as the music.

The traditional rites were discontinued in 1938, because of the passing of the most elderly full-bloods and because of the lack of interest of the present generation. The Salishan tribes on the Colville Reservation also held the Blue Jay dance every year until some time in the middle 1930's.

The following information about the ceremony of the Salish and Kalispel, recorded in 1920 by Bon Whealdon, was given by Chief Mose Michell, Alex Beaverhead, John Delaware, and Thomas Eulopsen—elderly full-bloods; and by Tom MacDonald, Joseph MacDonald, Antoine Morigeau, and Harry Burland—educated mixed bloods.

The myths that follow, obtained from some of the same old men, seem to explain why the Blue Jay was thought to give such strong sumesh or spirit power to the shamans.

> When we were young men, the Blue Jay or Kwas-Kwee rite was held each December or January, when Sumesh power is strongest. It was always observed in a large medicine tepee or log cabin away from the presence of curious white men, small children, and Indians who were evil in their living and unclean of habit and person; for Blue Jay would not demonstrate its work if undesirable people were present.
>
> Before the ceremony began, those who were to participate went through a process of purification. This cleansing was done for a three-day period prior to the actual meeting. It consisted of numerous sweatbaths, chanting of spirit songs, invocations to the Ekone beings (celestial beings interested in man's welfare), and fasting.
>
> For some reason long forgotten, the sitters, while in session, must not have any objects of metal on their bodies or in their clothing. So they had to wear buckskin clothes or drape robes and blankets about them.
>
> In the old Salish language we would chant for a long time: "Come, power bird. We are prepared. Show thyself. Prove thy power."
>
> Then the Blue Jay would come into the center of the tepee and do many things for us: Cure disease, tell us where to hunt and trap, tell us of enemies.
>
> The last night, the third one, Blue Jay would give different powers to different people: Some men to have dream visions; some men to walk, with feet bare, on burning

coals—no red come, no blisters or burns on skin; some to take flaming embers to hold in hands—no red, no burns come; some men to go long way in snow and freezing—no cold, no sickness come.

Yes we know the old way of Blue Jay and of our people. We speak not with forked tongues. It was good.

Old-Time Flathead Indians Had Varied, Delectable Diet

Told by: Not given
Writer: **Bon I. Whealdon**
Date: Not given

The writer was recently surprised, when a young Flathead Indian remarked: "My great grandfather's generation must have had a rough time of it, trying to subsist on a diet of deer, elk and buffalo meat." It was a pleasure to tell him that the old Indian's bill-of-fare was not restricted to meats. There were edible roots and bulbs, as well as various kinds of berries, which were gathered, processed and stored for winter use.

The bitterroot (spetlem) in particular furnished a starch substance in their diet. They were very fond of the roots of this plant and in May would dig, clean and store away great quantities of the bitter, tangy roots. When added to a meat-stew, or cooked with sweetened fruits or berries, the early whites who visited the region in 1847 found spetlem a pleasing acquisition to the menu.

In June the wild carrot (Slokem) crop was ready to be harvested. Dug during this proper season, wild carrots are just as tasty and nutritious as the varieties introduced by the white men.

In July, pstchelu or "white roots" were collected for winter consumption. Then in August, every available man, woman and child worked long, hard days, gathering vast amounts of the treasured camas (etwa).

Huckleberries on the mountainsides, service and elder berries, and even the chokecherries, were picked to be sun-dried for the months of deep snow. Then there were other edible berries, which were of too perishable nature to be stored away, but which were enjoyed while fresh.

Blue grouse, cottontail and snowshoe rabbits were plentiful in those days. These made occasional pleasing changes in the winter meat diet.

Annually bartering-visiting trips were made to the friendly tribes in Idaho. There they obtained supplies of dried and smoked salmon. The local Flathead streams (as yet unpolluted by white man's activities) teemed with native trout.

During the late fall months, our Salish went to the plains of eastern Montana for the bison-hunt. These great beasts provided the hunters and their families with an abundance of meat, some of which was smoked and dried. Pemmican was made by pounding dried buffalo or elk meat into a powder form. Often this meaty powder was mixed with marrow and dried huckleberries. This was a delectable food.

The bison, also, furnished other necessary articles. The skins were prepared for tepee-coverings and for some pieces of clothing. There was glue from hooves, cups and spoon-ladles from the horns. The sinews provided thread for sewing. The warm robes served as bed-coverings.

For seasoning certain food, they had the spicy, aromatic roots of the hoskirs or minnewac plant, procured near the quiet snow-fed pools in the highlands. Another condiment was shautemkan, or pine moss.

Truly Amotkan, great and kind God of the Salish, gave His children a sheltered, delightful region, bountiful in all things essential to their welfare. It is pathetic that a knowledge of an older happier way of life of a grand people is swiftly passing into the limbo of forgotten things.

Indian Boys' Balls, Toys, and Games
Told by: **Shot-His-Horse-In-the-Head**
Writer: **Bon I. Whealdon**
Date: June 3, 1942

All Indian boys loved to play, and they appear to have amused themselves with their balls more than do the white children today. As soon as they were old enough to toddle about the teepee, they began rolling their balls around. When they grew older, and were able to join companions at games, they were taught to play catch. They soon developed a contest with balls which they called, "Kick ball," where two opposing teams were engaged. There were goals well marked with poles for objectives, and two balls were used. The losers had to line up, bend over and rest the palms of their hands upon the ground, and then each received one swift kick on his seat by a victorious opponent. In hopes of revenge, the losers always insisted on another game.

Other than the name, a meager description, and the punishment inflicted upon the defeated team, an exact knowledge of formation and technique of "Kick ball" appears lost.

Balls for very small children were the inflated bladders of little animals. Often upon these balls were painted tiny, amusing, grotesque faces. Balls of the older boys were the bladders of large game animals. These were encased in coverings of doe skin. The balls for severe usage were covered with tough buckskin.

Sources of Flathead Dyes and Paints
Told by: **Lassaw Redhorn and Dominic Michell**
Writer: **Bon I. Whealdon**
Date: Not given

Our people required dyes and paints to adorn skins, robes, bags, and other craftwork. Then too, they frequently painted their faces and bodies in symbolical designs for the ceremonial rites.

Red was the color most commonly used. Red stains were easily obtained from ripe strawberries, raspberries and thimbleberries. However, stains quickly faded out, and therefore were not as desirable as dyes and paints. A pink-hued lichen which grows upon the rocks in the higher altitudes, was gathered in late August. When thoroughly dried and pulverized the substance from this lichen was a bright red powder. This was mixed with deer grease, or thick fish oil, and then used to paint animals, arrows, or forest scenes upon one's personal belonging. Alder bark, boiled down, furnished a beautiful shade of red dye. The very best red mineral paint (vermillion) was obtained from a cave near Helena, Montana, and some of the same material was procured through bartering with both the eastern Washington and British Columbia tribes. This paint was much in demand for the symbolic designs painted on face and body, and which portrayed personal experiences, war scenes, and contacts with guardian spirits.

It was believed that a person with face painted red was secure from physical, and spiritual enemies. That an ominous dream might not be actually fulfilled in one's life, the dreamer, upon awakening, immediately painted his, or her, face a brilliant red color. Red paint, upon one's face or body assured success in hunt or battle. A red circle painted around a wound hastened its healing. A snake's likeness painted upon an expectant mother's right hip was expected to give her safe delivery of a healthy child. A coiled snake, painted upon the belly of a slave woman by the head woman of the lodge, protected her from a philandering husband.

A large red circle, described upon the chest of an aged man or woman, symbolized a long full life. A boy, or girl, seeking unseen helpers and spirit songs, hoped to contact powerful, beneficial ones by painting upon his or her forehead a red triangle, and dusting the hair with red powder. An awkward gait in a girl's walk was corrected by painting her feet, ankles, legs, and knees red.

Yellow was another favorite skin paint. The brightest form of yellow was obtained from wolf's moss. This is a lovely lichen, growing extensively along the western slopes. It was either dried and pulverized into a powder, and then mixed with a grease for painting purposes, or dipped in water and then applied to skin by rubbing. This paint was also used in painting wooden articles and hides. Yellow, like red, was strictly an earth color.

A beautiful blue dye was obtained from boiling certain kinds of well-rotted wood.

This type of material was found in damp, swampy regions. Blue was used to represent objects of both the upper physical world (sky), and of the spirit land. Another rotten wood, thoroughly boiled, yielded a green dye. The deepest shade of green, and the most permanent on wood and hides was from "green slime"—a viscous mass of freshwater vegetation, moss green in color. This was dried in the sun, and then pulverized. Green, an earth color, was seldom used for facial designs.

White (clay and powdered fungi) was considered "the dead color." Its use was shunned by ordinary laymen, but occasionally a shaman would employ it to picture the death of an animal or a person, but never the spirit of either. The spirit of anything never died, therefore it was always represented by the "eternal blue."

Crude but effective paint brushes were made by tying a bunch of horse's tail hair to the end of a twig. Sometimes the paint was applied with the fingers and sticks. Frequently, designs were first painted upon the palm of one's left hand, and while still moist, were then applied, or stamped upon the face or body. In work that required accuracy, friends would lend their assistance.

Black, usually charcoal, powdered and mixed with grease, appears to have had but two uses. A hunter would paint his face and hands black out of respect for some animal, generally a bear, which he had slain. Often some wag would paint his entire body black for clownish imitations of a playful black bear. The Flathead deny that black was ever used by them in portraying night and forest scenes.

The knowledge of the sources of dyes and paints, and of the rich symbolism of colors is rapidly passing away.

Little Information Available on How Arrowheads Were Made
Told by: **Harry Burland, August Finley, and Dave Finley**
Writer: **Bon I. Whealdon**
Date: Not given

It is not known just when the Flathead came into possession of sufficient guns and ammunition for hunting and war purposes, so they could discontinue the use of bows, arrows and spears. When they arrived here in 1841 the missionary priests found the tribe with a few rifles, and many of the old weapons. The loss of arrows and spears in hunts and battles required a constant supply of new ones, so it is safe to assume that the arrow-makers were busy at their ancient craft as late as 1835. From that date onward, our Indians, through their contacts with traders, had little difficulty in exchanging pelts for the coveted arms of the whites.

No living Indian knows the exact method by which his forefathers manufactured their arrowheads. He may recall that his elders spoke of the kind of rock, and the water drip that was used, but that is the extent of his knowledge of the subject.

The late Harry Burland, Flathead Indian, gave the clearest account, as he had the story from the older Finleys who in their lifetimes had frequently visited an old arrow-maker. His camp was located three-fourths of a mile north of the present site of Ronan. At this spot, upon the east bank of Spring Creek, the aged man dwelt and plied his trade as late as 1830. He, it appears, had always been an arrowhead and spearpoint maker. Occasionally a close inspection of the ground still rewards the researcher with a faulty arrowhead and few flint chips. This particular artisan used an extremely hard flint rock, grayish-black in color.

August and Dave Finley told how the old man would first scratch a crude arrowhead design upon a flat piece of flint which he then placed in a low fire. When it was ready for the shaping process, he raked it out from the red hot coals and onto a slightly warmed flat stone. Then he flaked it into desired form and size by using his water drip, which was a wooden bowl affair with a tiny hole in its bottom, and attached handle. With this primitive equipment he deftly deposited a drop of water on the heated flint, just where he wished a flake or chip to loosen and fly off the parent body. Often an invisible seam in the flinty material would expand, resulting in a faulty point, which was thrown into the discard pile.

Another location, often visited by local people in search of arrowheads and chips, is a sand bank near Mud Creek, southwest of Ronan. After a windstorm has shifted the top sand, one may have the good fortune to find several specimens of excellent workmanship. These are pure-white flints with reddish streaks through them. A rare find, several years back, was a lovely moss-agate, which had been shaped into an arrowhead. Another evidence of the antiquity of the site is the piles of fresh water husk shells, scattered about the area.

Flathead Names of Long Ago
Told by: **Harry Burland, Tony Barnaby, and Antoine Morigeau**
Writer: **Bon I. Whealdon**
Date: Not given

A long time ago the names of Indians were derived from dream experiences. Something that came as a vision in a dream, was considered lucky for him, and he was named for it. These visions, he believed, came from his guardian spirit. Often his spirit helper would give him two names—one for use in his tribe, and the other a secret, spirit name to be used only when calling for help from his guardian spirit.

Other names were given by admiring friends to commemorate brave deeds. Names repugnant to the bearer were dropped at once. Unfriendly rivals or competitors might give a man contemptuous names, but these were not used by his friends. Out of modesty, Indians often adopted names contrary to their character or exploits. Humorous names were sometimes given to white men or Indians by their friends. Unfortunates with physical deformities were often given names describing their afflictions. Most names contained adjectives denoting numbers, sizes, shapes, colors, etc.

Hereditary names were often bestowed on children by their parents. Names known to one tribe were not recognized by other tribes and away from his own people an Indian usually had another name. When the "Black Robes" baptized an Indian, he gave him a Christian name, and white men often gave the Indians nicknames on their own account.

Often an Indian would adopt a name quite at variance with any personal characteristic, such as his property status, or exploits, so we have him being called "Weak Heart," "No Kill," "Small Elk," "Little Bear," "No Horse," "Small Robe," "One Elk," "Buffalo Calf," etc.

A very few names, generally applied affectionately by friends to their fellow braves, a well-liked white man, or a child, were of a humorous nature. Thus, occasionally we find such names as: "Head-Like-A-Peeled-Turnip," "Big-Cabbage-Head," "Red-Fire-On-His-Face," (a white man with a fiery red beard), "Beak-of-a-Hawk," "Old-Stinking-Goat," "Small-Dirty-Calf," and the like.

Some feminine names convey a poetic path. A small girl, crippled in her feet, was called "Little-Flower-With-No-Roots," another unfortunate child was named "Red-Fern-Wind-Blew-Over;" a small dumb girl was known as "Song-Not-Come," a little blonde white girl, greatly loved by the Indian women, was called "Little-White-Violet," and some times "Flower-Of-The-Snow."

The unfortunate with a physical deformity, or with some peculiar irregularity of face or figure was certain to be given a nickname which called attention to his defect.

Many names were hereditary, but others were passed on to the children only if the parents wished it. There has been much difficulty in establishing the identity of some early braves, because of an individual being called by several names. Among the Flathead were Indians from neighboring tribes—Crees, Pend Oreilles, Couer D'Alene, Spokanes, Kootenais, and even a sprinkling of Iroquois. It often happened that in addition to the names given to him by his spirit helper or parents, some friend of another tribe would call him by a new name. Then, too, if he had a blood brother, he was certain to be given a name by him, expressing admiration of some valorous exploit or characteristic. When "Black Robes" baptized him he was given a Christian name. Later, some white settler, unable to pronounce Indian names, might give him still another name.

A good example of how the Indians chose names is this: The son of an early white settler had his hair cut short, and then his head shaved. His bald head amused his Flathead friends very much. Whenever he met them, they would ask him to remove his hat, so they might see his head. This always resulted in much hearty laughter. Soon they were calling the boy "Head-Like-A-Peeled-Turnip," a nickname by which he was known all the rest of his life.

Indian Tribes Were Noted for Loving Care of Children
Told by: **David Finley**
Writer: **Bon I. Whealdon**
Date: Not given

The Flathead, in common with their good neighbors the Pend Oreille, Kootenai and Couer d'Alene possessed a very deep and lasting regard for their children. Indeed their love for the young was an outstanding characteristic of all Salishan people. To this esteem is attributed the fact that the children of their bitterest enemies were never put to death when captured. The small persons were usually adopted into the homes of childless Flatheads, and reared as members of the tribe. There were many instances when little ones of sufficient age to remember and grieve, were actually returned to their own people.

However, despite this tender love for this issue, the old Flatheads did not indulge them to the extent of coddling, and so unfitting them for the stern realities of primitive existence. With thoughtful, ever watchful affection, the parents sought to instruct their young in tribal crafts and pursuits, and to harden them to endure under conditions where weaklings could not survive.

This strenuous process began the moment a child was born. The midwife, or some other attendant immediately carried the infant to a cold, running stream, where it was quickly bathed. After this chilly ablution the youngster was roughly spanked upon its rump to toughen its skin in that portion.

If the mother's milk flow was small, the child's diet was enlarged by feeding it weak broth from meats and vegetables, that at such an early age would have killed the ordinary white child.

It was clothed in the softest of robes—rabbit furs, fawn skins, and beaver pelts.

For a journey the child was wrapped in a spotlessly clean robe and lashed to a cradleboard, which the mother carried upon her back. When the destination was reached, it was removed from the cradleboard and put in a criblike carrier, which served as the infant's bed while in the teepee. Sometimes, during a temporary stop for rest or lunch while on a trip, the cradle, or carrier-board, was suspended from a tree branch, or was leaned against a rock or dirt bank at an angle comfortable for sleeping.

Acting upon the old belief that there was much strengthening value in the meat broths, a puny weak infant was frequently bathed in such liquids. Some frontier white settlers were imbued with the same idea, and if a child was frail would dip it into a vessel of meat and vegetable broth, which they called "pot-licker."

Imperfect vision was rare among Indian children, but when a case did occur the child's weak eyes were moistened with its own urine to which water from a running stream had been added. That a child might be assured a thick growth of hair, its scalp was massaged with oil, or grease, and the hair thoroughly brushed. Children were never permitted to care for their own hair—in fact were forbidden to even touch it. When a boy reached the stage of puberty his hair was tied in a single knot at the nape of his neck. A girl attaining the same age, had her hair tied in a knot back of each ear.

During the period of adolescence boys and girls were given a severe course of training. They were instructed regarding the nature of sex, their duties and obligations, and sex relation.

At this time the child was taught the essential value of physical health and endurance. Nor was the spiritual welfare of the youngster neglected, for the elders instructed both the boys and girls how to obtain sumesh (medicine powers) and how to make their contacts with unseen helpers.

Along an Ancient Trail—1908
Told by: Not given
Writer: **Bon I. Whealdon**
Date: Not given

In North Crow Creek canyon is an old Indian pathway, worn smooth by countless generations of moccasin-covered feet. It leads one into the very heart of beautiful Mission Range, where there are many scenic and historical attractions to admire and to ponder over.

If one desires to catch occasional glimpses of big game, there is a region in upper North Crow where elk, deer, black and grizzly bear, mountain goat, and cougar roam. If on fishing bent, North Crow Creek up to the last falls teems with sporty, but elusive members of the finny tribe.

If weary of the trials and disappointments of the white man's busy, dizzy world, tarry awhile—a few days, a week, or a month—in any one of the many appealing camp sites by creek or bubbling spring. Here, drop that needless burden of worldly cares and enter into the kindly, soothing, healing spirit of Nature that permeates the area. Restoration to a glorious outlook on life is one's reward.

The lover of the virgin forests is bountifully delighted in the yellow pines, firs, spruces, and tamaracks, which arch and shade the way from canyon gate to the summit, magnificent specimens through the branches of which the sunlight filters and mellows. Amotkan's mighty cathedral, where beauty, majesty and harmony reign supreme.

Flanking a nearby gorge, chiselled wide and deep by the snow water of the ages, shapely birches with limbs looped by purple clematis neighbor with graceful aspens that gently shake their leafy robes as though tremulous from some deep inner joy. Dainty white spiked blossoms atop the tall stems of bear grass thrive among the glossy green clumps of dwarf laurel, while dense mats of creeping kinnickinick ablaze with crimson berries transform each jagged stone heap into a thing of vivid beauty. Other mountain flowers mingle with ferns and bracken from highest peaks to the huge, mist-sprayed, moss-covered boulders at the water's edge. Tiny Princess pines, used as a blood purifier, and gloriously hued "marsh brilliants" fringe the quiet snow-fed pools in the upper meadows. Here the Indians have come, from time immemorial, to dig the spicy roots of the Husk-kus, or minnewac plants, which are used for smoking, chewing and medical purposes.

Nearby in a sequestered vale is an old, old camping site with fuel for fires, water, and sweet mountain grass for the ponies. To this spot in early autumn will come our Indians with a long string of pack and saddle horses. Then the erstwhile lonely glen suddenly awakens to the activities of huckleberry pickers—bark-basket making, the trampling of ponies, the play and laughter of happy children and the incessant barking of many dogs. Pine squirrels and chipmunks scold and berate these intruders. Timid, squealing rock-bunnies scurry to refuge in the shale-slides.

Over the Gray Guards, as the towering ridge to the east is called, a pair of eagles lazily float as they keep watch o'er the sky-pointing peaks.

When evening silence broods like a gentle spirit over a still and pulseless world, the old men, wrapped in heavy mantles of race-old fancies and memories, sit by gleaming campfires. Finally stirred to speech by the owl's hooting in the dead spruce grove, or by the coyote's call from Mount E-tam-a-na's lonely brow, the patriarchs again relate the exploits and glories of the tribe. For a time the ancient past with its intriguing powers of medicine men, the half poetical mythology of the race, wars, buffalo-hunts and horse-raids holds sway.

In Mount E-tam-a-na, so called by an early people of Salishan stock, [one] once again touches on the long ago. To this lofty peak came an Indian youth (for whom it was named) to fast and to pray for a revealing of his spirit-helper. This unseen being, when so obtained, played an all important role in the life of its protege—an ally in battle, director in hunts and a healer of sickness.

Indians Find New Use for Flour

Told by: **Oliver Gebeau**
Writer: **Bon I. Whealdon**
Date: Not given

In 1938, old Oliver Gebeau, formerly Indian policeman on the Flathead Reservation, told me the following incident. Evidently it took place in 1891 shortly after Chief Charlo was forced to give up his ancestral home in the Bitterroot Valley and lead his band of Salish to the reservation in the Jocko Valley. To help them establish their new homes, the Government issued them rations of food and some other supplies.

Charlo's band of about 200 were very resentful because of their eviction from the land they so passionately loved, the land of their forefathers. The elders regretted that they had not heeded the words of Chief Joseph of the Nez Perces, who, not many years earlier, had said to them: "Come, Salish friends. Join with my band. Together we will be strong, and we will go in peace to the country of the white Queen. If you tarry here, many white people will soon come to take your land. Then the Government will move you to poor lands."

Oliver's father had stood near the Nez Perce chief and had heard his words. The Salish had refused to accompany Chief Joseph, they had remained on peaceful terms with the whites during the Nez Perce War, but they had later lost their land, just as Joseph had predicted.

So it was a very sullen company of Indians who, on horseback, rode to the Jocko Agency for that first issue of food, bolts of cloth, and army blankets. The agent and his helper surrounded by so many bitter faces were nervous. The Government interpreter, not used to such taciturn companions, was uneasy and seemed unable to explain how to use the foods. Silently the Indians loaded their pack ponies, mounted their riding horses, and rode away.

Coming to an opening near the Jocko River, they stopped to inspect their rations. The coffee and the sugar they were acquainted with and had acquired a fondness for. Likewise the salt. But the beans, rice and bacon were a puzzle. What would they do with such food?

And that strange white powder—some in big bags and some in little cans? What would they do with it?

Off went lids, and many an eager mouth was soon filled with baking powder. With wry faces they spat out the horrid-tasting stuff.

Chief Charlo spoke in anger, "The white boss man makes a bad-tasting joke with us. Tomorrow we will take it back and make him eat it."

Then some Indians tried the white stuff in one of the big sacks. It did not taste bad, but it formed a paste that stuck to their mouths and tongues, and it was difficult to swallow. But it must be good. Was it not like the wheat powder that the Clairmonts made at their strange grinding place near Stevensville? They made good loaves of bread from it. But how?

In the meantime, a man had become angry at his wife because she had laughed at his discomfiture when he had difficulty in swallowing the flour. He grabbed a generous amount of the white stuff in each hand, threw one handful at her face, threw another handful in her hair. It spread down over her features and gave her a startling change in color. Behold, she became a Suappi, a white person!

The Indians gazed in astonishment. They gasped. They laughed. They laughed hard. Soon the tension of the past unhappy weeks was swept away. They began a merry battle of flour, each one pelting another with the white stuff until all were Suappi. Even the ponies and the numerous dogs were transformed into ghostly creatures. Tears of unrestrained laughter streamed down the people's cheeks, leaving pasty streaks behind them.

The agent and Oliver Gebeau's father, riding down the trail, came upon the weird scene. For a moment they were puzzled. Who were these strange creatures making merry on the banks of the Jocko? Then they began to recognize familiar voices, and gradually they realized what was happening. They too began to laugh. They too lost the tensions of the past weeks. They and the Indians before them became friends.

Soon afterward, the good fathers of St. Ignatius Mission sent cooks to teach the Salish how to use the flour and baking powder, how to prepare the beans and rice and bacon.

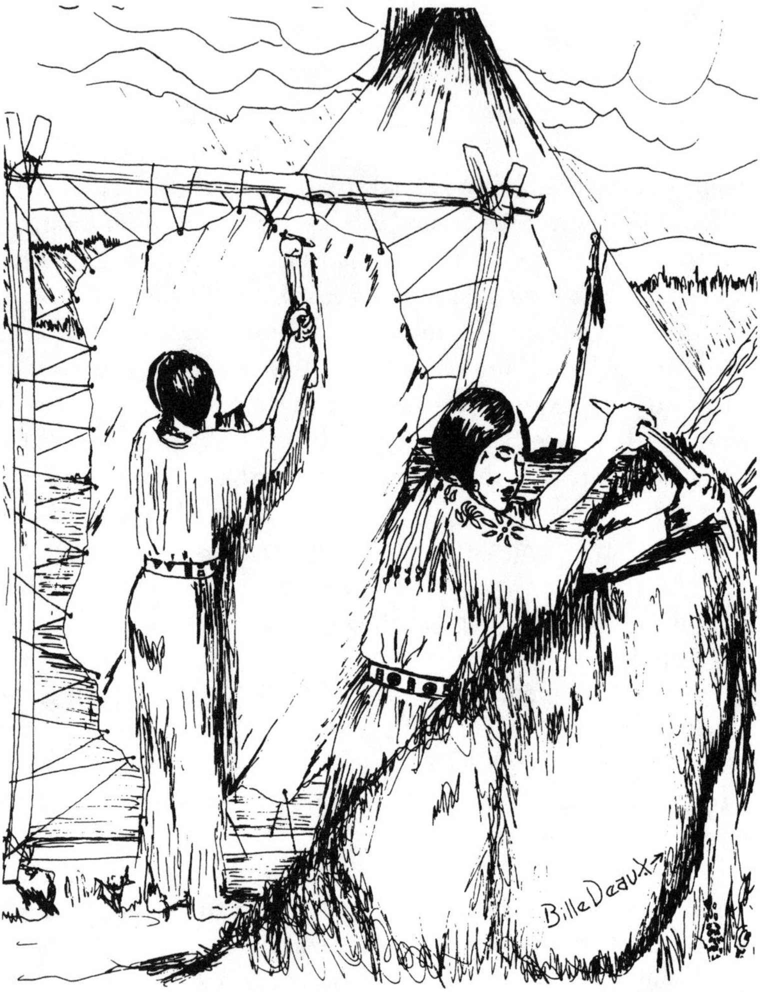
Bille Deaux

Chapter 10

Horses and Cattle

Wild Horses of the Toonachghaes
Told by: **Duncan McDonald via Will Cave**
Writer: **Mabel C. Olson**
Date: September 25, 1941

"My authority for the following story was Duncan McDonald, whose fund of Indian lore was inexhaustible.

"Before the white man set foot on land that was to become the state of Montana, a powerful tribe of Indians known as the Toonachghaes had their headquarters at the mouth of Rebate [Revais] Creek, about three or four miles west of Dixon. I won't vouch for the correctness of the spelling of the name, as I had it only by word of mouth, but it was pronounced To nak is.[1]

"Late in the 16th century, possibly about 1782, an epidemic spread rapidly through the tribe. The disease was so deadly that at its cessation the Toonachghaes, once 3,000 strong, were practically wiped out. The few survivors scattered among the neighboring tribes, the Blackfeet, Kootenais, Crows, Nez Perces, and Selish, the greatest number with the last named.

"Before the epidemic laid low the tribe, they had accumulated many horses. But while the masters were ill and dying, these horses wandered without curb, and became wild. The bands increased in number, and when the white man came to western Montana, he found many of them as wild and swift as deer. Prairie du Chevaux, or Horse Plains, was named for them.

"While Alexander Ross was camped near the site of Missoula, debating whether to traverse the canyon or attempt the Bitter Root route, the party killed 27 elk, 32 small deer, and four wild horses, the last being considered a greater exploit and causing more excitement than the killing of the other game. This was in February of 1824. Ross describes these horses as having long, fanlike, white tails. They were doubtless descended from the band owned by the Toonachghaes at the time of the epidemic.

"Long after, the Selish captured some of these wild horses." (See 'The Last of Montana's Wild Black Horses,' from *The Pioneer* (Missoula, MT), June 29, 1872, page 1, col. 5-7. The contributor was unnamed, but was probably Duncan McDonald.)

"The Indian pony is small, the full-grown animal weighing 400 to 800 pounds. The average is 600 pounds. They are often scrawny creatures, although some are beautiful. Frank Higgins of Missoula, when a boy, owned a beautiful, fiery, little dark baby pony, Marengo, that made him the envy of the rest of us. Marengo weighed about 450 pounds.

"Joseph Lomphry, a Frenchman who married a squaw, had a great band of cayuses which ran within 10 miles of Stevensville." (Lomphrie came to the Bitter Root with Father DeSmet. He was one of the traders on the Emigrant Road, and later became one of the first farmers and livestock men of the Bitter Root.) "In 1878 he sold about 1500 of them, as near as I recall the number, at $15 a head, to a Nat ———, who had sold a mine near Helena for $40,000." (Fifteen hundred is probably an exaggerated figure; Mr. Cave was uncertain on that point.)[2]

Notes

1. Frederick Webb Hodge, ed., *Handbook of American Indians North of Mexico,* Bureau of American Ethnology Bulletin No. 30 (Washington, DC: U.S. Government Printing Office, 1907–1910) does not mention such a tribe as the Toonachghaes. [See, however, the following references to a band of either Salish or Kootenai Indians called the Tona'xa: James A. Teit, "Traditions and Information Regarding the Tona'xa," *American Anthropologist,* vol. 32, no. 4 (Oct.-Dec. 1930), pp. 625-32; and Harry Holbert Turney-High, *The Flathead Indians of Montana,* Memoir of the American Anthropological Association No. 48 (1937), pp. 5-6.—Bigart Note]

2. Will Cave, 530 East Main Street, Missoula.

Horses
Told by: **Henry Burland and Frank McCleod [McLeod]**
Writer: **Bon I. Whealdon**
Date: October 22, 1941

It appears almost impossible to determine the exact date when horses were first brought into the lower Flathead Valley. Prior to 1840, our Indians may have acquired a start of horses through their frequent raids into the Piegan country. There is some historical basis for this claim.*

The Hudson Bay Company's records reveal that there were long strings (trains) on the route between this trading center on Post Creek and Fort Hall, Idaho, and Fort Vancouver, Washington, as early as 1847. Then too, the Mission Fathers, under the supervision of Fathers De Smet and Ravalli, were bringing in supplies from both Fort Hall, Idaho, and old Fort Colville, Washington, in 1843 and 1844. Also, Donald McCleod [McLeod] brought in horses in 1847.

From these pioneers' herds, the Indian quickly developed bands of their own. They found horses, both riding and packing, almost a necessity in their buffalo hunts and wars. They were helpful, too, in hunting and trapping trips into our own mountainous regions. Soon horses became indispensable.

The completion of the Northern Pacific provided a mode of transportation to horse markets in the eastern states. Buyers of horses for various branches of Governmental service; for construction contractors; and for Midwestern agricultural regions came flocking into the valley. Local owners of horses held great roundups, and thousands of head were shipped out. About this time, the raisers began using brands, some registered, while others were some locally distinguishing marks, or brands, usually the owners' initials.

Michel Pablo was a pioneer horse raiser. He was a lover of fine horses, and was known as an expert in judging a horse's merits and capability. For Pablo to admire a horse meant its purchase, if possible. Money being a minor consideration, he was known to have paid as high as $650.00 for a mount that just suited him.

Cutting horses, night herd horses, roping horses, riding horses, Pablo owned them by the hundreds—all branded

MP

He, in fact, had so many, that he said: "I've quit naming them. My riders can do that, just so long as they never abuse a horse, or call it a bastard"—a word Mr. Pablo despised.

Pablo's favorite son-in-law, Tony Barnaby, was, also, a horse lover. He had a beautiful all around Arabian named and branded H P. This horse was the envy of every cattleman and Indian rider upon the reservation.

Mr. Pablo repeatedly offered Tony a handsome size price for this mount; and just as often as he did, Tony would say, "No, my father, no man can ever buy my horse. H P represents, Tony's soul and Tony won't sell himself."

To which, Pablo always replied, "Yes, Tony, you are a real soul, and that is why you can say that."

Note
Flathead horses, during pioneer days, ran largely to cayuses (mustangs) and percheron.

Bigart Note
*Most sources have concluded that the Salish got their first horses from the Shoshoni during the eighteenth century. See Harry Turney-High, "The Diffusion of the Horse to the Flatheads," *Man,* vol. 35 (Dec. 1935), pp. 183-85.

How Wild Horse Island Got Its Name
Told by: **Duncan McDonald via Dean A. L. Stone**
Writer: **Mabel C. Olson**
Date: January 29, 1942

"Duncan McDonald had a fund of stories that he could tell when the spirit moved him. But he was of Scotch and Indian people, neither of which are communicative, and to those who asked him for a tale, he would usually reply, 'I'll tell you that sometime.' He had a reluctance to give his words to print.

"To illustrate this reluctance: I first met him in 1892. Not long after, I asked him to meaning of 'Missoula.' He put me off, promising to explain later. Twenty years after, I was returning from a three-week news assignment in the Kootenai country and in Glacier Park. The roads were poor, and the August sun beat down unmercifully. I had crossed the lake by boat to take the stage for Ravalli. At Polson Creek we changed horses. I was uneasy about the time, and told the driver he would never make the train. He assured me we would, and told me just to hang on tight. That was a wasted direction, for I was clinging for very life. The stage was pulled by six horses, only two of which had ever had harness on before. We made Ravalli in plenty of time, only to find that the train was three hours late.

"The station was fiery hot, and I waded across to an island in the Jocko. I had been there but a short while when I heard a crackle in the brush, and Duncan McDonald joined me. He squatted down beside me, and after he had lit a cigarette and I had filled my pipe, he said: 'Didn't you once ask me about the meaning of the word "Missoula"'?

"Upon that, I got my Scotch up, too, and said, 'Did I?' Twenty years, I thought, was somewhat long to wait for an answer.

"Not only was it hard to start him on a story, as often as not he would, during the telling of it, return to his somber reticence, and there the story would end. So that the fund of tales I drew from him were of a patchwork nature, seldom finished at one visit.

"One of these stories concerns the naming of Wild Horse Island, on the western arm of Flathead Lake. This is a long, narrow body of land, rather densely wooded with pine, fir, and cottonwood. It contains 2,164 acres and rises to a height of about 1,200 feet. There is no water there, except for the lake itself.

"To this island the Selish brought from the Eastern range a big band of horses they had captured from the Crows. They made the raid in winter, and crossed the horses over on the ice from the mainland. During the winter they rode herd on the band to prevent their escape. When the channel opened in the spring the horses were safely corralled by the expanse of lake around them.

"These horses were of very superior stock, solid blacks and bays. The Selish left them alone for a long time, and they multiplied, breeding handsomely.

"Later when the fur traders came in, the Selish began to tap their supply of horse flesh.

"The medium of exchange with the Indians was seldom money: the horse was the unit of measure. These horses kept on Wild Horse Island were much superior to the average run of Indian ponies, and the Selish soon found that each of them was worth three of the stock owned by the Indians to the West of them, where the Umatillas, Chinooks, and Cayuses had the smaller pintos and 'glass eyes' that were given the name of the latter tribe.

"So, trading on the basis of one for three, the Selish worked off their capital until they had depopulated Wild Horse Island.

"The first Montana horses were brought in by the Crows on a speculative date, probably in the 1700s. The Crows were the roving nation of Montana aborigines, and made not infrequent expeditions into Colorado and New Mexico, from where they returned with big bands of these superior horses. Raiding Selish and Blackfoot tribes were instrumental in spreading portions of these bands to other parts of Montana. These horses, when marketable, brought the highest prices in the Indians' intertribal merchandising.

"One tribe which became rich in these native horses was the Tonachghaes (spelling uncertain). (See article, 'Wild Horses of the Tonachghaes,' dated September 25, 1941.) It is believed that many of the bands which ran wild in northwestern Montana had at one time belonged to them. McDonald called them the 'Lost Tribe of the Selish.' He was never positive why they left their original habitat, but was sure that there was no quarrel between them and other tribes of the Selish nation. Some of the Old Ones thought that they fled East at the time of the first smallpox epidemic, which broke out about 1780 or 1790. The refugee bunch stopped for a time in the Prickly Pear Valley, below Helena. From there they vanished. Whether they moved on to the Southwest and mixed with the Utes and Shoshones nobody knew."

Horse Raising
Told by: **Alex McCleod [McLeod]**
Writer: **Bon I. Whealdon**
Date: December 19, 1941

"My grandfather, Donald McCleod [McLeod], brought into this region a considerable number of horses when he arrived in 1847. All transporting of supplies, food stuffs and equipment to our post and the shipping of pelts and buffalo robes and hides to Pacific coast shipping points had to be done with packtrains.

"Grandfather realized that there must be a constantly increasing supply of horses to meet the ever expanding activities of his company. He owned a number of mares (Cayuse breed), but had no stallion, so from a Mr. Blair of Victoria, Canada, he purchased two. Soon he had many hardy horses, suitable for packing and riding purposes.

"When my father, Frank McCleod [McLeod], Sr., and family were allotted valuable land, here in the Flathead Valley, they immediately turned their vast acreage into a horse ranch. They had a band of the original Cayuse horses; and for a while they served all ranch work, cattle herding and transportation very well.

"Realizing that eventually our valley must become a farming community, where a heavier breed of work horses would be required, father bought a few Percheron Mares and a stallion. His brand was FM.

"From 1890 to 1898, horses were so plentiful in the valley, and there was so little demand for them, that their possession was considered a detriment instead of being an asset.

"The spring of 1892, father, Allen Sloan and T. Finley rounded up 600 head of their choicest horses, Percheron and Cayuses. While they still had them in the corrals, they heard that there was a good market for horses among the farmers in North and South Dakota and Minnesota. Hiring a few bronc riders, among whom was Pete Finley of Polson village, they drove the herd across the Continental Divide on their selling trip to Minnesota.

"The prairies, covered with brush and buffalo grasses, afforded the animals an abundance of fattening feed, so the men leisurely drove them through the Dakotas. They were fortunate in selling them, a few here, and a few there, at fair prices. When they had reached the Minnesota State line, they had but six head left.

"In 1893, they drove large herds of horses north into Canada, where they found lively horse markets.

"Grandfather had a speedy Arabian riding horse that he called 'Selim.'"

Horse Roundup
Told by: **Joseph Marion**
Writer: **Bon I. Whealdon**
Date: October 29, 1941

"For some forty odd years prior to 1894, the Nez Perces and other Indians from Idaho, Oregon and Washington had been visiting friends and relations among the Flatheads and Pend Oreilles. Invariably, when they left the valley each fall, they neglected to take all their horses with them. These mustangs joined the already large herds of local horses.

"By the spring of 1895, the herds had become so numerous they constituted a serious menace to the cattle and buffalo range. Some of our leading stock growers were called together by such men as Michel Pablo and Chas. Allard, Sr., and others interested in keeping the free, open pasture lands for cattle, buffalo, and the horses rightfully belonging here.

"Michel Pablo stated the proposition in a few brief words: 'Neighbors, we must free the range of these alien cayuses, either that, or cut down upon the number of our own stock.'

"As if in keeping with some plan they hoped to devise, a Mr. Cory came to the valley. This affable gentleman posed as a Government official sent to supervise protective measures for the range. Now Mr. Pablo, a keen judge of mankind, said to friends: 'Personally I think Cory is a fraud come hither to fleece the Indians, now, we will work with him upon a legitimate scheme.' Immediately Mr. Cory was invited to join forces with the local cattle-raisers.

"Under his leadership, large corrals and a roundup camp were established in Oliver Gulch, west of Pend Oreille [Flathead] River. That was during the summer of 1895.

"Ranchers donated their services in an effort to rid the range of mustangs. Some bronc riders were hired. They very soon had 3,000 head of horses rounded up. In addition hundreds of horses and cattle, belonging to local Indians, were corralled. Here is where Mr. Cory cashed in on the deal. This Indian property was released to owners at so much per cow or horse.

"Of the 3,000 horses, a number were sold to individuals who did not live upon the reservation. These animals were promptly removed from the territory. Mr. Cory charged these buyers $150 to $250 per head.

"Two thousand were driven into Pablo's buffalo pasture corrals, near the Alphonse Clairmont Indian allotments upon the east bank of Mud Creek. Here, they were kept several months, in order to give the Nez Perce Indians who had been notified, time to come after their horses. No one presented a claim, and as the animals were becoming thin and weak, the local ranchers drove them many miles off the reservation where they scattered, never to return.

"The congenial Mr. Cory, whatever had been his original scheme, had performed a helpful function, and departed this region, his pockets well lined with greenbacks."

Pioneer Business in the Flathead
Told by: **Tony Barnaby, Andrew Stinger, and Allen Sloan**
Writer: **Bon I. Whealdon**
Date: October 21, 1941

Cattle raising in the Flathead Valley was commenced by the Mission Fathers, and a few individuals, like Angus McDonald on Post Creek, along in "the sixties." During that initial stage, the production of beef cattle was not considered so much as a commercial venture, as it was to assure the increasing population an abundance of meat.

As a natural result of the wanton slaughter of the great bison herds in Eastern Montana in that gory period between 1865 and 1875, our Indians were deprived of their principal food supply.

The good Fathers at St. Ignatius Mission saw that this acute shortage of meat was soon going to cause terrible suffering among their charges. They sought a way to forestall their privation. They realized that the Indians must begin to adapt themselves to a new manner of living. Being farsighted and resourceful men, they saw in cattle raising the possibilities of a permanent food source.

Even, as they had pioneered in bringing the Salish the Bread of Life, they now devoted their attention to bringing them material succor. With that in view, they encouraged and aided the progressive members of the tribe in obtaining a few "starter head" of cattle.

The Indians soon found that range cattle were a very good substitute for the buffalo; and within a few years time, they had a large herd roaming all over the valley.

The completion of the N. P. R. R. to Ravalli, Montana, placed cattle raising in this region on a commercial basis. This gave them access to Chicago and other markets.

Beef markets, also, created another payroll of local magnitude. The cattlemen had to have many cowboys for the spring and fall roundups. Herders were required during summer seasons, for the inevitable rustlers appeared upon the scene. Additional help was required at shipping time. Then, men were hired to accompany train loads to Chicago. Money in a golden stream poured into the Flathead. Everyone had plenty of it. The cowboys of that period were all Indians, and excellent riders and generous spenders of their wages.

Note

The predominating breeds of cattle in this region during the pioneer period were Galloway, Hereford and Shorthorn.

Route of DeMers Drive

Told by: **Dave Couture**
Writer: **Griffith A. Williams**
Date: November 18, 1940

Route of DeMers Drive from Lewiston, Idaho, to south of Kalispell, Montana, in 1879

Dave Couture, who, as far as we know, is the only Pony Express rider still living in Montana, described this route from Lewiston, Idaho, to north of the Flathead Reservation near Kalispell, which took place in the year 1879.

Dave, who at 15 years of age was a Pony Express rider, had resigned his position and gone to work for "Jack" DeMers as a rider.

The cattle, to the number of 1,100 head of Herefords, were purchased in Lewiston, Idaho, and were in charge of Telesphore G. DeMers, the oldest son of "Jack" DeMers. A youth in his teens, he was about the same age as Couture. There were a few older riders, experienced men, along with a number of Indians engaged for the drive, but young DeMers was the representative of his father.

When the drive had reached the Coeur d'Alene country the Indians refused to go any further without getting paid, thus necessitating young DeMers starting out alone for Frenchtown to obtain the money. On reaching Cameron's Crossing near St. Regis, Mr. Cameron advanced him $300 and he started back on his lonesome ride.

In a previous article for the Livestock Industry* we read of him being knocked from his horse in the dark by an overhanging branch of a tree and thinking he was about to be robbed. However, he arrived safely, paid the Indians, and no further interruptions delayed the drive.

The route from Coeur d'Alene was through the Lookout Pass and over the Mullan Trail to St. Regis, where the herd was made to swim across the river, and then on to Frenchtown, the home of "Jack" DeMers at the time. From Frenchtown the cattle were trailed through Arlee and north through Ronan to Dayton to be pastured. The Indians objected to the presence of this large herd on their reservation, so they were moved over

194 "I Will Be Meat for My Salish"

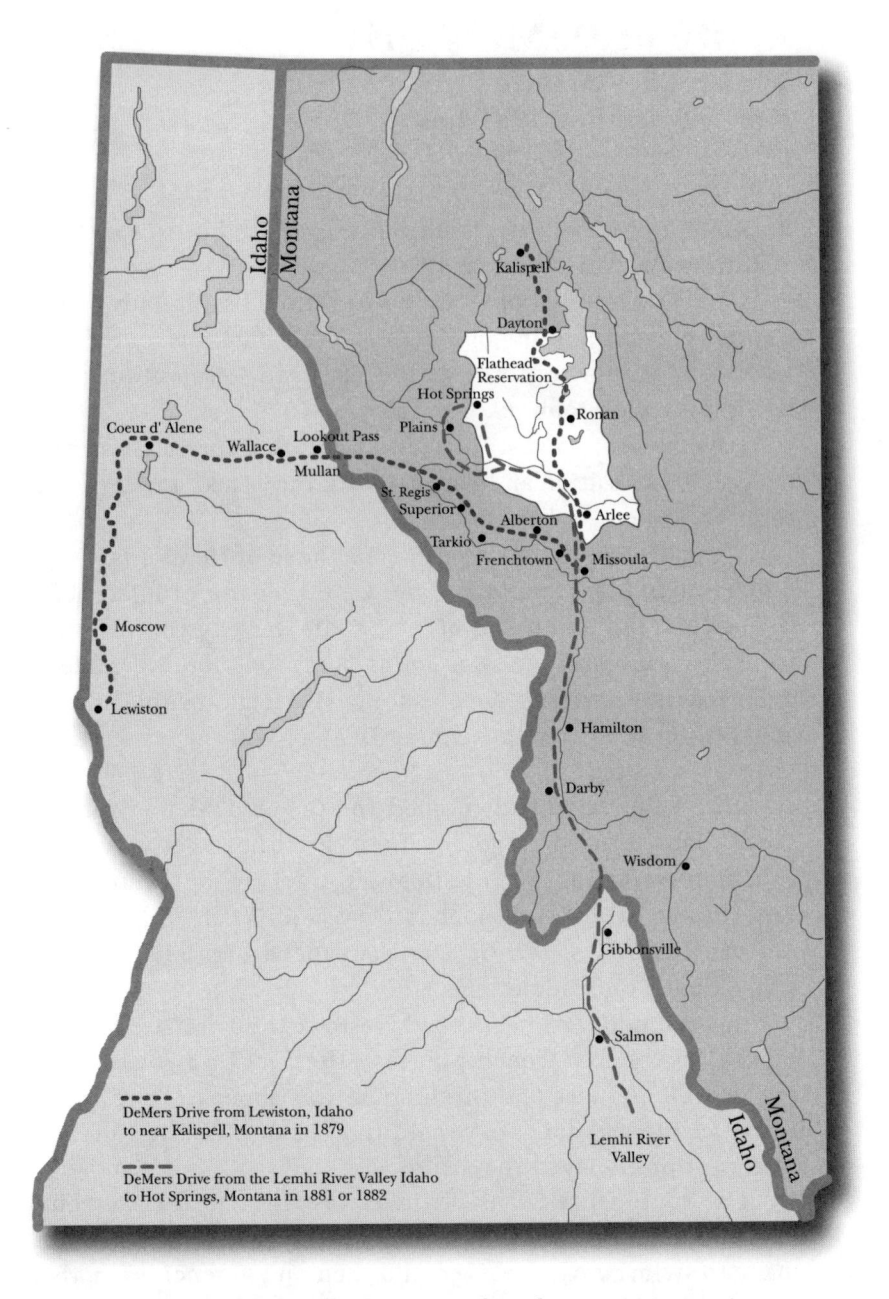

- - - - - DeMers Drive from Lewiston, Idaho to near Kalispell, Montana in 1879

──── DeMers Drive from the Lemhi River Valley Idaho to Hot Springs, Montana in 1881 or 1882

Bigart Note: DeMers cattle drive map, based on two manuscript maps in "Sanders County—Biography," box 62, WPA Records, collection 2336, Merrill G. Burlingame Special Collections, Montana State University Libraries, Bozeman, MT.

the line to the neighborhood south of the present town of Kalispell, after a journey of several weeks.

Note
How long the drive took is not recollected by Mr. Couture, whose memory, now that he is 76 years old, is somewhat dimmed, especially as to dates.

Bigart Note
*See Williams' biographical sketch of Jack Demers in Chapter 11 below.

Route of DeMers Drive Lemhi Valley to Hot Springs, Montana, 1881 or 1882

According to Dave Couture, it was in 1881 or 1882 that "Jack" DeMers purchased about 400 head of cattle in the Lemhi Valley in Idaho.

The route was directly north through the famous old mining camp of Gibbonsville, over the Continental Divide and into the Bitterroot River through Hamilton and Florence to Missoula. From Missoula the cattle were trailed, via Evaro, Arlee and Ravalli to Perma, where they forded the Flathead River; thence through Camas Prairie, skirting Dog Lake, now known as Rainbow Lake, to Hot Springs, where they were put out to pasture.

These cattle were mostly stock cattle—cows and calves—with about 100 head of yearling steers included, and were of Durham or Shorthorn breed.

Young T. G. DeMers and Dave Couture were considered experienced riders, both of them being practically raised on horseback. They both participated in this drive.

Cooperative Methods of Roundup

Told by: **Dave Couture**
Writer: **Griffith A. Williams**
Date: December 16, 1940

When these large herds, sometimes as many as 15,000 were rounded up from the ranges, the riders held the rounded-up animals until all the cows had found their calves and settled down. This did not take long. Then about ten riders would go through the center of the cattle, following each other in a line, perhaps 40 or 50 feet apart, until the leading rider was through the herd. In this way the herd was divided into approximately two halves. Thus they kept half of the herd away, leaving the remaining half lying quietly, until there was perhaps half a mile between them. Then the riders circled the cutout cattle until they quieted down.

The same performance was repeated until the second half of the herd was divided. Then the fourth of the whole was driven about a quarter of a mile way and they started to cut out the beeves. When this quarter of the herd was finished, two good men were put with the cut, which was the beef stock, and these were sent to the beef herd. The stock cattle were then turned loose to go back to the range. The second fourth went through the same process of elimination. Then came the remaining half with the same procedure, until finally the beef cattle for the market were in one herd.

These beef cattle, of course, had all been branded in the spring with each owner's brand. They could then be sold cooperatively, which was most often done, or each owner could then cut out his own stock and market individually, as was usual in the case of the Lynches. In case of cooperative selling, each outfit had its own riders go along with the trail to the destination, as was the case when Billy Irvine made his drive to Cheyenne. Billy was the superintendent or captain of the drive and riders or "reps" as they were called, represented the individual owners.

Note

This article was obtained December 4, 1940, in an interview with Dave Couture, who is still living at the age of 76 on his homestead, near Perma. Mr. Couture was a Pony Express rider at 15 and later was a top cow hand for "Jack" DeMers and took part in the semiannual roundup and on many long drives.

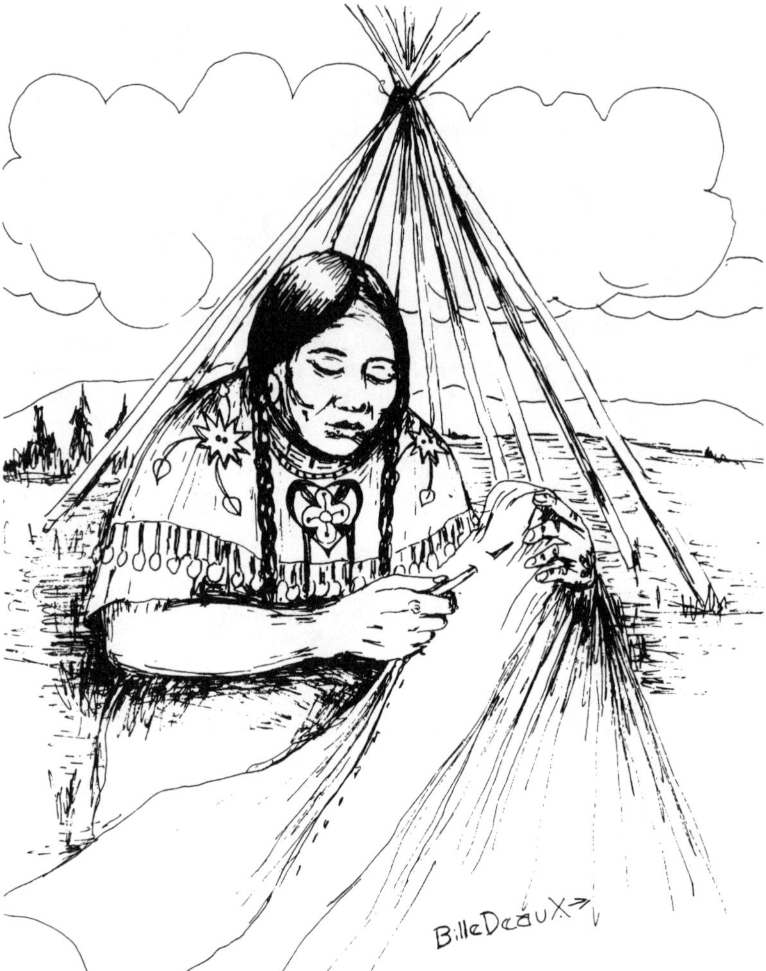
BilleDeaux

Chapter 11

Biographies

Joseph Barnaby
Told by: **Antoine Barnaby**
Writer: **Clarence A. Brown**
Date: November 24, 1939

Joseph Barnaby of French and Spokane Indian parentage, born in that country which in 1853 became Washington Territory, being a trapper and hunter, drifted around. As a young man he traveled across mountain ranges and valleys, bringing with him a few horses, locating first at Frenchtown, then on to the Bitter Root Valley and finally, upon reaching the Flathead Valley, decided it was ideal for hunting and trapping. Later he married and settled down there, acquiring a track of land and making his home at the foot of the hills about four miles north of where Arlee is now located.

To this union four sons were born, of whom Felixe and Antoine are still living. Felixe living at Arlee and Antoine about $1/4$ mile from Highway No. 93 just south of Mud Creek.

Joseph Barnaby never took to stock raising to any extent, never having more than 25 to 30 head of cattle besides a few head of horses. His brand was JB connected, taking his initials for his brand. He later died at Arlee.

Antoine Barnaby was born about 1873 while his parents were east of the Rocky Mountains during a buffalo hunt. While on these buffalo hunts it was not uncommon to be away from the home range for several years at a time. When Antoine was about three years of age, the band of Indians, returning from their hunt, passed near Helena; his parents being devout

Catholics desired that he be christened; a stop was made and he was taken to Helena for christening. This was done and placed on record.

When a young man he began raising cattle, increasing his herd until he had about 150 head. Then with the opening of the reservation to settlement in 1910, it became necessary to dispose of his herd due to a shortage of range. His brand was an inverted Y with a bar making a cross.

During the great buffalo roundup of the Pablo herd in 1907 Antoine rode as one of the cowboys, stating it was some of the wildest riding he had ever participated in.

Antoine remarked that in the buffalo roundup of the Pablo herd, he thought it was Professor Elrod of the University who came to the reservation to take some pictures of the roundup. He had succeeded in doing so as the buffalo were crossing the river, and then attempted to get back to camp, but the buffalo came so swiftly he did not have time and found it necessary to go up a tree. Not being able to take the large camera up with him, it was crushed as the herd of buffalo passed by beneath him.

Joseph S. Blodgett

Told by: Laura Blodgett Shultz, Hamilton, Montana;
   Leeson's *History of Montana,* **page 1299**[1]
Writer: Allis B. Stuart
Date: February 25, 1942

Joseph S. Blodgett was [born] in Hancock Co. Illinois December 27, 1835, as the son of Norman and Sally Blodgett. In 1847 the Blodgett family moved to Council Bluffs, Iowa, and settled on a farm. Joseph was then twelve years of age but he was expected to do about a man's work on the farm. He was out before daylight to feed the stock and to curry and water the horses and milk the cows. By sunup they yoked the oxen to a large breaking plough and he and his brother were out helping his father break and harrow sod. Joseph's job was to drive the farm yoke of oxen while his father held the plough steady in the furrow. His brother followed up with a team of horses and harrow.

Trudging along beside those oxen swinging an ox gad and keeping them moving was no light task and, as soon as supper was over and the chores done, he was glad to get to bed and was sound asleep as soon as he hit the hay. He attended school in the winter months, sometimes three and sometimes four months in a term.

Wheat was the money crop in those days and corn for feeding stock. Every farm raised hogs and corn was the best hog feed. Norman Blodgett and his two sons got in twenty acres of wheat and nearly ten acres of corn besides a good garden. The wheat was cut with a cradle and bound by hand and threshed with a horsepowered machine.

The Iowa summers were scorching hot and the winters had very severe low temperatures and high winds.

They lived in a log house, white washed inside and out, as were the stables and cattle sheds. In April Norman Blodgett sold his Iowa farm and the family joined an emigrant train bound for Utah.

Most of the train were Welsh families direct from Wales. They were fine people. The Blodgett family had three wagons, each with two yoke of oxen, and there were ten milch cows and eight good horses with harness and saddles. The wagons were loaded with seed grain, potatoes, and navy beans, besides garden seeds, goose berry, raspberry, currant bushes, a few young apple trees, rhubarb, and horseradish roots, a few wild plums, rosebushes, lilacs, and snowball shrubs, etc. They took their household goods and farm machinery and tools. This entire train settled near Ogden, Utah. They were all hard working experienced farmers. The train was considered wealthy as compared with earlier Mormon trains that crossed the plains and did not suffer as some of the earlier ones did. They had to do without many things but were never threatened with starvation and the Indians did not trouble them.

The Blodgetts had their seed for first planting, cows, horses, harness, farm tools, corn meal, and flour to last until they could make a crop. People were not selfish, they worked together and shared what they had with those less fortunate. Best of all they were all good farmers and hard working men and women. It was no place for "drones" or "shirks."

The Mormon Church laid out districts and supervised the irrigation and that was a big help. It was only a few years until that was a well to do community.

There were churches and good schools from the very first. Every child had a chance for a good education.

In April Joseph Blodgett was on an Indian trading expedition to the Snake country. The Indians were poor and had no furs of consequence or anything to trade. He soon left the party and joined William McWhirt and John Jeffreys on a trip to Oregon. There they purchased a herd of beef cattle and drove them to California. After disposing of the cattle, he engaged in mining in the Orville district and remained there a year. Then he sold his claims and headed for Walla Walla intending to return to Utah. At Walla Walla he met Capt. C. P. Higgins and hired out to him to go to Fort Owen. Higgins had charge of the supply train for Governor Stevens' expedition. Stevens was on his way to make treaties with the Indians along a proposed route for a railroad. After a treaty with one of the tribes they became dissatisfied and broke up into war parties. Not knowing of this trouble, Captain Higgins left the fort with one wagon and seven men and about ten o'clock a band of Indians attacked them and as Higgins was not expecting trouble he was not prepared for it. Higgins took to the brush and kept up the fight until midnight when some soldiers came to their relief. They had a small cannon and one shot from that sent the Indians scurrying. The party returned to the fort with the loss of only two oxen.

Later the Indians returned and made an attempt to set fire to the fort. They were unsuccessful in this and, finding themselves surrounded, they surrendered when Gov. Stevens asked them to come in and make a new treaty. The Indians called all their head chiefs in and after a two day parlay another treaty was made that was satisfactory to all concerned.

While this treaty was being negotiated soldiers stood with guns in hand ready for immediate action should the Indians show signs of hostility.

In 1858 Mr. Blodgett leased a schooner and ran it between Cascade and the Dalles. But soon tiring of that, he sold his lease and went to the Bitter Root Valley and purchased a pack train from Major Owen. At this time there were but twenty-nine white men in the whole valley and no white women. The Indians were Flatheads and Nez Perces and they were a fine class of Indians too.

The Blackfeet came across the range on horse stealing raids quite frequently. They did not often kill a white man but they would clean up all the horses in the country. At that time the Bitter Root Valley was a timbered valley with here and there open patches of prairie, and along the streams coming in from the sides was thick brush, willows, alders and quaking aspen and groves of cottonwood. The timber was mostly yellow pine.

For five years Blodgett hunted, trapped, and traded, often joining Indian hunting parties and going out on the plains after buffalo. All the eastern plains country was black with buffalo and most of the hunting was with bow and arrow. It was an exciting sport and an exciting life. They were always running into hostile war parties that disputed every foot of the buffalo country. The tribes were never friendly or never came to any agreement as to their boundaries. There were certain sections called "The Flathead Country," "The Blackfeet County," "The Sioux Country," and "The Crow Country" but it was theirs only as they could keep others out. War parties raided hunting parties regularly and their battles were quite exciting and any white man in a hunting party entered into these frays with zest. Joe Blodgett had a good Sharp rifle and he was a good shot and a good horseman. The Flatheads were glad to have him with them.

In 1862 he decided it was time to settle down and improve him a farm. He returned to Utah and purchased wagons, harness, stock cattle and all necessary farm machinery, came back to Montana and settled on a piece of land below the present town of Corvallis. He had taken a Flathead Indian wife and they had two children, a girl and a boy. He built a comfortable log house, stables and sheds and proceeded to fence his land. All the land was then owned by the Flathead Indians.

In 1877 when the Nez Perce Indians came through the valley on the warpath, Blodgett joined Gen. Gibbon's command and was at the Battle of the Big Hole. In company with eight other men he was left at camp to await daylight when they were to bring the cannon into the field for use. They were attacked by Indians. One man was killed and two severely wounded. The others took to the timber and later reached the wagons.

Note

1. Michael A. Leeson, *History of Montana, 1739–1885* (Chicago: Warner, Beers & Co., 1885), pp. 1299-1300.

More About Joseph Blodgett
Told by: **Alexander M. Chaffin and Allis B. Stuart**
Writer: **Allis B. Stuart**
Date: March 13, 1942

"Yes, I knew Joe Blodgett. He was in the Bitter Root Valley when my father arrived here. He was married to a Flathead Indian woman and lived on a ranch below Corvallis. There were several Blodgett children, a girl Sarah and two boys. Newman and Joe went to school with us at Corvallis. Later Blodgett sold his ranch to the Chaffins and moved up to the Sleeping Child Creek. He took up the ranch and afterwards sold it to Fred Leavitt. I do not think he ever farmed much, about enough to have something to eat.

"His brother Lyman Blodgett was a good farmer and had one of the best ranches in the country; had good stock and a well improved ranch, good buildings and fences and all kept shipshape.

"Joe did not have a 'turn' for farming. He liked to hunt and trap or act as guide for some little military expedition that came along and go with the Indians.

"He was in the expedition that went from here after the Nez Perce when they went through on the warpath in 1877. He was one of the party that was in charge of the cannon that Gen. Gibbons had along and before they got it to where they could use it, the Indians captured it and killed one man and wounded some more. Blodgett took to the woods and made his escape, but it was such a close call that he lost his taste for Indian campaigning.

"When Charlos' band of Flatheads left the valley for the Flathead Reservation, Joe Blodgett sold out and went with them and since that time I have lost track of him. I do not know what became of the children. I suppose they are on the reservation, as they would have allotments of land through their mother. I don't doubt but they are doing well down there."

Note

Talk with Alex Chaffin, March 10th, 1942.

****

I first knew Joe Blodgett in 1886. He lived on Sleeping Child Creek, first where the creek flows into the Bitter Root River. There was one girl, Sallie Blodgett, who rode horseback very well and was often on picnics and fishing excursions with the other young people of the valley.

I used to envy Sallie Blodgett the beautiful spot where she lived and the fact that her people didn't consider it their Christian duty to yank everything out by the roots and plant it to alfalfa.

The old Blodgett place, as it is in my mind today, was the most beautiful spot that I have ever seen.

On the south side of the creek there is a cliff of rock, all moss covered and with a fringe of ferns along the creek bank. There was a log house with a dirt roof all so overgrown with wild roses and clematis that you could hardly see it. The canon is very narrow and to the east is the main range of the Rockies and west the towering Bitter Roots with the beautiful Como Peaks. The Sleeping Child Creek, a clear cold mountain stream tumbling over great boulders like a miniature cataract, a gravel bar along the Bitter Root River covered with pine and cottonwood trees right in front of the house. There was an old fashioned rail fence completely covered with clematis and wild roses. Joe Blodgett or his wife must have loved those wild flowers and trees and shrubs for they never disturbed a thing, not even the dogwood and syringas that grew in the path. The path wound around them.

When Marcus Daly came, he took a larger irrigation ditch out of the river almost in front of the Blodgett house and graded the road so that it passed between the big ditch and the river. Marcus Daly had an eye for the beautiful and he did not whack down the trees or dig the rosebushes and dogwood out but allowed them to stand along the bank of his ditch, and there was never a man or woman passing along that road with a camera that did not stop and take a picture. It was the most beautiful spot that I have ever seen. It is painted in my memory just as it was then, even to the little white picket fence around the lone grave on the hillside. That too was pathetically beautiful.

The river, the mountains, and the canyon are still there but Fred Leavitt was a farmer and when the place came into his possession, the way he tore into those rosebushes, clematis, willows and dogwood is another story. Now there are about 200 acres of perfect fields of alfalfa, waving grain and beet field. There is a neat barbed wire fence all around the place that does *not* invite you to lean against *it* and chat about the weather. There is a large white farmhouse with a smooth green lawn and cement walks right straight up to the front door, with dressed up rosebushes, trim shrubs and regal lilies and gladiolas and neat weedless gardens, orchards, Jersey cows, and big red barns with hinges to the doors, and gates painted white, and an automobile. It is a marvelous ranch and there is much produce and milk and pigs marketed each year, but it isn't beautiful any more—just profitable.

There is the automobile and the worry about gas and tires, and will the water freeze in the kitchen sink, or the plumbing in the bathroom "bust."

The Blodgetts used to come tearing out of the brush on their spirited horses, gallop across the country without a moments' worry. If they didn't get back that day, they would the next, and the bunch grass in the pasture was knee high, and all the water was in the creek. No pipes to freeze. If it was too cold to bathe, you could wait until spring.

Who can truthfully say the life of the pioneer was one of hardship and privation? Wasn't it rather one of freedom, joy and beauty?

Allis B. Stuart.

Louis Courville

Told by: **Zephyr ("Swift") Courville**
Writer: **Griffith A. Williams**
Date: January 23, 1941

Louis Courville,[1] like "Jack" Demers, was a native of Montreal, Canada. In 1885 he settled on a ranch five miles north of the present town of Ronan, where for many years he maintained a herd of about 100 head of cattle and numerous horses. He never was a large operator.

According to his son, Zephyr ("Swift") Courville, his father had come to Frenchtown around 1864 and was engaged as a freighter by Demers, freighting in supplies from the railroad point at Corinne, Utah. He had the distinction of hauling in the first sawmill to Bonner from Fort Benton for A. B. Hammond.

An older son, Oliver Courville, and Dave Couture, both of whom are still living in Sanders County, also rode, freighted and packed for Demers as long ago as 1885, while Arthur Larivee [Larrivee], a stepson of Billy Irvine, then a boy in his teens, led the bell horse.

Zephyr Courville or "Swift," as he is always called, was a boy of ten when his parents came to the Flathead Reservation. Before he was 20, he was a range rider and a top cowhand for Charley Allard, who had married his sister. Before he was 26, on the advice of Allard, he invested his earnings in beef steers, and was the owner of about 700 acres on Camas Prairie, and at the peak of his operations he owned about 1,000 head of cattle. The opening of the reservation to settlement curtailed his operations because of the lack of range facilities, and most of his stock was disposed of in 1911.

Notes

"Swift" Courville, who until recently was a member of the Indian police at Hot Springs, is now living in Plains.

1. The information in this article was obtained in an interview with "Swift" Courville in Hot Springs on August 22, 1940.

Zephyr (Swift) Courville

Told by: **Zephyr (Swift) Courville**
Writer: **Griffith A. Williams**
Date: December 2, 1941

Zephyr (Swift) Courville, who is now town marshal and street commissioner of Plains, is a grandson of François Finlay, or "Benetsee," as he was called by the Indians, and who prospected for gold as early as 1852 on what was then Benetsee creek, now Gold Creek.

Finlay, according to his grandson, was of French-Scotch-Cree Indian ancestry. Finlay's daughter, Julia Finley, married Swift's father, Louis Courville, a French-Canadian, who came from Montreal to Frenchtown around 1864 and was engaged as a freighter by Jack Demers, freighting in supplies from the railroad point at Corinne, Utah. He also hauled in the first sawmill to Bonner from Fort Benton for A. B. Hammond.

At the time of his death, Finlay was making his home with a son-in-law and daughter, Mr. and Mrs. Joe Moran, near Frenchtown. He dropped dead on the way from the house to the barn one day. This was in 1876, according to the recollection of his grandson.

Swift, although he was but a small boy at the time, remembers his grandfather as a big sturdy six-footer with moustache, but no beard. He was of a genial, kindly disposition and was held in great esteem by both Indians and Whites.

Note
From an interview with Swift Courville December 1, 1941.

Sketch of Dave Couture

Told by: **Dave Couture, Frank Boyer, Arthur Larivee [Larrivee], and George Wurm**
Writer: **Griffith A. Williams**
Date: November 19, 1940

Dave Couture, now 76 years old and living on his homestead near Perma, is probably the only Pony Express rider in the State of Montana. He was born at Chewelah on the Colville Reservation, 75 miles north of Spokane, in 1864.

His father, Joseph Couture, a French-Canadian, was in charge of the Hudson Bay trading post there. When Dave was four years old, his parents trailed overland by way of Spokane to Sandpoint and thence along the Clark's Fork River to Missoula and finally to their destination in Frenchtown, where the father took up a homestead.

This was in 1868. Dave made the journey tied to a horse, led by his father, and from that time on he was literally tied to a horse for over half a century—and, by the way, he can still ride.

By the time he was eleven years old he was considered an experienced and responsible rider and at 15 he was riding the Pony Express route between Frenchtown and the Milk Ranch Station, near Iron Mountain.

"There was little time for schooling," says Dave. "Everyone had to work in those days. Besides I preferred riding to attending school."

The older Couture was engaged by the government to teach farming methods to the Indians on the Flathead Reservation and moved to Arlee in the late 1870s. He purchased 80 acres from the Indians, near Arlee, in exchange for two horses and four head of cows. He was adopted into the Flathead or Salish tribe, and, in this way, his family became eligible for allotments.

Dave claims the Indians received the name of Flatheads, not because of the shape of their heads, but because of their native stubbornness and limited intelligence.

Be that as it may, Dave remained in Frenchtown, resigned his job as Express rider and went to work riding and packing for "Jack" DeMers. At 15 he participated in the DeMers drive of 1,100 head of cattle from Lewiston, Idaho, to south of Kalispell. He was 17 or 18 when he took part in the DeMers drive of 400 head from the Lemhi Valley in Idaho to Hot Springs, Montana.

He scouted for the government when he was 18 years old and, during the building of the Northern Pacific in 1881–82, it was his duty to keep the whiskey runners off the reservation.

Note: Sources of Information

Dave Couture, address Perma, Montana, aged 76. Came to Montana with his parents from Washington state when only four years. Rode Pony Express when only 15 years old. Extremely alert and of interesting personality. Remembers incidents clearly, but is rather hazy as to exact dates. Was top cowhand for such outfits as those of "Jack" DeMers and the Lynches.

Frank Boyer of Plains, nearing 80 years old, but with good memory, alert and active and a pleasure to interview. He was one of the butchers who worked for the Lynches at the time of the hard winter of 1889–90, when many hundreds of cattle perished in the Pleasant Valley (Flathead County).

Arthur Larivee [Larrivee] of Camas, Montana. Old-time superintendent of the semiannual roundups. In failing health during the past few years, his memory is still good. He is a ready talker and has some good material in his recollections. He is a stepson of the late Billy Irvine.

George Wurm, who still operates a ranch on Camas Prairie and has been resident of Sanders County since the advent of the Northern Pacific in 1883. Mentally alert and eager to talk.

Joe Couture

Told by: **Louis Couture, his son**
Writer: **Clarence A. Brown**
Date: November 28, 1939

Joe Couture, of French-Canadian parentage, left Montreal, Canada, when he was a youth of 16 years of age, going with the Hudson's Bay Company to the Yukon where he remained with the company two years.

Later his travels took him through many new lands, including the Willamette Valley in British Columbia, then the Dalles in Oregon, where he with a group of ex-Hudson's Bay

Company's men made a trip to California. There they located gold in the streams in large nuggets. Their greatest hardship was caused by yellow fever which struck at that time. After recovery from the ravages of the fever the group left in 1849, returning again to the north and locating at the Colville Indian Reservation.

During the next few years Joe had acquired 35 head of good cattle and about 20 head of horses. Also during this time he had, like many early frontiersmen, taken as a wife a maid from the Indian village.

Mrs. Couture's father, then living in the Flathead Valley, being on a visit, explained the beauties, the advantages and how wonderful a country lay to the east across the ranges. Listening intently to the elder man tell of this veritable paradise created the desire to travel again, so in the spring of 1868, gathering his stock and such worldly possessions as could be carried, they set out for the new home, locating first at the head of Flathead Lake, known then to the Indians as "White Water." There they located for the winter on land now known as the Henry Therriault place. The spring of 1869 they were on the move again, traveling only as far as Frenchtown but again returning to the Flathead Valley, and located in the spring of 1870 near the present site of Arlee. There Mr. Couture acquired land and built up his home. To Mr. and Mrs. Couture were born three sons and one daughter: Dave, Emmerence, Mack, and Louis. He continued to increase his small herd to 75 or 80 head of cattle and from 30 to 50 horses; his brand was JC on the left ribs of cattle and left shoulder on horses, having taken his initials for his brand. He died about 1900.

Louis Couture acquired his allotment and settled on same about 1900, where he built up his home and continued with stock raising. His tract of land is located about $2^1/_2$ miles north of Polson on the west shores of Flathead Lake. Between 1900 and 1910 he had one of the large herds of the valley, running up to 1,200 head of good grade Herefords. His herd carried the ID brand. Some over 400 head of his herd came from the Flying U herds which he had purchased from Mr. C. Stimson of Polson, at a price around $27,000.

Mr. Couture found it compulsory to dispose of his herd following 1910 when the reservation was opened to settlement. The opening of the reservation took up all free range so that only actual holdings were available and on this he engaged in grain raising, which occupation he is still carrying on.

Mr. Couture married early and from this union there are five children living.

Jack Demers, Pioneer Stockman, Freighter, and Businessman
Told by: **Robert Demers, Missoula**
Writer: **Mabel C. Olson**
Date: February 13, 1941

"My father, Telesphore Jacques Demers, popularly called Jack, left Montreal for the California gold fields in 1849, at the age of 16. In the 1850s he went to Colville, Washington, where he engaged in freighting. There he married a quarter-breed Indian girl, to whom six children were born, two in Colville and the others in Frenchtown.

"He first came to Montana in 1856, to look the country over, and returned in 1862 to make his permanent residence in Frenchtown, whose founder he may be said to be. He owned practically the entire valley, and donated the sites for the church, one of the stones of which bears my father's and mother's names, and for the cemetery. We have a family vault, containing 14 or 15 bodies, which has been broken into many times (some of the bodies were petrified, hence the souvenir hunters).

"He owned three or four thousand acres, which he used for cattle range and for farming.

"When my mother, Leonie Demers, came to this country, my father was a widower. She came from Montreal with two nuns, Sisters of Providence. At that time there was no railroad here, and she came the roundabout way, to Corinne, Utah, on the Union Pacific, and from there made a trying trip by stage. She taught music in the convent established by the sisters until her marriage. I was the oldest of her five children, and was born at the agency in 1881. Mary and Peter Ronan were my godfather and godmother.

"My father was never quiet, but was always engaged in innumerable activities. After his arrival in Frenchtown, he continued his freighting, and also established stores at Frenchtown, Big Arm (north of Polson), at the agency, Cedar Creek, and, shortly before his death in 1889, at Demersville.[1]

"He owned the largest pack train in the territory, numbering 100 head of mules and horses, and kept them busy on the trails. He himself packed from Frenchtown into the Coeur d'Alenes, by way of Thompson Falls. He owned a ferry, on which he crossed his train. Along about 1868 or 1870 the cable of this ferry broke under the weight of a load of heavily-packed mules. All the animals drowned except five or six that were packed with tubs, the air under which buoyed them up. Along with them was drowned an employee of my father, a Frenchman whose name I do not remember.

"Father raised horses, mules, and sheep. He drove horses to the Northwest Territory to sell to the Mounted Police. His pay was in gold dust. Coming back from one of these drives one time, his men were held up by a gang of robbers, who killed three of them, and stole gold amounting to $60,000. Mother, who told me the story, gave the names of those killed and those who escaped, but I have forgotten them. Father for years had a claim on the government for the depredation, but nothing came of it.

"He traveled almost constantly, often on the road months at a time. On one occasion he was in the Northwest Territory. The intense cold was overcoming him, making him drowsy, and he wanted only to lie down. His men had to fight with him to keep him going; they knew that to sleep in that bitter cold would prove fatal.

"I do not know what year he trailed his first herd of longhorns, numbering 800 head, from Texas, but I am fairly certain that it was before 1868. They were brought up by William Dubray, Charley Allard, John Frasier, and Al Cobert. He ranged the cattle in Frenchtown Valley at first, and later in the Little Bitter Root, running over 1,000 head.

"He employed as cowboys David Couture, Charley Coulville [sic], John Frasier, Charley Allard, before the latter began his own herd, Alphonse Courville, and one of the latter's brothers. They worked the year round, for a wage of about $35 a month and keep.

"They fed the poorer cows during the winter, but never the steers. For hay they cut the wild grass, which grew rank and tall in those early years when June was counted as a month with 28 days of rain.

"When I was quite small, my father built my half-brother, Telesphore G. DeMers, a house at Camas Hot Springs, and gave him 100 head of cattle. The only fencing necessary in those days of free range was a pen where calves were weaned. Young as I was, I still have a vivid mind picture of that grass, so high that a steer lying down in it was completely lost to sight.

"Father's brand was the Diamond D.

There was a saying that the Diamond D horses were the best there were. His ring, which I now have, bears an inconspicuous gold

sunk in a square black setting, the band made of Cedar Creek gold.

"Mother has told me that when W. A. Clark had the contract to deliver mail between Missoula and Spokane, he negotiated with father for horses on credit. Clark was not then the prosperous man he was to become. His brother, Joseph K. Clark, was the carrier.

"Those were days of extensive credit; the country was just being settled, men were not yet established, and their assets were courage and enterprise, rather than ready funds. Mother showed me a bunch of notes given my father, about three inches thick. People, as a rule, were honest, and paid when they could; my father did not press them.

"Denver Lachlan told me of an instance of such credit, saying that he had never seen anyone so openhanded in his dealings, and that those in his debt were bound to repay him when he was so generous. Lachlan and his father owned a ranch at Paradise. He came into the store one day, and asked for a wagon, team of horses, and provisions, which he was given on credit. The next year Lachlan, in payment of the debt, drove 150 hogs from Paradise, up the river to Dixon and the Jocko, and south through O'Keeffe's Canyon.

"In his trade with the Flathead Indians, Father got furs from the Tobacco Plains district, Big Arm, and the vicinity of Demersville. The Indians were his friends, and would give him protection and anything in their power.

"The only Indian trouble I knew of resulted from an assessor's attempt to collect taxes from men who were part Indian. Jimmy Hess and 'Butch' Harding, Dwight Harding's stepson, under the assessor's orders, had taken over 150 head of cattle from my half-brother. Chief Michel decided to put a stop to the collections, which were made contrary to their treaty.

"I was then just a young boy staying with my half-brother. But I could talk the Indian language, and Michel sent for me to act as interpreter for a party of Indians the Chief sent to the assessor's deputies on Camas Prairie.

"Jimmy Hess had guns strapped on him, but he made no attempt to use them when the Indians took charge of the cattle. No further attempts at such collections were made.

"There was much rustling of cattle in those days. The biggest loss was to trusted men who used an easy opportunity to sell off small bunches from the herds in their charge, thinking that the few animals taken at a time would not be missed. My father, however, was very keen, and caught those who tried the scheme with him. He went several times a year to inspect his herds.

"He employed a large number of men. In Frenchtown Valley alone he had 10 or 15 men with his cattle. The year of his death, 1889, when I was eight years old, he kept a large dining room for his employees alone, and had two Chinese cooks, Te Lee and Charley. For the family he had a private dining room, which had no attraction for me; I always wanted to eat with the men.

"Many pioneers of Montana worked for him. Among them was Billy Irvine, who first saw my father in 1856, when he was here to look the country over. Baptiste Ducharme, a hunter and trapper who lived to be over 100 worked for him for years. Louis Courville, Sr., who came in 1861 or 1862, also did. Seymour Hurlburt was taking 200 head of horses for him to the Black Hills in 1889. He got to Butte when Father's death occurred. The horses were auctioned off in that city.

"Peter Scheffer, who later became a successful stockraiser at Huson, was one of Father's freighters. Louis Courville was another. His son, Oliver Courville, herded the horses at night. The freighting charge was an exorbitant amount per pound.

"The trip from Corinne required three months. Extra horses were taken along, so that one team could rest while another pulled the heavily-laden wagons over the rough road. The caravan consisted of from 10 to 15 wagons.

"With goods carried with such difficulty, Father was generous. The Michael Flynn family, good friends of his, called him the most kindly man in the country, and told of the many wagonloads of supplies he donated to the Sisters of Providence, who found their first years in the valley a struggle against want.

"Another good friend of Father's was David Hilger, custodian of the State Library in Helena, whom he saw on his frequent business trips there. Hilger was regretful that the State Library contained no picture of Father, whom he called a great man. He was pallbearer for my half-sister, who died in Helena in November of 1872, while attending St. Vincent's Academy. To reach her bedside, Father went horseback, changing to a fresh mount at intervals. But even so his pace killed one horse.

"He established the store around which Demersville grew, in 1882. (Robert DeMers does not profess to be very sure of his dates, and here seems to be in error: other sources, among them the *Kalispell News*, March 22, 1939,* place the date as 1887.) He turned the management of it to my brother-in-law, John Clifford.

"His constant activity had undermined his health, and he was taken ill in January of 1889. He and Mother set out for

Salt Lake City to consult specialists, but he was forced to enter the hospital in Butte, where he died in May of that year, at the age of 56.

Notes

1. He and John McCormick were post traders at the Missoula Military Post in 1879. Chattel Mortgages, Book B.

Source Note: Interview with Robert Demers, 517 Ford St., Missoula. (A follow-up by the Butte research assistant should be worthwhile: Mrs. Jack Demers, 79 years old, lives at 1101 West Broadway, Butte. Her son says she has many anecdotes to relate of the early days, many of which he has heard and forgotten; he would like for me to interview her, feeling that she would be more willing to talk when urged by him. However, she does not make her annual visit to Missoula until August.)

Bigart Note
*This item could not be located to verify the reference.

Add to Jack Demers Article

Told by: **Arthur Larivee [Larrivee], "Bill" Murray, and newspapers**
Writer: **Griffith A. Williams**
Date: August 30, 1940 to January 25, 1941

Arthur Larivee [Larrivee],[1] now living in Camas, near Hot Springs, who knew Demers intimately, taking an active part in the semiannual roundups on the reservation, describes him as a man of wonderful personality, wiry and vigorous, and generous to a fault. He was of medium height and build, light-complected, with full red beard. Considered as well-to-do at one time, he lost most of his money later because of leniency in dealing with those he freely extended credit to, especially in his mercantile operations at Frenchtown, Demersville, Arlee and Hot Springs.

His business interests were numerous, as can be gleaned from the following:[2]

A letter from Dalles City, Texas, dated March 3d, was received a day or two since by Mr. F. J. Demers [sic], of

Frenchtown. It contained the news that the latter gentleman's brother (William), who left here November 19, 1870, in company with Mr. W. Dubray, for the purpose of buying cattle, had a very narrow escape from poisoning at the above city recently. It appears that some of the gents who make a living by "ways that are dark and," happily in this instance, "tricks that are vain," learned that Mr. Dubray had a large amount of money, and introduced a dose of poison into his coffee, for the purpose of robbing him. They would have succeeded in their purpose but that they gave their victim an overdose, and, fortunately for him, a doctor was at hand to relieve his stomach of the same. He was doing well at last accounts. Mr. Demers says that cattle are now very high in Texas, large numbers having died there from the severity of the winter. He has purchased 800 head, and expects to arrive in Frenchtown with them on or about the 15th of October next.—*The Missoula Pioneer*, March 30, 1871, page 3, col. 1.

T. J. Demers of Frenchtown on Saturday last started a pack train of 43 animals for the Kootenai mines. The train was loaded principally with flour and beans.—*The Weekly Missoulian*, June 13, 1873, page 3, col. 3.

Advertisement: "Transportation to the Cedar Creek mines! T. J. Demers, Frenchtown, Montana. General Outfitting Store! Goods for the Cedar Creek mines stored in safe warehouses, and forwarded by pack trains to the mines at reasonable rate."—*The Missoula and Cedar Creek Pioneer*, January 5, 1871, page 1, col. 7.

Will Cave in an article in the *Mineral County Independent*, December 21, 1933, pages 17-19, and 23, tells of T. J. DeMers riding horseback, provisionless, with 12 others from Frenchtown, in the stampede to Cedar Creek in the fall of 1869.

The Grantor Index and Deed Record, Book A, shows that on July 9, 1870, he was still in Louisville. On that date he bought a house and lot on Main Street, Louisville, of Charles Conner and J. B. Hethier for $500. The building had been occupied as a saloon under the name of Hethier & Conner.

Although he returned to Frenchtown in 1870 or early in 1871, he kept his interest in the mining fields of Cedar and vicinity, as shown by purchases of claims on Cedar, Quartz and Packer Creeks to the amount of $5,900, and of mining locations made until 1888. In the 1880s he was interested with Louis Barrett, Cedar Creek's discoverer, and with Arthur P. and George Johnson. May 17, 1881, he bought the Moose Creek Ferry Ranch, about 20 miles west of Frenchtown; March 10, 1888, he sold it to Theodore Meunier.

His initials T. J. stood for Telesphore Jacques.[3] His oldest son, a pioneer of the present town of Hot Springs then called Pineville—in Sanders County—was familiarly known as "T. G.," his name being Telesphore Garcon. He died in Hot Springs many years ago. After the opening of the reservation he turned his allotment into town lots, which sold rapidly, being in close proximity to the now famous hot springs. His widow was for many years, and until recently, postmistress at Hot Springs for a number of years.

George Wurm of Camas Prairie tells of "Jack" sending his son over into the Nez Perce country to trail in a herd of cattle purchased there.[4] His helpers were Indians and after one day on the trail the Indians decided they wanted to be paid then and there. There was nothing for young Garcon to do but leave the cattle there and make the long ride back to Frenchtown alone to get the money. Fortunately, at Cameron's ferry, he obtained $300 in cash from George Cameron, starting back on the trail through the dark timber. With so much money on his person he was naturally apprehensive of being held up and when in the darkness, he was suddenly thrown from his horse, he thought it was "the end of the trail" for him. However, it proved to be only an overhanging branch of a pine tree, which in the darkness, he could not see, and which had caught him under the chin. Paying the Indians, he made the rest of the journey without any trouble.

"Jack" Demers also had a store in Arlee, which his brother Alec managed and which today is operated by descendants of the latter. William Demers, another brother, looked after his stock which ranged on the reservation near Arlee.

His first wife, Leonie [sic, Leonie, a white woman, was his second wife—Bigart Note.], was a half-breed Indian. He is survived by his second wife—not of Indian blood—who is now living in Butte.

Notes

1. Interview with Arthur Larivee [Larrivee] at Hot Springs on August 7, 1940. Larivee acted as superintendent of the semiannual roundups during the late 1880s

2. Information on business interests obtained from an article compiled by Mabel Olson, field worker in Mineral County.

3. Interview with Angelo Demers, a grandson of T. J., in Plains, August 8, 1940.

4. Interview with George Wurm, Camas Prairie, on August 29, 1940. Wurm is an old-time rancher in the Camas Prairie neighborhood and knew Demers intimately.

"Bill" Murray, one of the old-time cow punchers, remembers a story he heard concerning "Jack" DeMers and a Texas cowboy, who had come to Montana on one of the DeMers cattle drives.[1] They were camped out one night in early October, when it turned cold and started to snow, ending in a real blizzard. This was the first snowstorm the Texan had ever seen and he suffered intensely. DeMers woke the boy to go on guard that night. The Texan threw back his tarpaulin and when the snow rolled in on him he covered himself up again and told DeMers that he had already quit and someone else would have to herd in his place.

The next morning when they broke camp the Texan threw his bed in the wagon and was preparing to ride along with it when DeMers halted him. "You can't put that bed in that wagon and you can't go along with it. You quit last night, so you will need your bed with you."

"Hell, Jack, you're not going to put me afoot out here in the snow to carry my bed and saddle, are you?"

"No, I'm not going to put you afoot; you're already that way, its only about 15 miles to the nearest town. I guess you can make it in two or three days, if you hurry and don't freeze to death."

Mr. Murray says he understood that the Southerner made the town, but he back-trailed to Texas at the first opportunity.

An interesting sidelight on the breaking and training of cow horses is also provided by this same "Bill" Murray, who now resides in Plains. He says:

"When you find that a colt has what is known as good cow sense, it is always the best plan to shoe his hind feet, leaving the front ones bare. Then, when the horse stops suddenly, as a real cow horse has to do, he stops only on his hind feet and does his dodging on the fore feet. The reason he stops on his hind feet is because he has the shoes on them and can slam them into the ground without hurting himself. His front feet, being unshod and tender, keeps him from stopping on them.

"If you break a horse by jamming his forefeet into the ground, your horse will develop bad shoulders and won't be safe to ride, because he will stumble continually, and a horse that stumbles will fall eventually and he and his rider will become either crippled or killed."

Note

1. These two sketches were obtained in an interview with William (Bill) Murray on December 3, 1940. Mr. Murray, who now resides in Plains, was at one time a top cowhand and worked for several outfits, including that of the younger DeMers—Telesphore G. DeMers, a son of "Jack" DeMers.

François Finlay
Told by: **"Swift" and Oliver Courville**
Writer: **Griffith A. Williams**
Date: December 11, 1941

Further investigation of the history of François Finlay, or Benetsee, reveals the fact that he was married twice.

Following the death of his first wife, who was a member of the Flathead tribe, but whose name we have not yet learned, he married a Canadian Cree woman. Three sons were born to the first marriage—Basson, Joseph, and Abraham Finlay. They have long since passed away.

The second union with the Canadian Cree by the name of Mary Ashley produced eight children, six girls and two boys. All were married and most of them raised large families. All of them are dead with the exception of Peter Finlay, who is still living at the age of 84 on Camas Prairie, where he made his home for many years with the late Dave Couture.

The following is a list of the eight children by the second marriage: Mrs. Alex Morigeau and Mrs. Joseph Couture of Arlee; Mrs. Louis Courville (mother of "Swift" and Oliver Courville), Mrs. Joseph Palin and Mrs. Joseph Moran, all of Frenchtown; Mrs. William King of Colville; Peter Finlay of Camas Prairie and Basil Finlay, who died at Polson a few years ago.

All of these descendants, together with their children, were allotted land when the Flathead Reservation was opened and, according to "Swift" Courville, there must be over 200 descendants of François Finlay scattered over this western section.

Packed for Government

According to Oliver Courville of Hot Springs, who is older than "Swift," François Finlay must have gone to California around 1849. At any rate, he picked up his knowledge of placer mining there. He also packed for the government between Astoria, Oregon, and Fort Colville. He and a partner, whose name is not known, each having a 14 mule string for this purpose.

He came to Gold Creek or Benetese Creek, as it was called in 1852, to prospect and found light, float gold in small quantities.

He passed away suddenly at the home of his daughter, Mrs. Joseph Moran, near Frenchtown, about the year 1876 or 1877, as near as the Courvilles can figure out. Both were boys of tender age at the time.

Note

The foregoing article is the result of an interview with "Swift" Courville of Plains and Oliver Courville of Hot Springs at the latter place on December 9, 1941.

Bigart Note

The genealogical information in the Federal Writers Project interviews about the Finlay family does not agree with either church records or the information used for tribal enrollment on the Flathead Reservation. See the biographical glossary for a more detailed discussion of the differences.

François (Benetsee) Finlay

Told by: **Peter Finlay, Margaret Courville, and Z. Courville**
Writer: **Griffith A. Williams**
Date: February 10, 1942

It must have been around 1800 that François (Benetsee) Finlay, who was to become famous as the first, or at least one of the first, to discover gold in Montana in 1852 on Benetsee Creek, or what is now called Gold Creek, first saw the light.

According to most historians, François Finlay was a British subject of mixed Indian and Scotch blood. Such, however, is not the case, at least as far as place of birth is concerned.

The writer has done extensive research work during the past few months in an endeavor to learn more about the birth and antecedents of this famous Montana pioneer gold miner, through interviews with descendants of Benetsee.

From Miss Margaret Courville, the daughter and only child of Mr. and Mrs. Zephyr (Swift) Courville, who is a great granddaughter of François Finlay on her father's side, and who is particularly interested in the history of her antecedents, we learn that François Finlay was the son of Charles (Red Cloud) Finlay, a half-breed Kootenai Indian with Scotch-French blood in his veins, and Mary (Sitting Blanket) Finlay, half Spokane and half Pend d'Oreille Indian.

François Finlay was not born in Canada and was not a British subject, as we have been led to believe. He was born on Tobacco Plains, in what is now Lincoln County and where the town of Eureka now stands. We have this authentic statement from the lips of a son of François, Peter Finlay, who is still living on Camas Prairie at the age of 93. Peter says that although the Kootenai tribe ranged in British Columbia, Canada, Tobacco Plains across the border in the United States was also considered Kootenai country and that his father was born on this side of the border.

Benetsee Married Twice

Not much is known of his first marriage, although "Swift" Courville informs us that his wife was a member of the Flathead tribe and that three sons were born of this union—Joseph, Abraham, and Basson. We are not sure as to the correct spelling of the last named. It is given as it sounds. All three have long since passed away.

The second union with Mary Ashley, a Canadian Cree who also spoke Flathead and French (must have been mixed blood), produced eight children, six girls and two boys, of whom Peter is the only survivor. The following is a list of the eight children: Mrs. Alex Morigeau and Mrs. Joseph Couture of Arlee; Mrs. Louis Courville (mother of "Swift" and Oliver Courville), Mrs. Joseph Palin and Mrs. Joseph Moran, all of Frenchtown; Mrs. William King of Colville; Peter Finlay of Camas Prairie and Basil Finlay, who died at Polson a few years ago.

All of these children, or their descendants who survived them were allotted land when the Flathead Reservation was opened. According to "Swift" Courville, there must be over 200 descendants of François Finlay scattered over this western section. Be it remembered also that "Swift's" father, Louis Courville, who married Julia Finlay, Benetsee's daughter, was adopted by the Flathead chiefs as one of their members and was given an allotment years before the reservation was opened to white settlement.

Peter Finlay's Recollections

Peter Finlay is almost deaf and his eyesight has failed, but his mentality is good. He prefers to talk Indian or French, although he understands English, and through the courtesy of his nephew, "Swift" Courville, we were enabled to glean the following recollections:

> I was about 27 or 28 years old when father dropped dead at the home of my sister Ellen (Mrs. Joe Moran) near Frenchtown. They had a ranch there. He dropped dead on the way from the house to the barn. I am not quite sure, but I believe this was in 1876.
>
> I was but a year old when my father went to California to seek his fortune in the gold diggings. Of course, I do not remember anything about those days, but it was there he had his first experience in placer mining. He did not make much of a stake and soon returned to the land of the open range—the land of his fathers. He loved the wide,

open spaces and was really not a miner at heart, nor were any of the Indians or fur traders for that matter. They did not want the white man intruding into their country and tried their best to suppress all information pertaining to the discovery of gold. The fur traders, of course, wanted to keep the country as it was for their own selfish reasons, and the Indians wanted to keep what they felt rightfully belonged to them. My father loved to guide parties through the country so they would not be tempted to stay. He packed for the government at one time between Fort Colville and Astoria, Oregon.

He had a string of 14 mules for this purpose. He also acted as a guide when the government laid out the Flathead Reservation and always claimed they did not take in enough territory.

He was a very intelligent man and could read and write and the Indians of this western country, all of whose languages he could speak, trusted him implicitly. "Benetsee" was always called upon to settle disputes, for they recognized him as being fair and square in all things.

He was a big man in every way, about six feet in height, with piercing dark brown eyes that could flash fire at times, although he was of a gentle nature. He had shaggy hair and eyebrows like his Scotch ancestors, and a deep, broad chest. He had a mustache, but no beard. His appearance was always neat and he kept us that way when he was around, yet he was always kind and considerate, if firm, and was a hard worker and a mighty good provider.

I was but four years old when he prospected for gold, as he did as often as he took the notion. He found some in 1852 on what was then called Benetsee Creek—now Gold Creek—more gold than he was ever given credit for, for it was kept as much of a secret as possible, as I have mentioned before. He took it to Angus McDonald, who at that time was engaged in the fur trade and, like all the fur traders, feared that the news of the discovery of gold would bring in a hoard of whites and thus ruin his business. He urged my father to keep the matter quiet, which he did. How much he got out of McDonald I do not know, nor did he ever tell me, but it must have been quite a grub stake. McDonald sent the dust to the headquarters of the Hudson Bay Company in Victoria.

My father did return to his diggings and washed out more gold. Some of it he traded for supplies at Fort Owen and the rest he left with the company. It must have amounted to over $1,000.

He tired of his labor in the placer diggings, however, and returned to the life he really loved, guiding and packing, and spending the rest of his time with the Indians he loved and who loved and adored him.

Billy Irvine Memories
Told by: **Andrew Stinger, his partner**
Writer: **Bon I. Whealdon**
Date: December 18, 1941

"Mr. Billy Irvine had the very finest cattle spread in the entire Flathead Valley. He understood cattle and well he might, as he spent a lifetime with them, riding range, drifting cattle to distant shipping points, wintering herds in Canada, working for the biggest cattle outfits in Western Canada and Montana. His ranch was literally overflowing with fat range stuff and splendid horses. He and Emily were both unequaled bronc busters and 'buffalo boys.'

"In connection with his home ranch, Billy controlled an immense body of hay and grazing land, as well as an entire hillside of pasture.

"It was a delight to any westerner to visit the Irvine Ranch, for there Billy and Emily dispensed true Montana hospitality in generous fashion. The Irvines were courteous, well-informed, splendid appearing people. Billy and Emily's lives had been crowded with colorful experiences; and both delighted in recounting their thrilling adventures in vividly fascinating style. They were clean, fearless living people.

"Billy enjoyed helping needy folks. Always his purse and his well stocked larder were open to the unfortunate. Many a struggling homesteader had ample reason to praise the names and innate goodness of Billy and Emily Irvine. Patterned on a magnificent scale himself, Billy could not tolerate smallness of caliber in others. When a certain group of affluent, but miserly, foreigners began coming into the valley, Billy, seeing their greedy, grasping ways, felt that the West he knew and loved was ending. He always referred to these folks from that particular alien shore as 'right rumped trash that should have been dumped into the Atlantic.' 'Great Gods and little green apples,' he would say, 'by the very nature of these Mongrels, they can never be Americans! By permitting them to settle among us, we are shoving a nest of Yellow-jackets into our shirt bosom and feeding them on the honey of our land. Someday they are going to start stinging the eternal daylights out of us.'"

Billy Irvine

Told by: **Mrs. Mary Blood, his sister, and Harry Burland**
Writer: **Bon I. Whealdon**
Date: November 14, 1941

William Irvine, a son of Peter Ervine [Irvine], Hudson Bay Company employee, and Angela Ashley, Salish Indian woman, was born near old Fort Connah in 1856.

William, or "Billy" as he was affectionately called, was the oldest of nine children, so at a rather early age he was obliged to step out and shift for himself.

His first job, as cattle wrangler for a neighbor, was the beginning of a very busy career upon the range. He was an expert roper and bronc rider and his skill secured him employment as top hand for some of the largest stock raisers in Montana.

In 1876, he, in company with eleven other Flathead cowboys, drifted 1,200 head of local cattle to Cheyenne, Wyoming. Their route took them through Butte, Idaho Falls, across a corner of Utah, Laramie, thence to Cheyenne, from there they were shipped to Chicago, Illinois. They very leisurely made eight to ten miles per day in "drifting" the cattle. This enabled the cattle to prime fatten upon the free range.

Their caravan for this trip consisted of a covered chuck wagon, a diner, and a "pullman" for the cowboys. The outfit was drawn by four oxen.

The drifting of beef cattle to Cheyenne was such a profitable venture, that he took charge of the herds to that shipping point in 1877, 1879, and 1880.

In 1881, he went to Alberta, Canada, where he worked for the Pat Burns Company and for the George Lane outfit, two of the biggest cattle companies in all Canada. During the Riel Rebellion, Billy served the Canadian government in the capacity of supervisor of the cavalry horses.

Because of a scarcity of Flathead grazing in 1895, he drove some 600 head of cattle to Alberta. After fattening in good shape during the summer and autumn of that year, the severe Canadian winter killed every last one of the herd.

Billy finally located upon a valuable ranch, $17^1/_2$ miles west of Polson. Here with a small herd of cattle given to him by his old friend Charles Allard, Sr., Billy devoted attention to this nucleus band until it had increased to 3,000 head.

It is estimated that in addition to his own cattle, Billy, during his 84 years of life, handled untold thousands for others.

John Silverthorne, the Reticent
Told by: **Mrs. John M. Brechbill**
Writer: **Mabel C. Olson**
Date: December 2, 1941

"My father, John Silverthorne was born in Pittsburgh, Pennsylvania, in 1816. His ancestors were among the Englishmen who migrated from Wiltshire, in southwestern England, to Holland, and who later came to America. His father, Gabriel Silverthorne, descended from Oliver Silverthorne. There are members of the family scattered from New York to Washington, D.C., some doctors, some teachers, etc., descendants of the three brothers, Gabriel, William, and John who came to America from Holland. John returned to England, William came to the West, never to be heard of again, and my grandfather Gabriel moved to New Jersey from Pennsylvania. He came to Stevensville for a visit in 1871.

"Father used laughingly to call himself a Pennsylvania Dutchman. He did have some Dutch characteristics, but his appearance and bearing were distinctly English. He was tall and slender, and walked very erect. His features were fine, his complexion medium dark, his hair and eyes dark. In later years his hair became white, which, together with his name, led his friends to call him 'Silver.' At that time I was still quite young, but I remember well how angry it made me to hear him called 'Old Silver.' Nor did I like it at all when I was referred to as 'Miss Silver.'

"Father was always very quiet, and very reticent about himself. People who knew him remarked about it. He belonged to no society. (He belonged to the Fort Owen Grange in 1886. Miscellaneous Records, Book B, page 338. Office of the County Clerk, Missoula.) And yet there was nothing surly nor ill-natured about him. He was, on the contrary, humorous and witty. As a child, his quietness seemed a matter of course to me, but when I grew older I often wondered if he had experienced some sorrow to make him so.

"He was neat and particular about everything he did. I can still see him cooking the meals for us, his four children, pipe in mouth, or mending the boys' clothes, not saying a word for hours.

"He came to the Bitter Root Valley in 1852, when he was 36 years old. I do not know where he had been just previous to that date, whether or not he had taken in the gold rush in California. However, I am sure that he did not, as Judge Woody states, first come in 1856, although he may have been among the party who came that year from Utah with Fred Burr.

"He was among those who rebuilt Fort Owen, contracting that work on the two adobe buildings in 1857. He also freighted for Major John Owen, being in charge of the pack train in 1858. In 1860 he got out saw logs for Owen.

"Various histories and articles have broached the question of his possession of gold at different times, and some authors have explained that he secured it from François Finlay. It is possible that he did handle some for Finlay, of whom I do not recall hearing before. Some of it at least he mined himself, on Gold Creek, in Alder Gulch, and on Big Creek, below Victor. He took considerable gold out of the mine on Big Creek, about whose location and richness he would not talk. I used in later years to ask him why he did not go up there and dig out some more gold. He always replied, 'Maybe I will someday.' But he was getting too old at that time.

"He used to trade in horses, although he never kept many at a time. I remember I always loved the pacers he would buy, and I begged him to let me have one of these, a beautiful sorrel. He promised that when he died the sorrel would be mine, a promise which he kept.

"He also had a few cattle. One of his cows, a longhorn, gave birth to a calf the same day I was born. Like many of her kind, that cow could not be restrained by any fence: she seemed to have springs in her legs. She disliked strangers, and would make a fuss when one approached her. I sometimes think now that it was strange we children felt no fear of her. She knew us, and would bellow when we came within her sight.

"Father's main occupation, however, was farming. He raised wheat, oats, and buckwheat. In that day most farmers who raised grain at all went in for buckwheat.

"At that time practically all labor was hand work. Grain was scythed by hand, bundled and ricked by hand. It was hauled to a shed, where it was threshed by the treading of horses. The slatted floor enabled the kernels of grain to fall free from the stalks. Next the grain was hauled to the community fanning mill at Stevensville, to be rid of the chaff.

"I lost my two older brothers in the Spanish American War, and my remaining brother, Jefferson, died 20 years ago. My father died in 1887, at the age of 71, of lung trouble, the result, I imagine, of flu. He was active until a short time before his death.

"Several places in the Bitter Root have been named for him: Silverthorne Station is on Silverthorne Spur, which is run off from the main road from the mill. It has been taken over by the Missoula Mercantile Co. Silverthorne Ford is a crossing of the Bitter Root River. (Mrs. Brechbill does not recall a Silverthorne Creek, above Fort Owen, mentioned in *The Weekly Missoulian*, July 7, 1875.*)

"I have been told that there are pictures in a Dillon attic, one of which shows my father and his freight team. I do not know in which building they are.

"In 1934 while with my foster mother, Mrs. Robert Lander, in Stevensville, I met Mrs. Devenpeck, whom Major Owen employed, first as housekeeper in the spring of 1865, and later in that year to make bolting cloth for the mill. (Mrs. Brechbill does not know Mrs. Devenpeck's initials, nor does Owen give them in his journal.) I could not remember her at all. She spoke of having once made a shirt for my father from a blanket."

(Although Mrs. Brechbill has been blind for many years, she is cheerful and fun-loving. She is a short, plump woman, her round, placid face framed with heavy white hair.)

Notes
County Records

John Silverthorne sold to William L. Church for $300, on August 4, 1871, the Chambers, or LoLo Ranch, adjoining Fort Owen. Deed Records, Book A.

On December 21, 1875, Silverthorne mortgaged 12 horses. They were described as iron gray with white stripe; bays marked with white; sorrel with flax mane and tail. Mortgages, Book A, page 404.

On December 12, 1877, he mortgaged to S. C. Tyler 21 horses, branded JS on the left hip, right hip, or right flank. They were on his ranch, $2\frac{1}{2}$ miles from Stevensville. Mortgages, Book B.

He mortgaged, on May 21, 1880, seven horses with various brands, two of which were S on the right shoulder. The horses were described as cream, mouse-colored pinto, buckskin, dark bay, light bay. Mortgages, Book B, page 337.

On January 12, 1881, he mortgaged six horses, one a spotted blue, branded S and JS on the left flank. Mortgages, Book M, page 431.

Alfred Cave administered Silverthorne's estate. The court hearing began December 4, 1888. Gust Moser bought the ranch for $2,250. Deed Records, Book K, page 477.

The Silverthorne ranch consisted of 160 acres, fence-enclosed, on the west side of the Bitter Root River, about $2\frac{1}{2}$ miles from Stevensville. Mortgages, Book A, page 81.

Published Sources

1. Tom Stout, *Montana, Its Story and Biography* (Chicago: The American Historical Society, 1921), vol. 1, pp. 185-86.

2. Robert Vaughn, *Then and Now; or, Thirty-six Years in the Rockies* (Minneapolis, MN: Tribune Printing Co., 1900).

3. *The Journals and Letters of Major John Owen*, edited by Seymour Dunbar and Paul C. Phillips, (New York: Edward Eberstadt, 1927). Mention of Silverthorne is scattered throughout the two volumes.

4. *The Pioneer*, published in Missoula. Two or three brief items which really tell nothing of the man.

Bigart Note
*The Weekly Missoulian, July 7, 1875, contains several references to John Silverthorne's work in the Democratic Party but no reference to a Silverthorne Creek. The *Weekly Rocky Mountain Gazette* (Helena, MT), May 21, 1873, p. 3, c. 3-4, tells about a Silver Creek named after Silverthorne, but the article does not clearly identify the location.

Biographies

"I Will Be Meat for My Salish"

Biographical Glossary of Flathead Indian Reservation Names

by Eugene Mark Felsman and Robert Bigart

The Biographical Glossary is limited to those people mentioned in the manuscripts who were members of a Flathead Reservation tribe, married to a tribal member, or residents of the Flathead Indian Reservation. The biographical information below was based on Eugene Mark Felsman's twenty years of genealogical research on the Confederated Salish and Kootenai Tribes. Much of the information was abstracted from the Bureau of Indian Affairs censuses from 1886 to 1961. Sources other than the Federal Writers Project interviews and Felsman's tribal census research are noted at the end of each entry. Many sources have conflicting information. The information in the entries can only be as accurate as the sources available. We have been as careful as possible, but mistakes have certainly crept into the biographical sketches. We apologize for the errors.

Special thanks are due David C. "Chalky" Courchane for his genealogical work on the Finlay family in *Jocko's People*. We have relied heavily on his work for many of the biographical sketches below. The sources available use Finlay and Finley interchangeably. The biographical sketches keep the spelling found in the sources, so both forms will be found in the sketches.

Abbreviations for Sources

AS   *The Anaconda Standard* (Anaconda, MT)

BR Trails III   Bitter Root Valley Historical Society, *Bitter Root Trails III* (Hamilton, MT: Bitter Root Valley Historical Society, 1998)

Buffalo Roamed   Velma R. Kvale and Margaret Sterling Brooke, *Where the Buffalo Roamed* (St. Ignatius, MT: Mission Valley News, 1976)

CIA   U.S. Commissioner of Indian Affairs

CIA Report   U.S. Commissioner of Indian Affairs, *Annual Report of the Commissioner of Indian Affairs* (year of report)

Courchane   David C. Courchane, unpublished research materials, 1999

Demersville   Carle F. O'Neil, *Two Men of Demersville* (privately published, n.p., 1990)

DM   *The Daily Missoulian* (Missoula, MT) and *Missoulian* (daily) (Missoula, MT)

Enrollment   U.S. Bureau of Indian Affairs, *Selected Records of the Bureau of Indian Affairs Relating to Enrollment of Indians on the Flathead Indian Reservation, 1903–08,* National Archives Microfilm Publication M1350

FC   *The Flathead Courier* (Polson, MT)

Fort Owen   George F. Weisel, ed., *Men and Trade on the Northwest Frontier as Shown by the Fort Owen Ledger* (Missoula, MT: Montana State University Press, 1955)

FR   *The Federal Reporter*

Frontier Woman   Mary Ronan, *Frontier Woman: The Story of Mary Ronan as Told to Margaret Ronan*, ed. by H. G. Merriam (Missoula: University of Montana Publications in History, 1973)

Historic   Anonymous, *Historic and Scenic Missoula and Ravalli Counties: Souvenir of the National Irrigation Congress* (Missoula, MT: n.p., 1899)

Ind Census   U.S. Bureau of Indian Affairs, *Indian Census Rolls, 1855–1940,* National Archives Microfilm Publication M595

Jocko's People   David C. Courchane, *Jocko's People: The Descendants of James Finlay and His Son, Jacques Raphael Finlay* (privately printed, n.p., 1997)

Joseph Allard   June Allard Green and Joe Green, *Joseph Allard, 1876–1964: Pioneer, Cowboy, Stagecoach Driver, Rancher: Biographies and "His Life and Times"* (privately printed, n.p., 1986)

LCV   *Lake County Vista* (Polson, MT)

Leeson   Michael A. Leeson, ed., *History of Montana, 1739–1885* (Chicago: Warner, Beers & Company, 1885)

Miller   Joaquin Miller, *An Illustrated History of the State of Montana* (Chicago: The Lewis Publishing Co., 1894)

MHS	Montana Historical Society, Helena, MT
MVN	Mission Valley News (St. Ignatius, MT)
NA	National Archives, Washington, DC
NAmf	National Archives Microfilm Publications
OIA LR	U.S. Office of Indian Affairs, *Letters Received by the Office of Indian Affairs, 1824–81,* National Archive Microfilm Publication M234
OPA Archives	Robert C. Carriker and Eleanor R. Carriker, eds., *The Microfilm Edition of the Pacific Northwest Tribes Mission Collection of the Oregon Province Archives of the Society of Jesus* (Wilmington, DL: Scholarly Resources, 1987)
OPA Archives Guide	Robert C. Carriker and Eleanor R. Carriker, eds., *Guide to the Microfilm Edition of the Pacific Northwest Tribes Mission Collection of the Oregon Province Archives of the Society of Jesus* (Wilmington, DL: Scholarly Resources, 1987)
Partoll	Albert J. Partoll, "Angus McDonald, Frontier Fur Trader," *Pacific Northwest Quarterly,* vol. 42, no. 2 (Apr. 1951), pp. 138-46
RP	*The Ronan Pioneer* (Ronan, MT)
Sanders	Helen Fitzgerald Sanders, *A History of Montana* (Chicago: The Lewis Publishing Co., 1913)
Settlers	Hot Springs Historical Society, *Settlers and Sodbusters* (St. Ignatius, MT: Mission Valley News, 1976)
Silverthorne	Frank F. Reed, *History of the Silverthorne Family* (Chicago: Silverthorn(e) Family Association, 1982)
Stout	Tom Stout, *Montana: Its Story and Biography* (Chicago: The American Historical Society, 1921)
UM	Toole Archives, Mansfield Library, University of Montana, Missoula, MT
WM	*The Weekly Missoulian* (Missoula, MT)
Zontek	Kenneth S. Zontek, "Saving the Bison: The Story of Samuel Walking Coyote," (master's thesis, New Mexico State University, Las Cruces, NM, 1993)

Biographical Glossary

Allard, Charles, Jr. (1878–1930) The second eldest son of Charles Allard, Sr., and Emerence Brown Allard was in charge of the Pablo buffalo roundup of 1908. Charles, Jr., attended the College of Montana at Deer Lodge and the Montana State University at Missoula. A prominent Flathead Reservation rancher and tribal member, he was also known for his race horses and management of some of the first rodeos in western Montana. In 1905 he married Lula Spurgeon, a white woman adopted into the tribes, and in 1922 he married Emily Glover, a tribal member. He had no children. [*The Montana Record-Herald* (Helena, MT), June 28, 1930, p. 11, c. 1-2; *RP*, July 3, 1930, p. 1, c. 6]

Allard, Charles, Sr. (1852–1896) Confirmed as "Louis Charles Allard," this prominent part-Indian Flathead Reservation rancher and businessman was the more business oriented of the two partners who purchased the Pablo-Allard buffalo herd from Sam Walking Coyote in 1884. He was most famous as a buffalo owner, but he also worked as a cattle rancher and operated a stage line between Ravalli, Polson, and Demersville. In 1875 he married Emerence Brown, who was part Pend d'Oreille, and the couple had six children of whom only Joseph Allard and Charles Allard, Jr., survived to adulthood. After the death of his first wife, he married Louise Denise Courville, a tribal member, in 1892, and they had two daughters. Louise Anna Allard died at nine years of age in 1905 and Eva May Allard lived from 1894 to 1971. Charles Allard, Sr., died in 1896 in Chicago while seeking medical care for an injured knee that he had failed to have treated in time. [*Joseph Allard*, pp. 8-20; *DM*, July 22, 1896, p. 1, c. 5-6]

Allard, Eva May (1894–1971) The eldest daughter of Charles Allard, Sr., and Louise Courville Allard, Eva May attended college in Helena. She was one of the earliest tribal members to work as a nurse and retired as Superintendent of Nursing at the San Francisco City Hospital in San Francisco, CA. She died in San Francisco. [J. H. Green, Sun City, AZ, letter to Bigart, Nov. 25, 1996]

Allard, Joseph (1876–1964) The eldest son of Charles Allard, Sr., and Emerence Brown Allard, Joseph Allard operated his father's cattle ranch, stagecoach line, and other businesses after 1896. He attended the College of Montana at Deer Lodge and private schools in Oregon and Connecticut. Joseph was one of the riders in the 1908 roundup of the Pablo buffalo herd. In later years he served in several capacities in the Flathead Reservation tribal government. In 1898 he married Adeline Paulin, a tribal member, and they had six children. [*Joseph Allard*, pp. 3-7; *Historic*, p. 71]

Allard, Louise Anna (1895–1905) Daughter of Charles Allard, Sr., and Louise Courville Allard, she died of pneumonia in 1905 at nine years of age. [*DM,* Apr. 10, 1905, p. 7, c. 2]

Archibald, Billy. The interviews identify Archibald as one of the cowboys who worked on the roundup of the Pablo buffalo herd. No further information was found.

Aubrey, Charles (1845–1908) See "About the Writers" below.

Barber, Elizabeth "Lizzie" (1898–1947) The daughter of Oliver Gebeau and Rosalie Finley Gebeau, Lizzie was born in Arlee. A mixed-blood tribal member, she married a non-Indian, Samuel Barber, in 1914. She died along with three other relatives in an explosion and fire at a family reunion near Pablo in 1947. [*Jocko's People,* vol. 1, p. 232; *RP,* June 19, 1947, p. 1, c. 1]

Barnaby, Antoine "Tony" (1875–1945) The third son of Joseph and Lizette Mel-lu-seh Barnaby, Antoine was born in 1875 while his parents were on a buffalo hunt on the plains. He married Mary Pablo, a mixed-blood daughter of Michel Pablo, and operated a ranch near Ronan. [*Enrollment,* rl. 1, fr. 56, #2028; *RP,* Mar. 1, 1945, p. 1, c. 2]

Barnaby, Felix [or Felixe] (1867–1941) He was the son of Joseph and Lizette Mel-lu-seh Barnaby of the Jocko Valley. Half Indian, of Spokane and Kalispel descent, he married Mary Louise Two Crows, a full-blood Flathead, in 1894. Three of their children lived to adulthood, two boys and one girl. The family lived in Arlee where Felix operated a hotel that burned in 1929. [*Enrollment,* rl. 1, fr. 29, #1014; *MVN* (St. Ignatius, MT), June 6, 1984, p. 6, c. 1-7; David C. Courchane, *The de Forests: A Collection of Genealogies* (privately printed, n.p., 1997), pp. 390-91]

Barnaby, Joseph (1831–1921) Of Spokane and French descent, Joseph Barnaby married Lizette Mel-lu-seh (one half Kalispel) in 1850. They settled in the Jocko Valley and raised four boys to adulthood, including Antoine and Felix. In 1885 he had 20 acres under fence and a crop of 200 bushels of wheat and oats. [*Enrollment,* rl. 1, fr. 2, #40; *CIA Report* (1885), pp. 126-27]

Bartlett, W. A. See "About the Writers" below.

Beaulieu, Fred. The interviews identify Beaulieu as a pioneer settler on the reservation. Presumably he was an early white homesteader, possibly near the Flathead River. No further information was found.

Beaverhead, Alex (1874–1946) He married Louise Cumcumpoo in 1893 and the couple had eight children. Both Alex and his wife were full-blood Pend d'Oreille. In 1920 he related Salish legends and traditions to Bon Whealdon. [*Enrollment,* rl. 1, fr. 31, #1093]

Blodgett, Joseph Smith, Sr. (1835–1903) Born in Ohio, Joseph S. Blodgett spent the 1850s working on pack trains for John Owen, the Bitterroot Valley trader; for Gov. Isaac I. Stevens' 1855 treaty expedition; and others. In 1862 he located a ranch near Corvallis in the Bitterroot Valley. During the late 1850s and early 1860s, Joseph joined the Salish Indians in trapping, trading, and hunting buffalo. In 1860 he married Ella McLeod, of Pend d'Oreille and Salish Indian descent. In 1877 he fought with the U.S. Army against the Nez Perce Indians at the Battle of the Big Hole. He moved his family to the Flathead Indian Reservation when Charlo removed from the Bitterroot Valley. [Leeson, pp. 1299-1300; *DM*, Dec. 1, 1903, p. 8, c. 3]

Blodgett, Joseph Smith, Mrs. (?–1880) Ella McLeod, Pend d'Oreille and Salish Indian, married Joseph Blodgett, a white man, in 1860. They had at least eight children. They lived on a ranch near Corvallis in the Bitterroot Valley. [*Enrollment*, rl. 1, fr. 28, #981 and #989; "Pioneer Dies Near Missoula," undated and unidentified newspaper clipping, Society of Montana Pioneers Records, MS 68, box 1, folder 3, MHS]

Blodgett, Joseph Reeves, Jr. (1877–1950) The youngest son of Joseph S. Blodgett, Sr., and Ella McLeod Blodgett, Joseph Reeves was born in Stevensville in 1877. The family moved to Arlee with Charlo's band. He was a farmer and member of the Confederated Salish and Kootenai Tribal Council. He married Maggie McLeod in 1902. [*RP*, Mar. 30, 1950, p. 1, c. 5]

Blodgett, Lyman (1833–1908) In 1868 Lyman Blodgett, a non-Indian, started a ranch at Corvallis in the Bitterroot Valley. In 1871 he purchased a herd of cattle in Utah. His brother, Joseph Smith Blodgett, Sr., was already located near Corvallis and married into the Salish tribe. Lyman married a white woman from Wales and they had eleven children. [Leeson, p. 1300; *BR Trails III*, p. 153]

Blodgett, Newman (1863–1933) The eldest son of Joseph S. Blodgett, Sr., and Ella McLeod Blodgett, Newman was a tribal member born in the Bitterroot Valley. He died at Arlee. [*Enrollment*, rl. 1, fr. 28, #981; *LCV*, Apr. 27, 1933, p. 6, c. 1]

Blodgett, Sarah "Sally" [dates unknown] Daughter of Joseph S. Blodgett, Sr., and Ella McLeod Blodgett, Sally was part Salish and lived in the Bitterroot Valley. She did not survive her father who died in 1903. [*DM*, Dec. 1, 1903, p. 8, c. 3]

Blood, Mary (1875–1961) Mary Irvine Blood, part Kootenai Indian, was born in Frenchtown in 1875 to Peter Irvine and Angelique Ashley Irvine. Billy Irvine, the Flathead Reservation cattleman, was her brother. Mary died at St. Ignatius. [*DM*, Jan. 6, 1961, p. 8. c. 1; *RP*, Mar. 8, 1956, p. 8, c. 1]

Brechbill, John M., Mrs. (1866–1954) Ellen Silverthorne Brechbill was the daughter of John Silverthorne, a white man, and Lizette Finley Silverthorne, a Salish Indian. She was born in Stevensville. In 1884 she married John M. Brechbill, a white carpenter. Her husband was construction superintendent for some major building projects in Missoula and western Montana. He handled the construction of the county courthouse, Masonic temple, and Elk's temple in Missoula. The couple had three children. Ellen died in Missoula. [*Jocko's People,* vol. 3, pp. 60-61; *Enrollment,* rl. 2, fr. 74-85; *DM,* Dec. 12, 1945, p. 1, c. 4 and p. 6, c. 4; *DM,* Apr. 7, 1954, p. 6, c. 3]

Brown, Clarence A. (1888–1974) See "About the Writers" below.

Brown, Louis (1811–1889) Born in Quebec, Louis Brown had a varied career in the west as a fur trader, farmer, flour mill operator and expressman. He went to California in 1849 to mine gold. In 1860 he moved his family from a farm in the Colville Valley to Frenchtown, near Missoula. He was known for his devout support of the Catholic Church. His wife was Emily Goetsche, a Pend d'Oreille Indian. Two of their daughters married Moses Reeves, another married Joseph Houle, and yet another married Charles Allard. [*Joseph Allard,* pp. 24-30, 233; *Courchane*]

Burland, Harry Henry (1873–1939) Most of the references in the interviews to Harry Burland seem to refer to this Harry, who was the father of Henry Arthur Burland. This Harry was part Indian and born to Baptiste and Rosalie Morigeau Burland at Fort Colville, WA. At the age of 16 he moved to Jocko Agency to live with his relatives, the Oliver Gebeau family. He attended school at St. Ignatius Mission where he learned carpentry. In later years he worked as mechanic, carpenter, and blacksmith at the Agency and in Ronan. He was a noted musician. Harry Henry was married twice and had at least ten children. [*RP,* Feb. 9, 1939, p. 8, c. 2-5]

Burland, Henry Arthur (1903–1981) The Henry or Harry Burland who was a child of about ten years old when he joined his grandfather August Finley in the hunt for the remnants of Pablo's buffalo herd was Henry Arthur Burland (1903–1981), son of Harry Henry Burland (1873–1939). Henry Arthur's mother was Philomene Granjo Burland who died in 1906 when he was still very young. August Finley was probably his grandfather by Indian custom. Henry Arthur Burland was a tribal judge for the Confederated Salish and Kootenai Tribes. In 1925 he married Margaret Howlett, another tribal member. The couple had three children. He died in an automobile accident near Pablo in 1981. [*DM,* Dec. 19, 1981, p. 10, c. 2-3]

Cave, Will (1863–1954) See "About the Writers" below.

Charlo, Chief (1830–1910) Charlo or Little-Claw-of-a-Grizzly-Bear succeeded his father, Victor, in 1870 as chief of the Salish Flatheads. Charlo continued Victor's efforts to maintain the band's home in the Bitterroot Valley in the face of growing pressure from the government and economic competition from the surrounding white community. As the buffalo declined, he worked hard to expand the band's farms and stock herds and avoid conflict with the whites.

He had only limited success, and finally in 1891 poverty and drought forced him to remove to the Jocko Valley on the Flathead Reservation. Father Palladino characterized him as "a man of a quiet yet firm disposition, a true representative of his race and a thorough Indian. His conduct during the Nez Perces outbreak gained him the admiration of all, and proved once more the loyal friendship for the whites on the part of the Flat Heads [sic] .... But while friendly toward the whites, he surely is not in love with their ways ... Charlo is a sincere and practical Christian." He died in the Jocko in 1910 as the government was forcing the tribes to sell much of the reservation land to white homesteaders. [L. B. Palladino, S.J., *Indian and White in the Northwest: A History of Catholicity in Montana, 1831 to 1891*, 2d ed. (Lancaster, PA: Wickersham Publishing Company, 1922), pp. 85-90; J. Verne Dusenberry, "Samples of Pend d'Oreille Oral Literature and Salish Narratives," In Leslie B. Davis, ed., *Lifeways of Intermontane and Plains Montana Indians* (Bozeman, MT: Museum of the Rockies, Montana State University, 1979), pp. 109-20; *Frontier Woman*, pp. 145-53]

Clifford, John E. (1862–1936) Born in Missouri, Clifford was working at the Missoula Mercantile Company in Missoula when he caught the eye of entrepreneur T. J. DeMers. In 1887 T. J. hired Clifford to manage a new general store at the head of Flathead Lake at Demersville. In the same year Clifford married his employer's daughter, tribal member Delima DeMers. Clifford ran the business into the ground with high expenses and excessive accounts receivable. In 1891 he was elected Mayor of Demersville, but later that year the Great Northern Railroad bypassed the town and it was doomed. Clifford's excessive drinking caused Delima to sue for divorce in 1893. In 1900 Clifford was arrested and sent to prison for grand larceny in Butte. After serving his time, he dried out, went to work for the Anaconda Mining Company in Butte, and remarried. [*Demersville*, pp. 59-100]

Conko, Eneas Michel (1874–1954) Born in the Bitterroot Valley, Eneas was a full-blood Salish Indian. He was part of the 1891 removal to the Flathead Reservation with Chief Charlo. Eneas was married several times and had at least six children. In the 1930s and 1940s he served two nonconsecutive terms on the Confederated Salish and Kootenai Tribal Council. His efforts were aimed at protecting tribal resources and rights and limiting government control over the lives of individual Indians. In his later years, Michel enjoyed taking young people hunting with him and his family. One of the young people he befriended, Thurman Trosper, remembered him as a gentle, fatherly figure who liked to tell stories about the old days. In the 1930s and 1940s he lived on a small ranch southeast of Ronan. [*FC*, Sept. 16, 1954, p. 6, c. 4; Robert Bigart and Clarence Woodcock, "The Rinehart Photographs: A Portfolio," *Montana The Magazine of Western History*, vol. 29, no. 4 (Oct. 1979), p. 28]

Cory, F. M. (on the Flathead Reservation 1895–96) Little is known about F. M. Cory except that he was a white man who appeared on the Flathead Reservation in August 1895 with a forged letter of introduction as a Secret Agent of the U.S. Treasury Department. During the short period before he was discovered and arrested in January 1896, he investigated complaints about the guardianship of an elderly Indian woman and whiskey smuggling on the reservation. He also helped with a roundup of trespassing cattle on the reservation and directed a roundup of trespassing horses. The official reports indicate that he turned almost all of the fines he collected over to Agent Joseph Carter. When arrested, he refused to explain his motives. [John Lane to CIA, Jan. 29, 1896, LR 4,991/1896, RG 75, NA; Joseph Carter to CIA, Jan. 29, 1896, LR 4,996/1896, RG 75, NA; *AS*, Jan. 30, 1896, p. 10, c. 1]

Courville, Alphonse (1867?–1937) Born in Frenchtown, Alphonse was the son of Louis Courville, Sr., and Julia Finley Courville. According to the Federal Writers Project interviews, he worked as a cowboy for T. J. DeMers. He was survived by his wife, Eliza, and two children. [*RP*, June 10, 1937, p. 1, c. 6]

Courville, Julia Finley (1843–1904) A daughter of Patrick [not François "Benetsee"] Finley, Julia married Louis Courville, Sr., in 1861 at Fort Colville. They moved to Frenchtown in the 1870s. She was part Kootenai Indian and in 1885 the couple moved to a ranch on the Flathead Indian Reservation near Ronan. They had at least eleven children. [*Enrollment*, rl. 1, fr. 46, #1641; Jerome D'Aste, S.J., Diary, July 25, 1904, In *OPA Archives*, rl. 30, fr. 86; *Jocko's People*, vol. 2, pp. 431-33]

Courville, Louis, Sr. (1828–1922) Born in Quebec, Louis Courville first came to the Flathead Valley in 1859. During the 1860s and 1870s he worked variously as a gold miner, teamster, and rail splitter in Montana and California. He married Julia Finley, who was part Kootenai Indian, at Fort Colville in 1861. The family homesteaded near Frenchtown in 1878 and in 1885 moved to the Flathead Indian Reservation. Louis was a prominent stockman near Ronan and was adopted into the tribe. One of his daughters married Charles Allard, Sr. He was survived by seven sons, including Alphonse, Oliver, and Zephyr, and one daughter. [*DM*, May 10, 1922, p. 7, c. 3-4; *Enrollment*, rl. 1, fr. 46, #1641; Frenchtown Historical Society, *Frenchtown Valley Footprints* (Missoula, MT: Mountain Press Printing, 1976), pp. 23-24]

Courville, Margaret (1915–?) The only daughter of tribal member Zephyr Courville and Edna Helterline Courville, a white woman, Margaret was born in Plains, MT. In 1950 she married Mariano Villarin, a native of the Philippine Islands. They had a daughter in 1951 in San Francisco, CA. [*Jocko's People*, vol. 2, pp. 479-81]

Courville, Oliver (1863–1946) A tribal member rancher at Hot Springs, Oliver got his start herding horses for his father, Louis Courville, Sr., while his father was freighting for T. J. DeMers. Oliver was born in Frenchtown. He was survived by his second wife, Ella, and two children. [*DM,* Nov. 30, 1946, p. 2, c. 1]

Courville, Zephyr "Swift" (1873–1961) Zephyr, the mixed-blood son of Louis and Julia Finley Courville, was born in Frenchtown. He rode in the Pablo buffalo roundup and was a brother-in-law to Charles Allard, Sr. Most of his life he worked as a range rider and cowhand, but he also worked in the trucking business and served as town marshal and street commissioner at Plains. In 1913 he married Edna Helterline, a non-Indian woman from Plains. They had one daughter, Margaret. [*DM,* Nov. 26, 1961, p. 15, c. 1]

Couture, Dave (1864–1941) Dave Couture, the son of Joseph and Catherine Finley Couture, was born in the Colville Valley, WA. In 1870 his family moved to Arlee. He worked driving cattle and delivering mail. In later years he served on the Confederated Salish and Kootenai Tribal Council. When he died in 1941 he was living on Camas Prairie on the Flathead Reservation. [*Jocko's People,* vol. 2, p. 407; *LCV,* Nov. 6, 1941, p. 1, c. 6]

Couture, Emerence (1870–1942) Emerence Couture Bouchard Clairmont was the mixed-blood daughter of Joseph and Catherine Finley Couture. She had two sons by her first husband in the 1890s and six more children, including five daughters, by her marriage to Louis Clairmont, Jr. [*Jocko's People,* vol. 2, pp. 419-20]

Couture, Joseph (1824–1889) Joseph Couture was a French Canadian farmer who worked for the Flathead Agency in the 1870s. He first came to western Montana in 1868 and settled at Arlee in 1870. His third wife was tribal member Catherine Finley and the couple had twelve children. [*Jocko's People,* vol. 2, pp. 387-88; *Courchane*]

Couture, Joseph, Mrs. (1842–1912) According to David Courchane's research, Catherine Finley Couture was the daughter of Marie Gasper [not Mary Ashley] Finley and Patrick [not François "Benetsee"] Finley. She was part Kootenai Indian and married Joseph Couture, a French Canadian farmer, in 1860. After 1870 the couple lived at Arlee and had six daughters and six sons. [*Jocko's People,* vol. 2, pp. 387-88]

Couture, Louis (1862–1943) The son of Joseph and Catherine Finley Couture, Louis was born in Colville, WA. He moved with his family to the Flathead Reservation in 1870. A tribal member, Louis operated a farm on the west shore of Flathead Lake. He was married four times and had four children. [*Jocko's People,* vol. 2, pp. 388-89; *RP,* Sept. 30, 1943, p. 1, c. 4; *Courchane*]

Couture, Mack (1862–1926) Born in Colville, WA, Mack Couture was a son of Joseph and Catherine Finley Couture. The family moved to Arlee in 1870 where Mack lived until his death. Part Kootenai

Indian, he married Caroline Raymond, also a tribal member, and the couple had four children. [*Jocko's People*, vol. 2, pp. 394-95; *Courchane*]

Culligan, Josephine Della Sloan (1898–1972) A daughter of Allen Sloan and Cecille Morigeau Sloan, Josephine Della was born in Ronan. A tribal member, she was married twice and survived by a foster son and a foster daughter. Between 1932 and 1946 she carried the mail between Ronan and Hot Springs. [*Jocko's People*, vol. 2, pp. 270-71; *RP*, Dec. 21, 1972, p. 5, c. 5; *Buffalo Roamed*, p. 47]

Delaware, John (1863–1951) The son of Delaware Jim, John was born in the Bitterroot Valley of Delaware and Salish Indian descent. As a young man he was one of the Salish volunteers at Fort Fizzle at Lolo during the 1877 Nez Perce War. One of his bravest deeds was cutting the tether to a prize race horse in a Crow camp and stealing the horse. For many years he served as interpreter for other tribal members, but he grew deaf in old age. He died after being struck by a freight train at Schley south of Arlee. [*DM*, Apr. 7, 1951, p. 1, c. 4 and p. 2, c. 5-6]

Delaware, Moses (1876–1929) As a young man, Moses tended the loading chutes leading to the railroad cars during the roundup of the Pablo buffalo herd. On the tribal rolls as three-quarters Salish, he could write and served as Salish interpreter for some of Bon Whealdon's interviews in the early 1920s. Moses was enumerator for the 1910 federal census for all of the Flathead Reservation except the part in Flathead County. His father-in-law was a white employee of the Flathead Agency. [*Enrollment*, rl. 1, fr. 49, #1751; United States, *1910 Census of Population*, MT, Msla Co., Flathead Indian Reservation sheets 1-34, and Sanders Co., sheets 34-39, NAmf T624, rl. 834-35; *RP*, Dec. 19, 1929, p. 1, c. 3]

DeMers, Alexander L. (1849–1928) A younger half brother to Telesphore Jacques DeMers, Alexander was born near Montreal in 1849. He came to Montana in 1880. He operated a general store at St. Ignatius for a number of years before moving to Missoula in 1901 to operate a harness and saddle shop. Between 1907 and his retirement about 1920 he operated a general store in Arlee. Alexander married Grace E. Lambert, another non-Indian, in 1881 and they had seven children, including Lambert Demers. [*Sanders*, vol. 2, pp. 1138-39; *DM*, Nov. 10, 1928, p. 3, c. 3-6]

Demers, Angelo Frances (1889–1980) Son of tribal member Telesphore Garcon DeMers and his first wife, Alma Brosseau DeMers, Angelo was born in Hot Springs. He worked for a grocery store in Plains and later operated the DeMers Grocery for many years at Plains. [*Settlers*, p. 44; *Char-Koosta* (Pablo, MT), Feb. 15, 1980, p. 21, c.2]

DeMers, Clara Rivet (1843–1879) Clara was the first wife of Telesphore Jacques DeMers, a leading western Montana entrepreneur during the 1870s and 1880s. She was born in Oregon in 1843 to Anthony Rivet or Revais, a Frenchman, and Mary Xixitelixken, a Salish Indian. Her blind brother, Michel Revais, was the interpreter at Flathead Agency for thirty years. T. J. and Clara lived in Frenchtown after 1868. They had at least eight children, including Telesphore Garcon DeMers, before her death in 1879. [*Demersville*, pp. 1-32]

Demers, Lambert L. (1897–1990) A non-Indian, Lambert was the youngest son of Alexander DeMers, longtime merchant at St. Ignatius and Arlee, and Grace E. Lambert. He studied accounting at the University of Montana and returned to Arlee to operate the Demers Mercantile with his father and later his brothers and brother-in-law. They sold out in 1959. During the 1960s he worked as a rural mail carrier in Arlee. [*DM*, Feb. 27, 1990, p. B3, c. 5; *RP*, July 16, 1959, p. 1, c. 1-3]

DeMers, Leonie Garnot (1861–1947) Leonie was the second wife of Telesphore Jacques DeMers, prominent Frenchtown merchant and businessman. She was a white teacher of music at the Catholic school in Missoula who married in 1880 when she was 18 years old and her husband was 44 years old. They had five children including Robert Demers. Widowed in 1889, she moved to Missoula. After a few years, she moved to Butte to support her four surviving children by teaching French in the public schools. She died in Butte in 1947. [*Demersville*, pp. 33-47]

Demers, Robert J. (1882–1942) The oldest son of T. J. or Jack DeMers and his second wife Leonie, Robert was an accountant in Missoula. He was a non-Indian, but as a young man he learned to speak Salish while staying with his half brother, Telesphore G. DeMers, on the reservation. He died in Butte while visiting his mother in 1942. [*DM*, Jan. 16, 1942, p. 1, c.3]

DeMers, Telesphore Garcon (1863–1930) Son of Frenchtown merchant Telesphore Jacques "T. J." DeMers and Clara Rivet DeMers, a Pend d'Oreille Indian, T. G. DeMers directed his father's cattle drives from Idaho to western Montana in 1879 and 1881. In 1884 T. G. married his first wife, Alma Brosseau DeMers, a white woman who was adopted into the Confederated Salish and Kootenai Tribes. His father gave him cattle and a house at Camas Hot Springs on the reservation. After his first wife died in 1907, he married a local white school teacher, Myrtle Cole, in 1909. In addition to ranching on the reservation, T. G. also ran a hotel for many years at Hot Springs. ["The Passing of a Pioneer of the Camas Hot Springs," *Camas Hot Springs Exchange* (Camas, MT), Feb. 18, 1930, clipping in scrapbook at Hot Springs Public Library, Hot Springs, MT; *Settlers*, p. 44]

DeMers, Telesphore Garcon, Mrs. (Myrtle Cole DeMers Myler) (1908–1966) This was the second wife of Telesphore Garcon DeMers, a tribal member stockman and hotel operator at Hot Springs. A non-Indian, she was a teacher before marrying the widowed T. G. DeMers in 1909. In addition to their three sons, Myrtle had ten stepchildren from her husband's first marriage. She survived her husband by 36 years. The couple operated a hotel in Hot Springs, and he sold his allotment in town lots. She married Walker Myler after T. G.'s death in 1930. For many years she was postmaster at Hot Springs and even served one term as mayor of Hot Springs in the early 1950s. [*Settlers,* p. 44; *RP,* Aug. 11, 1966, p. 2, c. 3]

DeMers, Telesphore Jacques "T. J." (ca. 1834–1889) One of the most dynamic entrepreneurs of early western Montana, T. J. or Jack DeMers was born near Montreal. In 1857 he married a Pend d'Oreille woman, Clara Rivit, or Revais, at Colville. The couple moved to Frenchtown in 1868. They had at least eight children before Clara's death in 1879. T. J. was involved in a variety of businesses around western Montana, including freighting, cattle raising, retailing, flour milling, lumber milling, ferrying, and hotel management. In 1879 he was the fourth highest taxpayer in Missoula County. Between 1875 and 1878 he was a member of the Missoula County Commissioners. In 1880 he married Leonie Garnot, a white woman, with whom he had five more children. Demersville, a former town at the head of Flathead Lake, was named for him. He was only 55 years old when he died in 1889. [*Demersville,* pp. 1-57]

DeMers, William (1832–1876) Amable Guillaume "William" DeMers was a brother of Telesphore Jacques DeMers of Frenchtown. Born near Montreal, he moved to Frenchtown in 1869 to work in his brother's store and other business interests. He died unmarried in 1876 in Frenchtown. [*Demersville,* pp. 8-9, 28-29; *WM,* Jan. 9, 1877, p. 3, c. 4]

Ducharme, Baptiste (1781–1892) A French Canadian, Baptiste worked between 1800 and 1840 as a trapper and Indian trader across the Pacific Northwest. From 1840 to 1857 he farmed in the Willamette Valley in Oregon, and after 1857 he operated a farm near Frenchtown. He was part of the crew that whipsawed lumber to build the first flour mill in Frenchtown in 1859. He worked for many years for T. J. DeMers, the Frenchtown merchant. Baptiste had two different wives from the Salish tribes and at least ten children. [Leeson, p. 193]

Elizabeth (Nez Perce) This woman was the Nez Perce wife of an unidentified Pend d'Oreille man. About 1840 she used her medicine powers to drive off an attacking Piegan war party.

Eulopsen, Thomas (1866–?) A full-blood Pend d'Oreille, Eulopsen, married Ellen, half Spokane and half Kalispel. They had at least four children. [*Enrollment,* rl. 1, fr. 18, #633-34]

Finlay, Abraham (1819–1912) The interviews describe Abraham Finlay as a son of François "Benetsee" Finlay and an unnamed Flathead woman. Other sources give his parents as James Finley, François Finlay's brother, and Susanna Matilda Finley, a Kootenai Indian woman. Abraham was born in British Columbia and worked as a trapper and hunter for the Hudson's Bay Company. Later he carried mail dispatches and operated a ferry at the foot of Flathead Lake. He married Susan Whis-whis-topi, a Pend d'Oreille woman, and they had four children. Abraham died in Polson. [*Jocko's People*, vol. 1, pp. 27-28; *Enrollment*, rl. 1, fr. 39, #1412; *FC*, Jan. 12, 1912, p. 1, c. 3]

Finlay, Alex (1855–?) Tribal member Alexander Francis "Whole Coyote" Finley was born in 1855 to Alexander "Tum-no-ka" Finley and Isabel (Red Wolf) "Ta-nee" Pellew Finley. In 1887 he had a farm six miles east of St. Ignatius and bought $50 worth of fruit trees. He married Mary Sabine Walking Coyote after Samuel Walking Coyote's death in the late 1890s. After Mary Sabine's death about 1901, he was married two more times. [*Jocko's People*, vol. 3, pp. 8-10; *CIA Report* (1887), p. 138]

Finley, August (1852–1927) Part Kootenai Indian, August was a son of Miguam Jacques or Jacob Finley and Agnes Paul Finley. He was listed as a farmer and farm hand. At the time he was hired to hunt out the remnants of Pablo's buffalo herd, he was married to his third wife, Agnes Perdum Finlay. He was widely known for his generosity to friends in need of food and shelter. He died near Ronan. [*Jocko's People*, vol. 3, pp. 179-80; *RP*, Dec. 29, 1927, p. 1, c. 2]

Finley, August, Mrs. (*ca.* 1852–1939) Agate Perdum, a Pend d'Oreille Indian, married August Finley, a Kootenai Indian, in 1905. It was August's third marriage and Agate's third marriage. No children were recorded from the marriage. In 1914 Agate was rumored to be an heir to a large fortune from a relative in Kansas City. There is no record that she actually received the inheritance. She died in Ronan. [*Jocko's People*, vol. 3, pp. 179-80; *RP*, Feb. 20, 1914, p. 1, c. 5; *RP*, Nov. 23, 1939, p. 1, c. 3]

Finlay, Basil "Pial" (1859–1926) The interviews give François as Basil's father, but other sources give his parents as Patrick Finley and Mary Ashley Finley. A tribal member, Basil was born at Fort Colville, WA, and died near Polson. In 1882 he married Sophie Brooks Finley, a Flathead Indian woman, and the couple had seven children. Basil was a successful stockman, farmer and horse trader in the Polson area. [*Jocko's People*, vol. 2, pp. 501-03; *FC*, Feb. 25, 1926, p. 1, c. 4]

Finlay, Basson (1828–died before 1905) This is probably Jean Baptiste "Bassaw" Finley, the son of Patrick [not François "Benetsee"] Finley and Margaret Finley, who was probably a Flathead Indian woman. In 1867 a Blackfeet war party killed Basson's first wife and his sister-in-law at the head of Flathead Lake as they were preparing to harvest a field of barley. They also kidnapped Basson's son, Koonsa, who then lived among the Blackfeet until he was 22 years old. About 1879 Koonsa was brought back to the Flathead Reservation where in 1882 he murdered Frank Marengo. [*Jocko's People,* vol. 2, pp. 27-30; John W. Wells to CIA, Aug. 31, 1867, In *OIA LR,* rl. 488, fr. 788-90; *WM,* June 23, 1882, p. 3, c. 3]

Finlay, Charles "Red Cloud" (1847–1909) Born at Colville, WA, Charles, a Kootenai Indian, married Mary Louise "Sitting Blanket" Paul, a Spokane and Kalispel woman, in 1874. Charles' father was Joseph Finley and his grandfather's brother was François "Benetsee" Finlay, whom the interviews mistakenly identify as Charles' son. Charles and Mary's fourth child was François Finley born in 1893. Charles died at St. Ignatius. [*Jocko's People,* vol. 2, pp. 140-41]

Finley, Dave (1849–1927) A son of Miguam Jacques, or Jacob, Finley and Agnes Paul Finley, Dave was born in California in 1849. He and August Finley were hired by Michel Pablo to hunt out the remnant buffalo on the reservation. Part Kootenai Indian, Dave married Anne, a Flathead Indian woman, and they had three children. Anne died before 1908 and David died near Ronan. [*Jocko's People,* vol. 3, p. 178; *RP,* Mar. 17, 1927, p. 1, c. 6]

Finley, Feenom (1846 or 1847–1925) The T. Finley or Feenom Finley mentioned in the interviews was probably Joseph "Teenum" Finley, a tribal member born in Washington to Miguam Jacques Finley and Agnes Paul Finley. According to the interviews he worked on cattle drives and one source claims he was the one who brought the first buffalo calves to the Flathead Reservation. He married Philomene Penama, a Pend d'Oreille Indian woman, and they had eight children. [*Jocko's People,* vol. 3, pp. 176-77]

Finlay, François (1893–1928) Son of Charles "Red Cloud" Finlay and Mary "Sitting Blanket" Finlay, this François was a tribal member and the great grandnephew of François "Benetsee" Finlay. He married Felicite Delaware, a tribal member in Arlee, in 1895 and the couple had eight children. [*Jocko's People,* vol. 2, p. 151]

Finley, François "Benetsee" (ca. 1805–died before 1873) François was born to Jacques Raphael "Jocko" Finlay, a French Canadian, and a Chippewa Indian woman in Canada. François was a trapper and hunter for the Hudson's Bay Company and in 1849 mined for gold in California. He is best known as one of the first to discover gold in Montana. The Federal Writers Project interviews have confused François and his older brother Patrick. Patrick "Pichina" Finley (1802–1879) was also a trapper and hunter and died in Frenchtown. The interviews attribute Patrick's children and wives to François. [*Jocko's People,* vol. 2, pp. 1-13, and vol. 3, pp. 2-8; Paul C. Phillips and H. A. Trexler, "Notes on the Discovery of Gold in the Northwest," *Mississippi Valley Historical Review,* vol. 4, no. 1 (June 1917), pp. 92-95]

Finley, James. The interviews identify James Finley as Oliver Gebeau's aged grandfather. In fact, he was the grandfather of Oliver's wife, tribal member Rosalie Finley Gebeau. James Finley (1794–ca. 1853/1854), son of Jacques Raphael "Jocko" Finlay, died 12 years before Oliver was born. Oliver's father-in-law was James "Jemmi" Finley, Jr. (1843–ca. 1907), so it is possible in the interviews Oliver was referring to his father-in-law. [*Jocko's People,* vol. 1, pp. 24-27, and 230-32]

Finlay, Joseph (1830–?) This Joseph Finlay was a tribal member and son of Patrick [not François "Benetsee"] and Margaret Finley and a brother to Basson Finley. Joseph married another tribal member, Arzell Ashley, and the couple had nine children. He was a trapper and hunter. [*Jocko's People,* vol. 2, p. 41]

Finley, Louise (1830–1943) Born in the Bitterroot Valley, Louise Finley lived to be 112 years old. She remembered Father Pierre DeSmet, S.J., founding St. Mary's Mission and was among the first of the Salish to be baptized. She outlived four husbands and had seven children. During her later years she became blind. She died near Polson. [*DM,* Mar. 21, 1943, p. 1, c. 3-4; *FC,* Mar. 25, 1943, p. 1, c. 3; John J. O'Kennedy, "Sits-in-the-Corner," *Indian Sentinel,* vol. 23, no. 5 (May 1943), pp. 77-78]

Finlay, Mary Ashley (1819–1897) This Mary Finley was a Kootenai Indian and the fourth wife of Patrick "Pichina" Finley, the brother of François "Benetsee" Finley. The interviews mistakenly give François as Mary Ashley Finlay's husband. The couple had five children. Their first children were born at Fort Colville, WA, and their later children were born on the Flathead Indian Reservation. Mary Ashley Finlay was the daughter of Jean Pierre Asselin and Rosalie, a Cree Indian woman. [*Jocko's People,* vol. 2, pp. 1-13]

Finlay, Mary "Sitting Blanket" (1857–1905) Mary Louise "Emptoo-pee" [Sitting Blanket] Paul, a Spokane and Kalispel woman, married Charles "Red Cloud" Finley in 1874. Charles' grandfather's brother was François "Benetsee" Finlay, whom the interviews mistakenly identify as the son of Charles and Mary. The fourth son of Charles and Mary was François Finlay, born in 1893. Mary died in Montana. [*Jocko's People,* vol. 2, pp. 140-41]

Finlay, Patrick "Pichina" (ca. 1802–1879) Patrick was a son of Jacques Raphael "Jocko" Finlay, a French Canadian, and a Chippewa Indian woman. Patrick was born about 1802 and François "Benetsee" was born about 1805. Both were born near Edmonton, Canada, and lived much of their later lives in Montana. Most of the children attributed to François in the interviews were actually children of Patrick. Patrick was married four different times and had at least nineteen children between 1819 and 1862. Patrick worked for many years as trapper and hunter for the Hudson's Bay Company. He died in Montana and was buried at Frenchtown. [*Jocko's People,* vol. 2, pp. 1-13, and vol. 3, pp. 2-8]

Finlay, Peter (1852–1943) Peter "Tish-nah" Finlay, the son of Patrick [not François "Benetsee"] Finlay and Mary Ashley Finlay, was part Kootenai Indian born at Colville, WA. Peter was married twice and raised a daughter and a number of adopted children. In the 1880s Peter was a farmer and rancher in the Mission Valley and an Indian policeman. In 1892 he was seriously injured in a horse racing accident near Polson. He died at St. Ignatius. [*Jocko's People*, vol. 2, pp. 482-83; *CIA Report* (1885), pp. 126-27; Peter Ronan to CIA, Feb. 14, 1885, LR 3766/1885, RG 75, NA; Sam E. Johns Papers, SC165, UM, vol. 7, p. 110]

Gebeau, Henry (?–1906?) Henry, a white man, married Cecille Shaw from the Colville Indian Reservation who was half Spokane Indian. Their son, Oliver, taught at the government school at Jocko and also served as Indian policeman on the Flathead Reservation. [*Jocko's People*, vol. 3, pp. 241-42]

Gebeau, Oliver (1866–1941) Oliver was born in Frenchtown, to Henry Gebeau, a white man, and Cecille Shaw Gebeau, a Spokane Indian woman who was a descendant of François "Benetsee" Finlay. In 1882 Oliver moved to the Flathead Reservation and in 1888 married Rosalie Finley, a distant relative and descendant of James Finlay, François' brother. Oliver was Industrial Teacher at the government school at Jocko and later an Indian policeman. Oliver and Rosalie had twelve children. [*Jocko's People*, vol. 3, pp. 241-42; *FC*, June 26, 1941, p. 2, c. 1; *Enrollment*, rl. 2, fr. 305-28; "United States v. Higgins, County Treasurer (Circuit Court, D. Montana. August 30, 1901)," *FR*, vol. 110 (Oct.–Nov. 1901), pp. 609-11]

Grinder, Jim (1868–1977) A member of the Nez Perce tribe, Grinder arrived on the Flathead Reservation about 1900. He worked as a cowboy, rodeo rider, and rustler. He served a term in the Deer Lodge penitentiary for rustling. In 1915 he married Mary Pablo, a daughter of tribal member Michel Pablo. Grinder worked for Pablo for many years, including during the famous buffalo roundup. He died at Hot Springs at the age of 109. [*FC*, Oct. 27, 1977, p. 9, c. 7-8; *Settlers*, pp. 156-57]

Houle, Joseph, Jr. (1868–1952) Joseph Houle, Jr., was the eldest son of Joseph Houle, Sr., a French Canadian, and Rose Brown Houle, who was half Pend d'Oreille. Joseph, Jr., was born in Frenchtown and married Ellen Dubay in 1888. In 1895 he moved to Ronan and farmed until his retirement. He was one of the riders during the roundup of Pablo's buffalo herd. He was survived by four children. [*Enrollment*, rl. 2, fr. 384-86, 394-97, 420-21; *RP*, Mar. 27, 1952, p. 1, c. 3]

Irvine, Angela Ashley (1839–ca. 1880) Born in Canada to Jean Pierre Ashley and Mary Finley Ashley, Angela was part Kootenai Indian. She married Peter Irvine, a non-Indian Hudson's Bay Company employee, in the early 1850s. In 1855 she worked as a cook for the

Flathead Agency. One source indicates the couple had nine children. She died between 1877 and 1886. [U.S. Census, 1860, "Free Inhabitants in Bitterroot Valley, County of Spokane, Territory of Washington, September 14, 1860," typescript, SC188, UM, Dwelling #149; Richard H. Lansdale journals, Coe Western Americana Collection, Yale University Library, New Haven, CT, Dec. 14, 1855; *DM*, June 18, 1939, p. 4, c. 5-6; *Ind Census*, rl. 107, fr. 197]

Irvine, Emily (1851–1937) Emily Brown Irvine was the part Pend d'Oreille daughter of Louis Brown and Emily Goetsche Brown. She was born in Colville, WA, and moved to Frenchtown at the age of five. She survived the deaths of several husbands over the years before marrying Billy Irvine, a Kootenai mixed blood, in 1895. In addition to working for many years as a nurse, cook, and housekeeper, she was also an excellent horsewoman. She operated the first restaurant at Polson, and she rode in the Pablo buffalo roundup of 1908 with her husband, Billy Irvine. While fishing on the Jocko River she found the bodies of two murdered white men. She testified at the 1890 murder trial of La La See and Pierre Paul, who were hung in Missoula for the crime. [*FC*, Apr, 29, 1937, p. 1, c. 3-4; *Enrollment*, rl. 2, fr. 551; *Joseph Allard*, pp. 157, 233]

Irvine, Peter (1828–1889) Peter Irvine was born in Scotland and came to the Flathead Valley in the 1850s. He worked as Flathead Agency interpreter in the middle 1850s. He worked for the Hudson's Bay Company and also did some personal trading among the Pend d'Oreille. A Kootenai woman, Angela Ashley Irvine, was his wife and the famous cowboy, Billy Irvine, was their oldest son. During his later years he seems to have farmed or ranched on the Flathead Reservation. [*Fort Owen*, pp. 175-76; *Enrollment*, rl. 107, fr. 197; *Courchane*]

Irvine, William "Billy" (1856–1939) Billy Irvine, the eldest child of Peter Irvine and Angela Ashley Irvine, was part Kootenai and born in 1856 at Post Creek, MT. He worked as a cowhand for many of the major cattlemen in Montana and Alberta. At the age of twenty he was trail boss for a drive of 1,200 Flathead Reservation cattle to the railroad in Cheyenne, WY. In 1886 he returned to the Flathead Reservation and started a ranch west of Polson with the help of Charles Allard, Sr. Billy rode in the Pablo buffalo roundup in 1908. He became one of the principal cattlemen on the Flathead Reservation. His first wife was Louise Dupuis, a part Kootenai tribal member. In 1895 he married his second wife, tribal member Emily Brown Irvine. [*DM*, June 18, 1939, p. 4, c. 5-6; *Jocko's People*, vol. 1, pp. 137-41]

King, Mary Finley (1838–1925) Mary Anne Finley King was a daughter of Patrick [not François "Benetsee"] Finley, a French Canadian, and Marie Gasper Finley, a Kootenai Indian woman. She was born in Canada and lived most of her life in the Colville Valley, WA. She married Pierre [not William] King, a Frenchman, in 1853 at Kettle Falls, WA. The couple had eleven children before Pierre's death in 1885. Also known as Peter, Pierre King was a carpenter, blacksmith, and farmer and left his widow a farm which she operated between 1885 and 1918. Mary was also known for her beadwork and leather work. [*Jocko's People*, vol. 2, pp. 342-47; William S. Lewis, "Oldest Pioneer Laid to Rest," *Washington Historical Quarterly*, vol. 17, no. 1 (Jan. 1926), pp. 39-42; *Chewelah Independent* (Chewelah, WA), Nov. 5, 1925, p. 1, c. 1]

LaMousse, François (1826–1918) François' father, Ignace LaMousse, was a leader of the Iroquois fur traders and trappers who settled among the Bitterroot Salish in the early nineteenth century. Ignace married a Salish woman. In 1835 François and his older brother, Charles, were baptized in St. Louis. François was a very successful farmer in the Bitterroot Valley and was frequently called on to serve as interpreter during negotiations with Chief Charlo. In 1891, he moved to the Flathead Indian Reservation with the rest of Chief Charlo's band. He died on the reservation at the age of 92. [A. Sullivan, S.J., "Francois Saxa," *The Indian Sentinel*, vol. 1, no. 9 (July 1918), pp. 41-42; *Fort Owen*, pp. 63-65]

La Rose, John. The only John LaRose identified was the son of Xavier and Mary LaRose born in 1899. The parents were both half Pend d'Oreille. This John LaRose would have been only 41 years old in 1940, while the person interviewed by Bon Whealdon was "a very old man." [*Enrollment*, rl. 1, fr. 13, #475]

Larrivee, Arthur (1871–1945) Arthur was the only surviving child of Henry Larrivee, a non-Indian, and Emily Brown Larrivee, part Pend d'Oreille, who were married in 1866. In 1885 Henry died in an accident. Billy Irvine was Arthur's stepfather. Arthur managed his stepfather's ranch and drove a stagecoach from Ravalli to Demersville, at the head of Flathead Lake. During the late 1880s he supervised the semiannual cattle roundups on the Flathead Reservation. [*Enrollment*, rl. 2, fr. 547-61; *RP*, May 24, 1945, p. 1, c. 2; Stout, vol. 3, pp. 792-93]

Lewis, Bill (dates unknown) According to the interviews Lewis was a white man from Washington State and one of the most capable cowboys on the roundup of the Pablo buffalo. Lewis married Jennie Finley, a tribal member, in 1897 and they had one daughter. The couple divorced in 1926 and Lewis seems to have left the reservation sometime later. [*Enrollment*, rl. 1, fr. 48, #1720-21]

Lomphrey, Joseph (*ca.* 1806–1890) Lomphrey was a non-Indian trader in the Northern Rocky Mountains who came to the Bitterroot Valley in the 1840s with Father Pierre DeSmet, S.J. He traded horses along the emigrant trail to Oregon and California and then rested the exhausted stock in the Bitterroot Valley during the winter. In 1856 he settled down on a farm in the Bitterroot Valley. His wife was a Snake Indian. His descendants moved to the Flathead Indian Reservation in 1891 with Chief Charlo. [*Fort Owen*, pp. 59-61; *AS*, Aug. 22, 1890, p. 1, c. 5; *Missoula Gazette* (daily), Aug. 21, 1890, p. 8, c. 3]

McCrea, Robert A. (1884–1969) Part Colville Indian, McCrea was born in Chewelah, WA, and came to the Flathead Indian Reservation in 1910. Malcolm McLeod was his uncle. He married tribal member, Matilada Gebeau, a daughter of Oliver Gebeau, an Indian policeman on the reservation. He worked mostly in the Ronan area as a cook for mining, logging, and construction camps. [*DM*, Dec. 24, 1969, p. 7, c. 4]

McDonald, Angus (1816–1889) Born in Scotland, Angus was employed by the Hudson's Bay Company as a trader at various posts in the Pacific Northwest. Starting as a clerk, he eventually became a chief trader in charge of the Colville District. In 1842, he married Catherine, a Nez Perce/Iroquois Indian woman, at Fort Hall, ID. He also worked among the Montana Salish tribes for a number of years and joined in their hunts. When Chief Victor died in 1870, he willed his favorite war horse to Angus. Angus and Catherine raised a large family and many of their descendants now live on the Flathead Indian Reservation. [Partoll]

McDonald, Catherine (1819–1892) Catherine was the Nez Perce/Iroquois wife of Angus McDonald, the Scottish Hudson's Bay Company trader. About 1841 Catherine accompanied a trading expedition to the American Southwest. She married Angus in 1842 at Fort Hall, ID, among the Nez Perce. Catherine lived with her husband at various trading posts as he moved up the Hudson's Bay Company organization. Much of their time was spent at Fort Colville, WA, and Fort Connah on the Flathead Reservation. Among their twelve children were Duncan and Joseph A. McDonald. Catherine was closely related to a number of the Nez Perce chiefs involved in the 1877 war with the United States government. [Catherine McDonald, "An Indian Girl's Story of a Trading Expedition to the Southwest about 1841," *The Frontier* (Missoula, MT), vol. 10, no. 4 (May 1930), pp. 338-51; Partoll]

McDonald, Duncan (1849–1937) Of Scottish and Nez Perce descent, Duncan was the son of Catherine and Angus McDonald. He was born at Fort Connah near St. Ignatius, and spent part of his childhood at Fort Colville, WA, where his father was chief trader for the Hudson's Bay Company. As a young man, he joined the Pend d'Oreille Indians on buffalo hunts and war parties. In the late 1870s he operated a store near the Jocko Agency. Between 1888 and 1904, he operated a hotel, general store, livery, blacksmith, and stage line at Ravalli, MT. Through his mother he was related to the Nez Perce chiefs involved in the 1877 war, and he interviewed them for a history of the Nez Perce War published in a Deer Lodge, MT, newspaper in 1878. Duncan was frequently consulted as a spokesman for the Indians on the Flathead Reservation. [Leeson, p. 1313; *RP,* Sept. 11, 1925, p. 6, c. 2-4; *R. L. Polk & Co.'s Minnesota, North and South Dakota and Montana Gazetteer and Business Directory,* vol. 6-14 (1888–1904); Duncan MacDonald, "The Nez Perces: The History of Their Troubles and the Campaign of 1877," *Idaho Yesterdays,* vol. 21, no. 1 (Spr. 1977), pp. 2-15, 26-30, and vol. 21, no. 4 (Win. 1978), pp. 2-10, 18-28; *DM,* Oct. 17, 1937, p. 1, c. 6, and p. 6, c. 1]

McDonald, John (1891–1964) Son of Joseph McDonald and grandson of Angus McDonald, John was a tribal member born north of St. Ignatius. He ranched and farmed on the Flathead Indian Reservation and was known as an expert horseman and roper. He rode in the roundup of the Pablo buffalo herd. In 1911 he married Lydia Luddington, a tribal member, and the couple had eleven children. [*DM,* Apr. 19, 1964, p. 14, c. 6-8]

McDonald, Joseph (1866–1944) Joseph McDonald was a son of Angus and Catherine McDonald and a brother of Duncan McDonald. Joseph was born at Fort Colville, WA, while his father was chief trader there. Allotted on the Nez Perce Reservation, he spent most of his life in western Montana. He worked in the roundup of the Pablo buffalo herd. He married a Flathead Reservation tribal member, Lucy Deschamps, and the couple had nine children. [*RP,* Apr. 27, 1944, p. 1, c. 2]

McDonald, Tom (1858–1939) The son of Angus McDonald, who established Fort Connah in the Mission Valley, Tom spent most of his life at Post Creek. A tribal member, he was survived by his widow, Christine, a Piegan Indian enrolled on the Flathead Reservation, and seven children. Duncan McDonald was his brother. [*DM,* Oct. 23, 1939, p. 2, c. 2; *Enrollment,* rl. 1, fr. 16, #570-76]

McLeod, Alex (1884–1965) Of Scottish, Colville, and Kootenai descent, Alex was the grandson of Donald Angus McLeod, Sr., a Hudson's Bay Company trader who married into the Colville tribe. His parents were Frank McLeod, Sr., and Julia King McLeod. Alex was born in Arlee and, as a young man, worked in the roundup of the Pablo buffalo herd. [*DM,* Mar. 21, 1965, p. 14, c. 1]

McLeod, Donald Angus, Sr. (1804–1901) In 1847, Donald McLeod, a Scotsman, brought a herd of horses into the Lower Flathead Valley. The Hudson's Bay Company used the horses for pack trains to move supplies and furs in and out of the area. After leaving the Hudson's Bay Company, he operated a road house and ferry at Bearmouth near Deer Lodge, MT. He farmed at Colville, WA, before moving to the Flathead Reservation in 1885. In 1850 he married his second wife, Rosalie Morigeau, who was part Kootenai Indian, and the couple had at least nine children. [*MVN,* July 27, 1983, p. 7, c. 1-4; "Index to the Burials of Lake County, MT," unpublished manuscript, Missoula Public Library, Missoula, MT]

McLeod, Frank, Jr. (1882–1956) Frank, Jr., was a son of Frank McLeod, Sr., and Julia King McLeod. Of part Kootenai descent, he was born in Washington and moved to the Flathead Reservation in 1884. Alex McLeod was his younger brother. Frank, Jr., was a carpenter and rode in the roundup of the Pablo buffalo. In 1910 he married Janice Gardipe and they had seven children. [*Jocko's People*, vol. 2, p. 370; *DM*, Mar. 28, 1956, p. 11, c. 3]

McLeod, Frank, Sr. (1859–1921) Frank, Sr., was the son of Donald McLeod, Sr., a Hudson's Bay Company trader, and Rosalie Morigeau McLeod, a Kootenai woman. In the early 1890s he drove herds of horses from the Flathead Reservation for sale in the Dakotas, Minnesota, and Canada. He was foreman on the Jesuit farm at St. Ignatius Mission. Frank, Sr., married Julia King, who was also part Kootenai, and the couple had at least ten children. [*Jocko's People*, vol. 2, p. 370]

McLeod, Malcolm (1870–1944) Malcolm was one of the younger children of Donald McLeod, Sr., a non-Indian, and Rosalie Morigeau McLeod, a Kootenai woman. His mother died in 1880 in Colville, WA, and his father moved the family to the Flathead Reservation in 1885. Malcolm became famous for his skill as a cowboy. He worked for Charles Allard, Sr., for a number of years and in 1893 rode one of Allard's buffalo at Butte, MT. Breaking horses, rodeos, packing, and general cowboy work over the years took him to Canada, Washington, and across Montana. He took part in the roundup of the Pablo buffalo herd. Malcolm married three times and had several children. He died in Washington State. [Malcolm McLeod, "A Unique Family History" *MVN*, July 27–Oct. 19, 1983]

Marion, Louis Joseph (1873–1949) A non-Indian, Louis Joseph Marion was born in Missoula while his father was sheriff of Missoula County. His father, Joseph E. Marion, was an important figure in western Montana politics during the late nineteenth century. As a young man, Louis Joseph drove a stagecoach across the reservation. In 1892 he married Emerance Larrivee, part Pend d'Oreille from the Flathead Reservation. They had four children before Emerance died in 1900, the same year Louis Joseph began ranching near Polson. In 1905 he married another Salish woman, Annie Houle, and the couple had two children. Louis Joseph worked on the roundup of the Pablo buffalo. For six years he was a County Commissioner for Lake County, MT. [*DM*, Jan. 6, 1946, p. 2, c. 3-4; *FC*, Apr. 28, 1949, p. 1, c. 2]

Matt, Mrs. The interview with Henry Burland about his grandfather, August Finley, hunting the remnants of Pablo's buffalo did not give enough information to identify the Mrs. Matt who was part of the hunting party.

Matt, Alex (1852–1922) A son of Louis Matt, a French Canadian, and Killed-in-the-Lodge, a Piegan Indian woman, Alexander was born in northeastern Montana. In 1866 or 1867 Louis and his family moved to the Bitterroot Valley where his wife and children were adopted into the Bitterroot Salish tribe. Louis was a blacksmith and taught his trade to Alexander. In 1877, Alexander was captain of a group of Salish Indian volunteers who protected the Bitterroot whites during the Nez Perce War. Alexander and his family later moved to the Flathead Indian Reservation and started a store. After the store failed, he operated a blacksmith shop and ranch in the Jocko Valley. Alexander was married twice and some records indicate he had fifteen children. ["United States v. Higgins, County Treasurer (Circuit Court, D. Montana. July 2, 1900)," *FR*, vol. 103 (Sept.–Oct. 1900), pp. 348-52; *Jocko's People*, vol. 2, pp. 43-45; *DM*, Dec. 3, 1922, p. 4, c. 2]

Michel, Chief (1805–1897) Michel, or Michelle, was elected chief of the Upper Pend d'Oreille tribe after Alexander died about 1868. In the 1870s he lived near the Jocko Agency and became closely identified with the government agents and Catholic missionaries. During this period he lost much influence with his tribe because he was not physically able to accompany his people on the buffalo hunts. In 1864 one of his sons was hung by white miners for the murder of a white man. Despite his son's claims of innocence, Michelle declined to avenge the hanging because Michelle feared a war with the whites would hurt the tribe. In the 1880s, Michelle moved to a ranch near Ronan and grew grain and fruit. Towards the end of his life he opposed the efforts of Missoula County to collect taxes from mixed-blood tribal members. [John C. Ewers, *Gustavus Sohon's Portraits of Flathead and Pend d'Oreille Indians, 1854*, Smithsonian Miscellaneous Collections, vol. 111, no. 7 (1948), pp. 50-52; Arthur L. Stone, *Following Old Trails* (Missoula, MT: Morton John Elrod, 1913), pp. 133-34; *DM*, May 14, 1897, p. 1, c. 3]

Michell, Charley, Chief (1863–1929) Charley, or Sapiel, Michell succeeded his father, Chief Michelle, as chief of the Upper Pend d'Oreille tribe in 1897. He married Suzette, a Pend d'Oreille woman, in 1887 and the couple had five children including Moses Michell who became Pend d'Oreille chief in 1929. [*Enrollment*, rl. 1, fr. 31, #1096-1101; St. Ignatius Mission House Diary, Sept. 17, 1929, In *OPA Archives*, rl. 3, fr. 597]

Michell, Dominic. The interpreter for Chief Charley Michel could not be identified. There was a Michel Dominic Finley who lived from 1868 to 1929.

Michell, Mose, Chief (1886–1944) Although never officially recognized by the United States government, Mose Michell became chief of the Upper Pend d'Oreille tribe in 1929 at the death of his father. He was married twice and had two children. The wife mentioned in the interviews was Adeline Bigjohn Michell, half Flathead and half Spokane, who survived him. [*RP*, May 11, 1944, p. 1, c. 1]

Michell, Mose, Mrs. (1886–?) Adeline Bigjohn, of Flathead and Spokane descent, married Chief Mose Michel of the Pend d'Oreille in 1912 and again in 1934 after a period of separation. The couple had two children. After Mose Michell died in 1944, she married another tribal member, Louie Toweepa Quintah, and she survived Louie's death in 1957. [*RP,* May 11, 1944, p. 1, c. 1; *RP,* Jan. 24, 1957, p. 1, c. 3]

Moran [i.e., Marent], Ellen Finley (1855–1934) Margaret Ellen "Pish-nah" Finley was the part Kootenai daughter of Patrick Finley and Mary Ashley Finley. She was born in Colville, WA, and in 1885 married Joseph Marent, the white man for whom the Marent Trestle and Marent Gulch near Evaro, MT, were named. Joseph maintained a boarding house and saloon near the trestle during construction. The couple adopted a daughter. The Marent's were divorced in 1889. Margaret Ellen died at Arlee. [*Jocko's People,* vol. 2, pp. 11-13]

Moran [i.e., Marent], Joe (1836–1891) Born in Canada, Marent served in the Civil War and came to Virginia City, MT, in 1866. He married Margaret Ellen "Pish-nah" Finley, a Kootenai woman, in 1885. Marent operated a boarding house and saloon near Evaro, MT, just south of the Flathead Reservation. Both the canyon and the railroad trestle which spans the canyon came to be named after Marent. The couple adopted a daughter but had no other children. They were divorced in 1889. Marent died in a mysterious railroad accident near Ravalli. [*Jocko's People,* vol. 2, pp. 11-13; *AS,* Apr. 22, 1891, p. 1, c. 6; *AS,* Apr. 25, 1891, p. 8, c. 1]

Morigeau, Alex, Mrs. (1837–1932) Rosalie Finley, the part Kootenai Indian daughter of Patrick [not François] Finley and Marie Gasper Finley, was born in Canada. In 1856 in Washington she married Alexander Morigeau, who was also part Kootenai, and the couple had eleven children. Alexander was at various times a trapper, hunter, rancher and boardinghouse operator. The couple spent most of their lives in the Jocko Valley, where Rosalie died. [*Jocko's People,* vol. 2, pp. 253-54; *FC,* Sept. 22, 1932, p. 1, c. 1]

Morigeau, Antoine (1866–1949) Antoine, the part Kootenai son of Alexander Morigeau and Rosalie Finley Morigeau, was born in Colville, WA. In 1889 he married Mary Louise Clairmont, who was part Pend d'Oreille, and they had nineteen children. Antoine worked as an Indian policeman, rode in the Pablo buffalo roundup, ranched, and owned a hotel and butcher shop in Ronan in partnership with Andrew Stinger. [*Jocko's People,* vol. 2, pp. 283-85; *RP,* July 13, 1939, p. 1, c. 3-4; *RP,* Nov. 17, 1949, p. 1, c. 6-7]

Moss, Henry (1892–1970) According to the interviews, Moss tended the loading chutes during the roundup of the Pablo buffalo herd. In 1908 he was 16 years old. His father, William Moss, was an eighth Cherokee and his mother, Emma Munroe Moss, was half Kootenai and half Piegan. [*Enrollment,* rl. 3, fr. 224-48]

Murray, William "Bill" According to the interviews Murray lived in Plains in 1940 and had worked as a top cowhand for tribal member Telesphore G. DeMers among others. No further information was found.

O'Connell, Tom "Butch" The interviews identify O'Connell as one of the cowboys who worked on the roundup of the Pablo buffalo. No further information was found.

Olson, Mabel C. (1900–1956) See "About the Writers" below.

Pablo, Michel (ca. 1846–1914) Michel's father was Mexican and his mother was a Piegan Indian woman. He was born near Fort Benton. His parents died while he was young, and Michel lived in Colville, WA, and western Montana. He moved to the Flathead Indian Reservation about 1863 and worked for Angus McLeod, the Hudson's Bay Company trader. During the 1860s, he worked as interpreter at the Jocko Agency, and in 1864 he married Agathe Finley, a Pend d' Oreille woman who was the agency cook. After 1870 the couple ran a cattle ranch near what is now known as Pablo, MT. About 1883, Pablo joined with another cattleman, Charles Allard, Sr., in purchasing twelve head of buffalo. The buffalo herd grew and in 1907 was sold to the Canadian government. The roundup of the herd for shipment to Canada was detailed in the Federal Writers Project interviews. Pablo was widely known for his wealth and generosity. [George D. Coder, "The National Movement to Preserve the American Buffalo in the United States and Canada Between 1880 and 1920" (Ph.D. diss., Ohio State University, 1975), pp. 20-21; "United States v. Heyfron, County Treasurer (Circuit Court, D. Montana. April 24, 1905)," *FR*, vol. 138 (July–Sept. 1905), pp. 964-68; *Jocko's People*, vol. 1, pp. 311-14; *FC*, July 16, 1914, p. 1, c. 3]

Palin, Joseph [i.e., Hilaire], Mrs. (1856–1926) Angelique Rosalie "Mary Ann" Finley was the daughter of Patrick [not François] Finley and Mary Ashley Finley. A tribal member, she was born in Washington but lived most of her life in Montana. In 1871 she married a French farmer, Hilaire Palin. The couple lived near Frenchtown and had fifteen children. Angelique was a midwife. [*Jocko's People*, vol. 2, pp. 483-85; Miller, pp. 382-83; *Enrollment*, rl. 3, fr. 262-71]

Peone, Alvin (1894–1953) Louis Alvin Peone, the part Kootenai son of James and Maude Peone, was born in Polson. As a young man he worked on the loading chutes for the roundup of the Pablo buffalo herd. He was a farm laborer. He married Mary Antoine Clairmont, another tribal member, in 1925 and they were divorced in 1941. Louis Alvin died at St. Ignatius. [*Jocko's People*, vol. 1, pp. 95-96; *FC*, Nov. 6, 1941, p. 8, c. 2; *RP*, Apr. 9, 1953, p. 1, c. 2; *DM*, Apr. 7, 1953, p. 6, c. 3]

Peone, James (1862–1932) Born in Colville, WA, James Peone was the son of Louis Peone, a French Canadian, and Catherine Finley Peone, who was half Kootenai Indian. He came to the Flathead

Reservation and married Maude Bourassa, a Kootenai Indian woman in 1891. Between 1897 and 1906 the family lived in Danville, WA. James rode in the roundup of the Pablo buffalo herd and lost some aching teeth in an accident on the buffalo loading chutes. His occupation was given as farmer. James Peone had at least four children. He died at St. Ignatius. [*Jocko's People,* vol. 1, p. 95; *DM,* Sept. 25, 1970, p. 7, c. 4; *RP,* May 19, 1932, p. 1, c. 4]

Pierre, Peter (1900–1983) There have been a number of Pete Pierres on the Flathead Indian Reservation. The Pete Pierre interviewed by the Federal Writers Project was probably the man who died at Arlee in 1983. A lifelong Arlee resident and cattle rancher, he competed on the rodeo circuit as a young man and in later years was a respected tribal leader and interpreter. The interviews identify him as a Salish religious leader. He married Mary Moss in 1921 and they had eight children. [*DM,* Jan. 3, 1983, p. 12, c. 1]

Pierre, Phillip (1875–1949) Presumably this is Phillip Eneas Pierre, a full-blood Pend d'Oreille from Ronan who died in 1949. He was survived by his wife, Clarice, also Pend d'Oreille, and two stepsons, John Peter Paul and Mose Paul. [*RP,* July 21, 1949, p. 6, c. 5-6]

Que-que-sah (1850–1938) The biographical references in the interviews seem to refer to Joseph Quequesah (1850–1938). In the interviews Que-que-sah remembered Indian Samuel arriving on the Flathead Reservation in 1873 and refers to killing four buffalo with bow and arrows in 1889. Joseph was a Pend d'Oreille Indian who married Mary, another Pend d'Oreille, in 1875 and they had three sons, Joseph, Jr., Ignace, and Antoine. [*Enrollment,* rl. 1, fr. 24, #863-67]

Quee-teelt. The interviews identify this person as Angus McDonald's "old Indian friend" who aided in selecting the site for Fort Connah. No further information about Quee-teelt was found.

Ray, Arthur (1885–1956) A member of the Colville tribe, Ray came to Montana from Colville, WA, in 1903. He rode in the buffalo roundup for Michel Pablo and was a longtime rancher and cattleman in the Polson area. In 1908 he married Nellie Sloan, a tribal member on the Flathead Reservation and a daughter of Allen Sloan, and they had six children. [*FC,* Mar. 8, 1956, p. 8, c. 2]

Redhorn, Lassaw (1853–1934) Lassaw Redhorn was listed as Lassaw McDonald, Pend d'Oreille, in the 1905 Flathead Reservation enrollment. According to the interviews he went on summer buffalo hunts in the Yellowstone Valley as a young boy and knew Indian Samuel very well. He married Mary Louise, also Pend d'Oreille, in 1878, and the couple had three children. He died near Ronan. [*Enrollment,* rl. 1, fr. 40, #1435-36; *RP,* Aug. 9, 1934, p. 8, c. 3]

Reed, Clara Peone (1899–1970) Clara Peone, who was part Kootenai, was born in Danville, WA, to James and Maude Peone. The family moved to Ronan in 1906. In 1917 she married Arthur Reed, a white man, in Spokane, WA. The couple had eight children. Clara died in Ronan in 1970. [*Jocko's People*, vol. 1, pp. 95-96; *DM*, Sept. 25, 1970, p. 7, c. 4]

Roberts, Louise (1867–1929) Louise King Roberts, the part Kootenai daughter of Mary Anne Finley and Peter King, was born in Colville Valley, WA. She married Randolph Roberts, a non-tribal member, in 1885 and soon after 1900 they moved to the Flathead Reservation. She died in Ronan. [*Jocko's People*, vol. 2, pp. 384-85; *Enrollment*, rl. 3, fr. 398-402; *RP*, Feb. 14, 1927, p. 1, c. 4]

Ronan, Mary (1852–1940) Of Irish descent, Mary was the wife of Peter Ronan, Flathead Indian Agent from 1877 to his death in 1893, and mother-in-law of Joseph T. Carter, agent from 1893 to 1898. She married Peter Ronan, 14 years her senior, in 1873 and had many children. Her husband had various jobs in journalism and mining until 1877 when he was appointed as agent and the family moved to Jocko Agency. Mary got to know many of the Flathead Indian leaders during her years at Jocko and learned to speak Salish. In 1893 she moved to Missoula where she died. [*Frontier Woman*; *DM*, Apr. 11, 1940, p. 1, c. 3, and p. 3, c. 4-5]

Ronan, Peter (1838–1893) Ronan was born in Nova Scotia and came to Montana in 1863. He worked briefly in the gold mines and then took a job at a Virginia City, MT, newspaper. Between 1866 and 1874 he published a newspaper in Helena, which was finally bankrupted by a fire that destroyed the plant and office. In 1877 Ronan was appointed agent for the Flathead Indian Reservation and held the position until his death in 1893. He developed a reputation as an efficient and honest agent. His diplomatic abilities allowed him to work with traditional Indian leaders to keep the peace and foster agricultural and ranching development on the reservation. [Helen Addison Howard, *Northwest Trail Blazers* (Caldwell, ID: Caxton Printers, Ltd., 1963), pp. 203-45; Peter Ronan, *Historical Sketch of the Flathead Indian Nation*, reprint ed., (Minneapolis, MN: Ross & Haines, Inc., 1965]

Roullier, Fred (1859–1921) Born in Montreal, Canada, Roullier moved to western Montana in 1885. In 1886 he married Caroline Ethier, part Kootenai Indian and a member of the Burland family. In 1897 he moved to a farm near Ronan which he operated until his death. He was survived by his wife and five children. [*Historic*, pp. 71-72; *DM*, Aug. 26, 1921, p. 3, c. 3]

Shot-His-Horse-In-The-Head (150–1932) This full-blood Nez Perce Indian was adopted by the Flathead Reservation tribes in 1905. He had lived on the reservation for "many years." In later years he was known as Louie Head. [*Enrollment*, rl. 1, fr. 402; *RP*, Mar. 31, 1932, p. 5, c. 1]

Shultz, Laura Blodgett (1882–?) Schultz was the youngest daughter of Lyman Blodgett of the Bitterroot Valley. Some sources give her first name as Clara. She remembered her mother trading butter with the Indians for meat in the 1880s. In 1897 she married a white man named Shultz and they farmed in the Corvallis area for 37 years. A non-Indian, she was still alive in Hamilton in 1961. [Leeson, p. 1300; *DM,* Dec. 11, 1961, p. 6, c. 1-3; *BR Trails III,* pp. 386-88; "Clara Blodgett Shultz," Bitterroot Valley Pioneer Society Papers, SC 1053, folder 3, MHS.]

Silverthorne, Jefferson (1868–1922) The youngest son of John and Lizette "Losett" Finley Silverthorne, Jefferson was part Salish Indian and born in the Bitterroot Valley. In 1907 he married Anna Jones, a white woman, and they had seven children. Jefferson was a farmer on the Flathead Indian Reservation and his wife was a practical nurse. He died at St. Ignatius. [*Jocko's People,* vol. 3, pp. 61-62; *Silverthorne,* vol. 2, pp. 702-10; *DM,* Nov. 8, 1922, p. 2, c. 4]

Silverthorne, John (1816–1887) Born in Pennsylvania, Silverthorne came to the Bitterroot Valley in the early 1850s. In 1859 he married Lizette "Losett" Finlay of the Bitterroot Salish tribe, and the couple had six children. During the 1850s he paid some bills with gold dust and could have been the first white gold miner in Montana. The historical sources are inconclusive about how he obtained the gold. He operated a farm in the Bitterroot Valley until his death. [*Jocko's People,* vol. 3, pp. 58-59; *Fort Owen,* pp. 126-35; *Silverthorne,* vol. 1, pp. 489-512]

Skyenna, François. This source for a Salish buffalo legend in 1926 could not be identified.

Sloan, Allen (1850–1937) A Chippewa Indian from St. Cloud, MN, Sloan first came to the Flathead Valley in 1874 and started a ranch near Ronan. In 1884 he married Cecille Morigeau, of part Kootenai descent, and the couple had twelve children. Sloan ran a stage line from the railroad at Ravalli to Demersville, at the head of Flathead Lake, which he sold to Charles Allard. In 1906 he traded his ranch near Ronan for a house and land on the Flathead River. After moving to the Flathead River, he operated a ferry, store, hotel, livery barn, and stage line on the road between Ronan and Hot Springs. The area is still known as Sloan's Ferry. Sloan was a major stockman and early businessman on the Flathead Indian Reservation. [*Jocko's People,* vol. 2, pp. 264-71; *Buffalo Roamed,* pp. 46-49; "United States v. Heyfron, County Treasurer (Circuit Court, D. Montana. April 24, 1905)," *FR,* vol. 138 (July–Sept. 1905), pp. 968-69; *FC,* July 8, 1937, p. 1, c. 5]

Sloan, Allen, Mrs. (1862–1941) Cecelia Morigeau Sloan was the part Kootenai daughter of Alex Morigeau and Rosalie Finley Morigeau. She was born at Rollins on Flathead Lake and married Al Sloan in

1884. The couple ranched near Ronan and later operated several businesses at Sloan's Ferry on the Flathead River. The couple had twelve children. [*RP,* Nov. 6, 1941, p. 1, c. 3-4]

Stimson, C., Mr. (1841–1936) Curtis F. Stimson came to Flathead with the white homesteaders in 1911. Born in Ohio, Stimson was married twice and had two children before he came to Montana. He operated a private bank for many years in Nebraska. In Montana he made investments and loans on Flathead Valley lands. According to the interviews, in the early part of the twentieth century, he sold over 400 head of cattle to Louis Couture for around $27,000. He died in Polson at the home of his son, Walter. [*FC,* Mar. 26, 1931, p. 1, c. 5; *FC,* Feb. 6, 1936, p. 1, c. 4]

Stinger, Andrew (1871–1941) Stinger was born in Ontario, Canada, and moved to the Flathead Reservation in 1884. He worked as a stage driver and cowboy on the reservation. In 1897 he married Louise Courville Allard, a tribal member and the widow of Charles Allard, Sr., and managed the Allard cattle and buffalo ranch. During the roundup of the Pablo buffalo herd on the Flathead Reservation, he was responsible for transporting the buffalo from the pens to the railroad. In later years he operated a dance hall, hotel, meat market, and billiard parlor at Ronan. He lost several businesses and his home in the 1912 fire that destroyed much of the Ronan business district. In 1907, after the death of his first wife, he married Alice Roberts, a tribal member. He was survived by four children. [*Jocko's People,* vol. 2, pp. 444-50; *RP,* Oct. 2, 1941, p. 1, c. 1]

Stinger, Bias (1909–?) Bias Stinger was probably Leonard or Theodore Leonard Stinger, the son of Andrew Stinger and his second wife, Alice Roberts Stinger, a tribal member. In 1941 he was living in Ronan. [*RP,* Oct. 2, 1941, p. 1, c. 1]

Stinger, Louise Courville Allard (1868–1905) A tribal member on the Flathead Reservation, Louise Courville was born in Colville, WA, and was the second wife of Charles Allard, Sr., a part Indian French Canadian, between 1892 and 1896. The couple had two daughters. In 1897 she married Andrew Stinger and they had three children. Louise died at Ronan. [*Jocko's People,* vol. 2, pp. 444-50; *AS,* Nov. 27, 1905, p. 12, c. 4]

Stone, Arthur L. (1865–1945) See "About the Writers" below.

Stuart, Allis B. (1863–1947) See "About the Writers" below.

Taelman, Louis, S.J. (1867–1961) Father Taelman had a long career as an educator and Indian missionary. He was born in Belgium and first came to Montana in 1890. He taught at Gonzaga College in Spokane, WA, for many years and became president of the college in 1909. While in Washington, he ministered among the neighboring tribes. He spent fifteen years as a missionary to the Crow Indians. Between 1924 and 1940 he was stationed at St. Ignatius

Mission on the Flathead Reservation. He then served as missionary to the Spokane and Kalispel tribes in Washington until his retirement in 1952. [*OPA Archives Guide,* p. 48]

Thierrault, Henry (1857–?) Therriault was born in Maine and came to Missoula in 1879. In 1882 he moved to Salish, at the head of Flathead Lake, and farmed and operated a store. He married Lizzie A. Cyr, a white woman, in 1886. In 1890 he moved to Polson and opened a general store and hotel. In 1904 he relocated to Canada. The Therriaults on the Flathead Reservation today are not descendants of Henry but of two of his relatives who married into the tribes. [*Historic,* p. 71; *WM,* Oct. 23, 1886, p. 3, c. 5; *DM,* Apr. 6, 1904, p. 3, c. 3; Marie Cuffe Shea, *Early Flathead and Tobacco Plains: A Narrative History of Northwestern Montana* (privately printed, Eureka, MT, 1977), p. 111]

Vandenburg, Felix. The interviews identify this person as an 80-year-old man in 1942 who could translate picture writing on tepees and who had been a champion dancer in his earlier years. The name is usually spelled Vanderburg on the reservation. No other references to this person were found.

Walking Coyote, Samuel (1843–1897?) Whista Sinchilape, or Walking Coyote, a Pend d'Oreille Indian, was one of the principal characters in the drama of the founding of the Pablo-Allard buffalo herd on the Flathead Reservation. According to Charles Aubrey, a trader in the Marias River area of north-central Montana, in 1877 the married Walking Coyote had an affair with a Blackfoot woman. Fearing the fine and flogging that was the normal punishment for the offense, Walking Coyote tamed several buffalo calves and herded them back to the reservation as a peace offering. According to some reports his teenage son or stepson, Joseph Attahe or Blanket Hawk, assisted in the operation. The gift did not prevent the flogging but provided the seed for a small herd of buffalo near St. Ignatius Mission, which was later sold to Michel Pablo and Charles Allard. Walking Coyote's Pend d'Oreille wife was Mary Sabine or Wuh-Wah and the couple had three to five daughters in addition to their son, Joseph. [Zontek, pp. 78–82, 132–34; *Enrollment,* rl. 1, fr. 13, #462]

Walking Coyote, Samuel, Mrs. (1846– ca. 1901) Mary Sabine Walking Coyote or Wuh-Wah was the Pend d'Oreille wife of Samuel Walking Coyote and mother of Joseph Attahe or Blanket Hawk the Pend d'Oreille Indians who were responsible for taming and driving a small herd of buffalo calves to the Flathead Reservation in the late 1870s. Joseph may have been Samuel's stepson. The Walking Coyotes also had between three and five daughters. In 1879 she was the widow of a white man and sold over 200 head of cattle, depositing the money in a Missoula bank for her children's education. About 1879 she was shot in the shoulder by her husband while he was drunk. The sources do not indicate if the attacker was her first husband, the unnamed white man, or Walking Coyote, her second husband. The injury caused her continuing trouble until it was operated on in St. Patrick Hospital in Missoula in 1891. Mary married her third husband, Alexander Finlay, after Samuel Walking Coyote's death in the late 1890s. [Zontek, pp. 78-82, 132-34; *Enrollment,* rl. 1, fr. 13, #462; Marianne Farr, "Sisters of Providence and Health Care at St. Ignatius Mission and St. Patrick Hospital, 1855–1900," unpublished student paper, Dec. 12, 1997, pp. 20-21 and Appendix F; J. B. Monroe, "Samuel, the Pend d'Oreille," *Forest & Stream,* vol. 59, no. 1 (July 5, 1902), p. 6]

Whealdon, Bon I. (1889–1959) See "About the Writers" below.

Williams, Griffith A. (1882–?) See "About the Writers" below.

Wurm, George (1864–1948) Born in Illinois, Wurm came to Montana in 1883. He worked in Thompson Falls and Plains in western Montana as a miner and rancher. In 1910 he was one of the white homesteaders who located on Camas Prairie on the Flathead Indian Reservation. Over the years he expanded his ranch holdings until 1943 when he sold out and moved to Plains. [*Plainsman* (Plains, MT), Nov. 18, 1948, p. 1, c. 4]

About the Writers

Charles Aubrey (1845–1908)

Aubrey related the story of Samuel Walking Coyote in *Forest and Stream* in 1902. W. A. Bartlett quoted the entire story in part of his buffalo manuscript which is reproduced above in Chapter 4. In 1877 Aubrey operated a trading post on the Marias River. The Pend d'Oreille Indians were among his customers that winter, and one, Sam Walking Coyote, took a Blackfeet woman as his second wife. After the Blackfeet wife left, Aubrey suggested that Walking Coyote take a small herd of buffalo calves to the Flathead Reservation as a peace offering to the chiefs and missionaries. According to his account, Aubrey played a critical role in the origins of the Pablo-Allard buffalo herd on the Flathead Reservation.

Born in New York State, Aubrey came to Montana in the late 1860s after serving in the Civil War. After a brief stint mining in Alder Gulch, he went on to a variety of other enterprises. Between 1875 and 1885 he worked as a trader along the Missouri River in Montana.

Most of this time Aubrey traded among the Montana Blackfeet, but, during the middle 1880s, he operated a trading post for T. C. Power at Wolf Point on the Fort Peck Reservation. A major export from this store was dried buffalo bones.

In 1875 Aubrey married a Blackfeet woman, Louise Chouquette, and the couple had nine or ten children. After the middle 1880s, Aubrey raised cattle on the Blackfeet Indian Reservation and filled various jobs at the agency, such as agency farmer and freighter.

During the twentieth century he wrote accounts of many of his experiences on the plains for George Bird Grinnell in *Forest and Stream*. He died in 1908 under mysterious circumstances.

[U.S. Census, *Tenth Census of the United States, 1880,* MT, Choteau Co., p. 58B, lines 46-49, NAmf T9, reel 747; Charles Aubrey, "Montana's Buffalo: The Pablo-Allard Herd: The Origin of the Herd," *Forest and Stream*, vol. 59, no. 1 (July 5, 1902), p. 6; "Charles Aubrey," *Forest and Stream*, vol. 71, no 10 (Sept. 5, 1908), p. 377; LeRoy Barnett, "Ghastly Harvest: Montana's Trade in Buffalo Bones," *Montana the Magazine of Western History*, vol. 25, no. 3 (Summer 1975), pp. 2-13; Blackfeet Heritage Program, *Blackfeet Heritage, 1907–1908: Blackfeet Indian Reservation, Browning, Montana* (Browning, MT: Blackfeet Heritage Program, 1980?), p. 23; "Another Old-Timer Gone," *The Choteau Acantha* (Choteau, MT), Aug. 27, 1908, p. 1, c. 5; "About the State," *Missoula Gazette* (daily) (Missoula, MT), Nov. 17, 1890, p. 5, c. 2; "Those Lucky Indians," *The Northwest Illustrated Monthly Magazine*, vol. 11, no. 12 (Dec. 1893), p. 7; "Investigation Reveals Murder," *The Kalispell Journal* (Kalispell, MT), Aug. 27, 1908, p. 1, c. 1]

W. A. Bartlett

Bartlett was the Montana Writers Project author who wrote the manuscript for the history of buffalo in Montana, part of which is reproduced in Chapter 4 above. No further biographical information was located about him.

Clarence A. Brown (1888–1974)

In 1939 Brown wrote biographical sketches of two of the French Canadians who married into the Salish tribes: Joseph Barnaby and Joe Couture. The sketches were based on interviews with their surviving mixed-blood sons.

Brown was born in North Dakota and moved to Polson in 1912 with his parents. He served in the navy during World War I. In addition to working for the Montana Writers Project in the later 1930s, he worked at the Polson post office for many years.

["Clarence Brown," FC, Oct. 10, 1974, p. 9, c. 3]

Will Cave (1863–1954)

Cave related several of Duncan McDonald's stories for the Montana Writers Project. In 1941 he repeated McDonald's story about a battle between the Blackfeet and Salish in the Missoula Valley (Chapter 1) and wild horses in western Montana (Chapter 10).

Born in Alder Gulch, or Helena, in 1863, Cave's family moved to the Bitterroot Valley in 1865 and Missoula in 1872. He served as a volunteer at the Battle of the Big Hole in 1877, but refused to shoot women in the attack on the Nez Perce camp. In 1898 he organized a volunteer force for the Spanish-American War but did not go overseas.

He spent many years in Missoula County government. In 1891 he became the county's first auditor. He also served as county assessor, deputy county treasurer, deputy county clerk, and justice of the peace. He later had a land title abstract business, which he sold in 1943 at the age of 80. Cave was widely known for his knowledge and stories about Missoula history. A number of these stories appeared in the local newspaper over the years.

["Will Cave Dies at 90," DM, Mar. 2, 1954, p. 1, c. 4, and p. 10, c. 3; "Cave, Will," Montana Biographical Clippings File, UM]

Mabel C. Olson (1900–1956)

Olson was born in Norway where her mother, Oline Olson, was visiting. Her father was Anton C. Olson, who operated a store in Superior and was a longtime justice of the peace. Mabel attended school in Superior and Virginia City. She attended college in Dillon and Missoula and later taught school in eastern Montana. During the early 1940s, she conducted the interviews for the Montana Writers Project that are reproduced above.

In later years she wrote for a Portland newspaper and was a freelance writer for magazines and newspapers. Much of her writing was about nature in the Portland area. She died from injuries received from a speeding car while walking along a dirt road in the Portland area.

["Memorial Service to Honor Mable [sic] C. Olson," *The Mineral Independent* (Superior, MT), Apr. 19, 1956, p. 1, c. 2]

Arthur L. Stone (1865–1945)

A. L. Stone was a newspaperman in Missoula who related several of Duncan McDonald's stories to Montana Writers Project workers. He was born in Massachusetts and came west in 1884. Trained as a chemist, Stone was a field chemist for the Union Pacific Railroad and a teacher and school administrator in Montana before entering journalism. Between 1891 and 1907 he worked for the *Anaconda Standard*. From 1891 to 1904 he was the Missoula or western Montana correspondent for the *Standard*. During the period of 1907 to 1914 he was editor and manager of the *Missoulian*. In 1914 he became the first dean of the University of Montana School of Journalism. For half a century Stone was one of the most prominent figures in Montana journalism. He retired in 1942 and died in Missoula in 1945. His wife, Adelia Norwood Stone, died in 1917. They had six children.

[Robert George Raymer, *Montana: The Land and the People* (Chicago: The Lewis Publishing Company, 1930), vol. 3, pp. 567-69; "Montana Newspaper Hall of Fame," *Journalism Review* (School of Journalism, University of Montana, Missoula), no. 2 (Spr. 1959), inside front cover; "Dean A. L. Stone Dies: Private Service Today," *DM*, Mar. 20, 1945, p. 1, c. 4-5 and p. 5, c. 1]

Allis B. Stuart (1863–1947)

The writer for the interviews about Joseph Blodgett was the aged and impoverished widow of Granville Stuart (1834–1918). Allis was Granville's second wife and twenty-nine years his junior.

In 1858 Granville became famous in Montana history as one of the first white prospectors to discover gold. The news of the discovery caused a rush of gold miners in 1862. Granville and his brother, James, followed the mining rush around Montana but had little success. In 1867 he settled in Deer Lodge and opened a store and lumberyard. In 1862 he married a twelve–year old Shoshone woman. They had eleven children before she died in 1888. Granville had extensive cattle interests until the hard winter of 1886–87 wiped him out financially.

In 1890 Granville married Allis, a young white woman whose bigotry drove Granville's mixed blood children out of the Stuart home. Granville worked as Montana state land agent and U.S. State Department minister to Uruguay and Paraguay in the 1890s. Allis accompanied him on his travels, but the couple was always financially overextended. He worked as a librarian and in 1916 was commissioned to write a history of Montana which he never completed.

After Granville's death in 1918, his widow worked as a social worker, ranch cook, and in various other jobs. Between 1939 and her death in 1945 she was on public assistance in Ravalli County. She worked for the Montana Writers Project between 1940 and 1942 gathering material for a history of the livestock industry.

[Paul Robert Treece, "Mr. Montana: The Life of Granville Stuart, 1834-1918" (Ph.D. dissertation, Ohio State University, Columbus, 1974), pp. 415-69; Howard R. Lamar, ed., *The Reader's Encyclopedia of the American West* (New York: Thomas Y. Crowell Company, 1977), pp. 1147-48]

Bon I. Whealdon (1889-1959)

The writer who gathered most of the interviews reproduced in this book, Bon I. Whealdon, was born in Ilwaco in southwest Washington to Elizabeth and William David Whealdon in 1889. The Whealdons were a Quaker family who settled in Ilwaco, near the mouth of the Columbia River, in 1847. William David's father, Isaac Whealdon, made friends with the local Chinook Indians. Bon's father was variously a farmer, a county commissioner, and a teacher. He also bought and sold land. Isaac Bonnil (Bon) Whealdon had five brothers and sisters and two stepbrothers. The children attended local schools and Bon was listed as a high school graduate. In later life, Bon had excellent penmanship and wrote clear and well constructed sentences. He made reference to a number of literary and anthropological sources, so he must have read widely.

Known as a mystic most of his life, Bon held seances as a teenager and in his early twenties. In 1896 a Cree Indian woman led a seance at the Whealdon home in an unsuccessful attempt to locate a cache of gold rescued from a shipwreck in the 1850s and buried on the Whealdon farm.

Bon's mother died in 1905 and sometime after 1910 he and his still-grieving father, moved to the Flathead Reservation to homestead land. William later returned to Ilwaco and died there in 1918. According to the mortuary records, Bon left the Flathead Reservation to serve in World War I but returned in 1922.

Over the years on Flathead, Bon farmed, worked as a lumberman, and was the first caretaker of the Mountain View Cemetery in Ronan. In a 1932 letter he described surviving the depression on his farm near Ronan. He kept cows, pigs, and teams of horses, and grew a garden in addition to gathering local wild foods. Tribal elder Thurman Trosper was a teenager in Ronan in the 1930s and remembers Bon as a slightly built man about five feet eight inches tall who was always dressed up in a dark suit. Bon was well known in the Ronan area for interviewing local Indian and white residents about western Montana history.

During long periods of his life, Bon suffered from arthritis, spinal meningitis, and tuberculosis. During his last thirty years, he lived with

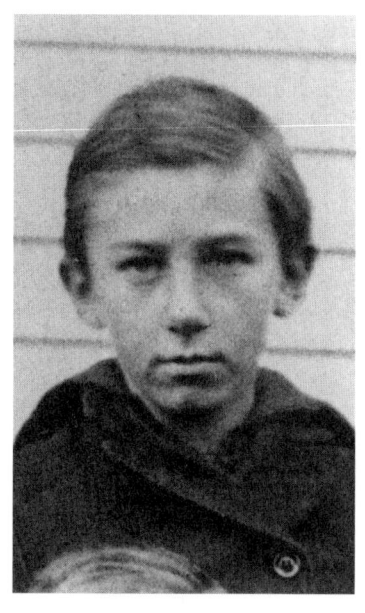

Bon Isaac Whealdon, 1907.

the Lawrence Thompson family. The Thompsons originally lived in Ronan but they and Bon moved to Hot Springs in the late 1940s. He never married.

A frequent letter writer, Whealdon had an extensive interest in family genealogy as well as Salish Indian history and customs. His surviving manuscripts tell much more about his Whealdon ancestors then they do about his own life. Nothing was found describing his relations with Mission Valley tribal elders. The dates noted in the Montana Writers Project manuscripts indicate interviews over a number of years including 1922, 1923, 1926, 1934, 1938, and 1941. The 1941 interviews were done specifically for the Writers Project. The interviews reproduced here suggest that Whealdon must have earned the trust of a number of elderly Salish Indians in the Ronan area.

Typed versions of many of his interviews were found in the surviving Montana Writers Project papers. Many more must have been lost with the disappearance of the Flathead Reservation files. The Montana Writers Project manuscript of Flathead or Salish stories, "Sunlight and Shadow: The Story of the Flathead Indians," seems to have relied heavily on Whealdon's material. A few chapters from that manuscript were published in the *Hot Springs Sentinel* (Hot Springs, MT) newspaper between 1954 and 1956. Between 1957 and 1959, Whealdon wrote a column of local news and commentary for the *Hot Springs Sentinel* entitled "Notes from Old Crip."

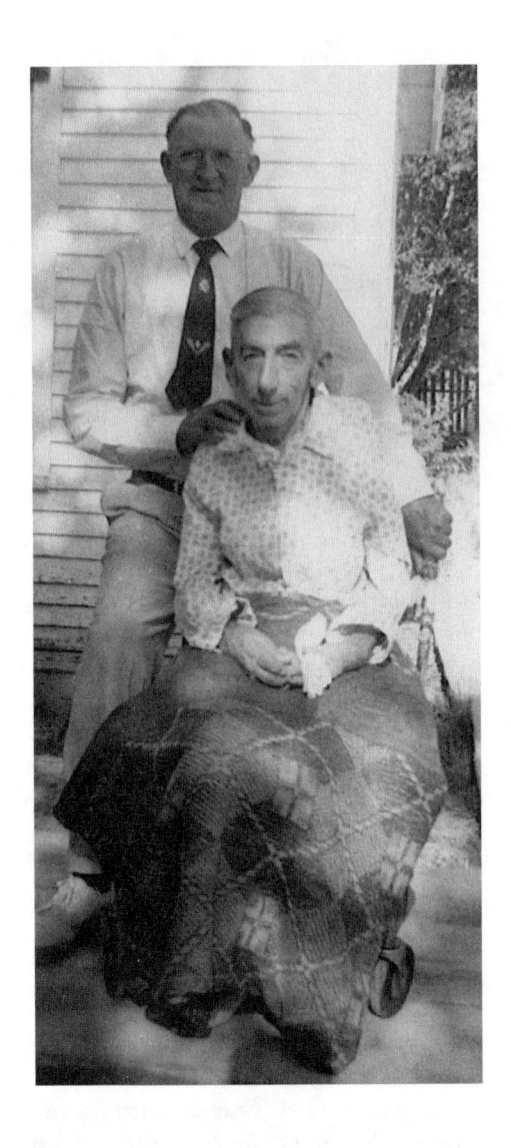

Bon Isaac Whealdon, sitting; Rev. John Russell Whealdon, a younger brother of Bon, standing, August 1957.

Bon Whealdon was a remarkable person in many ways. His interest in Salish Indian history and culture preserved the memories of many Salish elders of the 1922–41 period. We can only hope that more of his manuscripts will come to light in the future.

[Whealdon sometimes embellished his personal history and conflicts appear in the available biographical information below: David T. (Tom) Whealdon (Louisville, KY) personal letter to Bigart, Aug. 14, 1997; "Obituary Report," Shrider's Mortuary, Ronan, MT; Ruby El Hult, *Lost Mines and Treasures of the Pacific Northwest* (Portland, OR: Binfords & Mort, Publisher, 1957), pp. 134-43; "Whealdon Rites Today," *RP*, Jan. 29, 1959, p. 1, c. 5; Bon Whealdon (Ronan, MT) to Dan Whealdon, Apr. 14, 1932, copy in Rodney K. Williams (Long Beach, WA) personal letter to Bigart, July 16, 1997; Thurman Trosper, Ronan, MT, personal interview with Bigart, Oct. 28, 1999; "Notes from Old Crip," *Hot Springs Sentinel* (Hot Springs, MT), Jan. 29, 1959, p. 1, c. 1-2]

Griffith A. Williams (1882–?)

Some biographical sketches and other research reports from Plains and Hot Springs were written by Williams. He got much of his information from interviews with the Couture, Courville, and Larrivee families.

Williams was born and educated in England. In 1905 he came to Butte to teach in the Butte Business College. After a few years he moved to journalism. In 1915 he bought a Dixon, MT, newspaper and in 1918 he purchased the *Plainsman* in Plains, MT. As of 1921 he had both newspapers. No information was located about his life after 1921.

[Stout, vol. 2, pp. 46-47]

Name Index

Allard, Charles A., Jr. 87, 92, 116, 128, 239
Allard, Charles A., Sr. 70, 76, 78-83, 86-90, 92, 105, 108, 110, 112, 115-16, 119, 125, 129-30, 137, 190, 207, 213-14, 228, 239
Allard, Eva May 87, 239
Allard, Joseph 87, 239
Allard, Louise Anna 87, 240
Allard, Louise Courville. *See* Stinger, Louise Courville Allard
Archibald, Billy 94, 240
Aubrey, Charles B. 70, 75-76, 78, 81-82, 267
Ayotte, Alex 91, 95, 105, 134

Babtiste (Iroquois Indian) 104
Barber, Lizzie 28, 240
Barnaby, Antoine 61-62, 77, 83, 94, 96, 108, 119, 138, 174, 186, 191, 199-200, 240
Barnaby, Felixe 199, 240
Barnaby, Joseph 199, 240
Barnaby, Tony. *See* Barnaby, Antoine
Barrett, Louis 219
Bartlett, W. A. 69, 268
Beaulieu, Fred 141, 240
Beaverhead, Alex 149, 155, 163, 165-67, 240
Bedson, Col. 90
Blair, Mr. 189
Blodgett, Joseph, Jr. 204, 241
Blodgett, Joseph S. 200, 202-05, 240
Blodgett, Joseph S., Mrs. 203, 205, 241
Blodgett, Lyman 204, 241
Blodgett, Newman 204, 241
Blodgett, Norman 200, 201

Blodgett, Sally 200
Blodgett, Sarah "Sally" 204-05, 241
Blood, Mary 94, 135, 227, 241
Boyer, Frank 209-10
Branch, E. Douglas 75
Brechbill, John M., Mrs. 228, 231, 241
Brown, Clarence A. 199, 210, 268
Brown, Louis 116, 242
Burland, Harry H. *See also* Burland, Henry Arthur
Burland, Harry Henry 41-42, 44, 155, 166-67, 173-74, 242
Burland, Henry Arthur 22, 38, 43, 50, 54, 56, 142, 185, 227, 242
Burns, Pat 228
Burr, Fred 229

Cameron, George 193, 219
Cave, Alfred 231
Cave, Will 33, 183-84, 218, 268
Chaffin, Alexander M. 204-05
Champaigne, Baptiste 71-72
Champaigne, Michel 71
Charley (Chinese) 215
Charlo, Chief 180-81, 242
Church, William L. 231
Clark, Joseph K. 90, 214
Clark, W. A., Senator 90, 214
Clifford, John E. 216, 243
Conko, Eneas 155, 163, 165, 243
Conner, Charles 218
Conrad, Alicia D. 88
Conrad, Charles E. 87-88, 130
Cory, F. M. 191, 244
Courville, Alphonse 214, 244
Courville, Julia Finley 208, 222, 224, 244

Courville, Louis 128, 207-08, 216, 224, 244
Courville, Margaret 223, 244
Courville, Oliver 207, 216, 221-24, 245
Courville, Zephyr "Swift" 78, 92, 94, 110-11, 128-32, 207-08, 221-24, 245
Couture, Dave 78, 110-11, 193, 195-97, 207, 209-11, 214, 222, 245
Couture, Emmerence 211, 245
Couture, Joseph 209-11, 245
Couture, Joseph, Mrs. 211, 222, 224, 245
Couture, Louis 210-12, 245
Couture, Mack 211, 245
Cruzan, James A. 131
Culligan, Della Sloan. *See* Culligan, Josephine Della Sloan
Culligan, Josephine Della Sloan 126, 246

Daly, Marcus 206
Delaware, John 166-67, 246
Delaware, Moses 25, 94, 246
DeMers, Alex 219, 246
Demers, Angelo 220, 246
DeMers, Clara Rivet 212, 219, 246
Demers, Jack. *See* DeMers, Telesphore Jacques "Jack"
Demers, Lambert 29, 247
Demers, Leonie 212, 214, 217, 219, 247
Demers, Robert 212, 216-17, 247
DeMers, Telesphore Garcon 193, 195, 214, 219, 221, 247
DeMers, Telesphore Garcon, Mrs. 219, 247
DeMers, Telesphore Jacques "Jack" 29, 193, 195, 207-10, 212-21, 248
DeMers, William 218-19, 248

DeSmet, Pierre J., S.J. 29, 70, 184-85
Devenpeck, Mrs. 231
Douglas, Howard 91, 94-95, 134
DuBray, William 213, 218
Ducharme, Baptiste 216, 248
Dunbar, Seymour 231
Duvall, D. C. 51

Eaton, Howard 87
Edgar, Henry 28
Elizabeth (Nez Perce Indian) 43, 106, 248
Elrod, Morton J. 144, 200
Eulopsen, Thomas 166-67, 248

Finlay, Abraham 221, 224, 248
Finlay, Alex 76, 78, 249
Finlay, Basil 222, 224, 249
Finlay, Basson 221, 224, 249
Finlay, Charles "Red Cloud" 223, 250
Finlay, François (b. 1893) 223, 250
Finlay, François "Benetsee" 208, 221-26, 229, 250
Finlay, Joseph 221, 224, 251
Finlay, Mary Ashley 221, 224, 251
Finlay, Mary "Sitting Blanket" 223, 251
Finlay, Patrick "Pichina" 251
Finlay, Peter 189, 222-24, 252
Finley, August 41, 142-43, 173, 249
Finley, August, Mrs. 142, 249
Finley, Dave 142, 173, 176, 250
Finley, Feenom 78, 110, 189, 250
Finley, James 26, 251
Finley, Louise 157, 251
Finley, Mary. *See* King, Mary Finley

Name Index

Finley, Peter. *See* Finlay, Peter
Finley, T. *See* Finley, Feenom
Flynn, Michael 216
Ford, Joseph 79-81
Ford, Samuel 80
Forsyth, N. A. 97
Frasier, John 213-14

Garcia, Andrew 82
Garretson, Martin S. 81
Gebeau, Henry 181, 252
Gebeau, Oliver 22, 25-26, 28, 180, 252
Gibbon, John, Gen. 203
Gibson, O. D. 88
Grinder, Jim 94, 129, 252

Hammond, A. B. 208
Harding, "Butch" 215
Harding, Dwight 215
Hess, Jimmy 215
Hethier, J. B. 218
Higgins, C. P., Capt. 202
Higgins, Frank 184
Hilger, David 216
Houle, Joseph 94, 113, 125, 127-28, 252
Hurlburt, Seymour 216

Indian Samuel. *See* Walking Coyote, Samuel
Irvine, Angela Ashley 227, 252
Irvine, Emily Brown 94, 116, 135, 226, 253
Irvine, Peter 227, 253
Irvine, William "Billy" 94, 135, 196, 207, 210, 216, 226-28, 253

Jeffreys, John 202
John (Ceour d'Alene Indian) 120
Johnson, Arthur P. 219
Johnson, George 219
Jones, C. J. "Buffalo," Col. 89-90, 130
Jones, Tom 76-77, 86, 88

King, Mary Finley 31, 33, 39, 41, 222, 224, 253
King, William, Mrs. *See* King, Mary Finley

Lachlan, Denver 215
LaMousse, Francois 41-42, 254
Lander, Robert, Mrs. 231
Lane, George 228
Larivee, Arthur. *See* Larrivee, Arthur
La Rose, John 165, 254
Larrivee, Arthur 207, 209-10, 217, 220, 254
Leavitt, Fred 204, 206
Leeson, Michael A. 200, 204
Lewis, Bill 94, 129, 254
Lomphrey, Joseph 184, 254
Lomphrie, Joseph. *See* Lomphrey, Joseph

MacDonald, Angus. *See* McDonald, Angus
MacDonald, Duncan. *See* McDonald, Duncan
MacDonald, Joseph. *See* McDonald, Joseph
MacDonald, Tom. *See* McDonald, Tom
Many-Tail-Feathers (Blackfeet Indian) 82
Marion, Joseph 190, 257
Matt, Mrs. 142, 143, 257

Matt, Alex 80, 257
McCormick, John 217
McCrea, Robert A. 92, 116, 118, 126, 255
McDonald, Angus 103-05, 144, 191, 225, 255
McDonald, Catherine 104, 255
McDonald, Duncan 28-29, 34, 78, 104-05, 144, 183-84, 186-88, 255
McDonald, John 105, 256
McDonald, Joseph 70, 103, 106, 155, 157, 166-67, 256
McDonald, Tom 166-67, 256
McGowan, Camille 115
McGowan, Camille, Mrs. 115-16
McLeod, Alex 116, 189, 256
McLeod, Donald 185, 189, 256
McLeod, Frank, Jr. 39, 94-96, 133-34, 185, 257
McLeod, Frank, Sr. 189, 257
McLeod, Malcolm 94, 116-17, 129, 257
McWhirt, William 202
Meunier, Theodore 219
Mi-sum-mi-mo-na (Blackfeet Indian) 71-73
Michel, Chief 42, 215, 258
Michell, Charley, Chief 42, 77, 107, 155, 258
Michell, Dominic 21, 23, 29-30, 43, 48, 50, 52, 54, 56, 150, 170, 258
Michell, Michell, Chief. *See* Michel, Chief
Michell, Mose, Chief 47, 76, 106-07, 157, 166-67, 258
Michell, Mose, Mrs. 107, 259
Miller, Jock 79-80
Monroe, J. B. 76, 84, 89
Moran, Ellen Finlay 208, 222, 224, 259
Moran, Joe 208, 259

Morigeau, Alex, Mrs. 222, 224, 259
Morigeau, Antoine 79-80, 94, 111, 113, 138, 166-67, 174, 259
Moser, Gust 231
Moss, Henry 94, 259
Murray, William "Bill" 217, 220-21, 260

Nelson, Frank 80

O'Connell, Tom "Butch" 94, 260
Oliver, Frank, Hon. 91
Olson, Mabel C. 28, 33, 115, 183, 186, 212, 220, 228, 268
Owen, John, Maj. 203, 229, 231

Pablo, Michael. *See* Pablo, Michel
Pablo, Michel 61, 70, 76-87, 90-92, 94-96, 105, 108, 110, 112-13, 115-22, 125-30, 132-33, 135-38, 141-42, 185-86, 190, 260
Palin, Joseph, Mrs. 222, 224, 260
Peone, Alvin 94, 96, 136, 260
Peone, James 94, 96-97, 132, 136, 260
Pierre, Peter 25, 54, 56-57, 261
Pierre, Phillip 163, 165, 261

Que-que-sah 107, 120, 122, 150, 261
Quee-teelt 104, 261

Ravalli, Anthony, S. J. 70, 72, 185
Ray, Arthur 125

Name Index

Redhorn, Lassaw 36, 48, 50, 63-64, 149-50, 155, 160, 163, 165, 170, 262
Reed, Clara Peone 132-33, 136
Riel, Louis 228
Roberts, Louise 31, 33, 262
Ronan, Mary 213, 262
Ronan, Peter 213, 262
Roosevelt, Theodore, Pres. 90, 113
Ross, Alexander 183-84
Roullier, Fred 137, 262
Russell, Charley 91, 95, 97, 113, 134-35

Scheffer, Peter 216
Scott, Samuel 34
Short Coyote. *See* Walking Coyote, Samuel
Shot-His-Horse-In-The-Head 35, 109-10, 170, 262
Shultz, Laura Blodgett 200, 263
Silverthorne, Gabriel 228
Silverthorne, Jefferson 230, 263
Silverthorne, John 228-31, 263
Silverthorne, John [Uncle to John in Bitterroot Valley] 228
Silverthorne, Oliver 228
Silverthorne, William 228
Skyenna, François 48, 50, 263
Sloan, Allen 61, 91, 113, 125-26, 189, 191, 263
Sloan, Allen, Mrs. 157, 264
Smith, Jacob 80
Stevens, Isaac I., Gov. 202
Stimson, C., Mr. 211, 264
Stinger, Andrew 62, 77, 83, 109-10, 117-19, 134, 137, 144-45, 191, 226, 264
Stinger, Bias 137, 264
Stinger, Louise Courville Allard 87-88, 130, 137, 264

Stone, A. L., Dean 28, 186, 269
Strathcona, Lord 87
Stuart, Allis B. 200, 204, 206, 269

Taelman, Louis, S. J. 29, 265
Te Lee (Chinese) 215
Therriault, Henry 211, 265
Thompson, L. E. 30
Tyler, S. C. 231

Vandenburg, Felix 29, 265

Walking Coyote, Samuel 63, 70-83, 87, 103, 105-09, 112, 119, 125, 265
Walking Coyote, Samuel, Mrs. 71, 73-77, 106, 265
Wells, Samuel. *See* Walking Coyote, Samuel
Whealdon, Bon I. 21-23, 25-26, 28-29, 31, 33, 35-36, 39, 41-42, 44, 47-48, 50, 52, 54, 57, 61-63, 103, 106-09, 111, 116-20, 125-27, 132-38, 141-42, 144, 149-50, 153, 157, 160, 163, 165-68, 170, 173-74, 176, 178, 180, 185, 189-91, 226-27, 270
Williams, Griffith A. 110, 128, 193, 196, 207-09, 217, 221, 223, 273
Wissler, Clark 51
Woodrow, Judge 87
Woody, Frank H., Judge 229
Wurm, George 209-10, 219-20, 266

Yellow Wolf (Blackfeet Indian) 71

The Artist

The illustrations for this book are by noted Native American artist Dwight W. BilleDeaux, a member of the Blackfeet tribe who has married into the Confederated Salish and Kootenai Tribes. For more than twenty years, he has taught art students on the Flathead Indian Reservation. Galleries across Montana as well as Munster, Germany; New York City; Seattle; Washington, D.C.; Denver; St. Louis; Cambridge, Massachusetts; and Sacramento, California have exhibited his work. His illustrations have appeared in numerous books relating to the Blackfeet tribe and the Montana Salish tribes. He received his training at the Academy of Arts in San Francisco and the University of Montana at Dillon and Missoula.

The Editor

Robert Bigart is Director of the Salish Kootenai College Press and has worked at the college since 1979. He began researching Flathead Reservation and Salish tribal history in the late 1960s.